Applied Theatre

Applied Theatre:
International Case Studies and Challenges for Practice

Second Edition

Edited by Monica Prendergast and Juliana Saxton

intellect Bristol, UK / Chicago, USA

First published in the UK in 2016 by Intellect,
The Mill, Parnall Road, Fishponds, Bristol, BS16 3JG, UK

First published in the USA in 2016 by Intellect, The University of Chicago Press,
1427 E. 60th Street, Chicago, IL 60637, USA

A catalogue record for this book is available from the British Library.

Cover design: Holly Rose
Copy-editor: MPS Technologies
Typesetting: John Teehan
Production Manager: Katie Evans

ISBN: 978-1-78320-625-4
ePDF: 978-1-78320-626-1
ePUB: 978-1-78320-627-8

Printed and bound by Hobbs, UK.

Contents

Chapter Three: Story, Storytelling and Applied Theatre

Part Two: The Landscape of Applied Theatre

Chapter Four: Popular Theatre

Part Three: The Locations of Applied Theatre

Part Four: Challenges for Practice

Acknowledgments

The editors wish to thank the journals which did not charge for the use of articles and all the authors for permission to use their work. We also are grateful to our Intellect Books editors Claire Organ and Katie Evans for their detailed attention and eagle eyes.

"The Welfare State Theatre" by Theodore Shank. *TDR: The Drama Review*, *21*(1) (March 1977), pp. 3–16. ©1977 by New York University and the Massachusetts Institute of Technology.

"Walking in both worlds: Snuff Puppets at Barak Indigenous College" by K. Donelan and A. O'Brien. *ATR: Applied Theatre Researcher*, *7*(2), 2006. By kind permission of Applied Theatre Researcher/IDEA Journal.

"Duen Phen: Joker performance in the nightclubs of Bangkok" by Mary L. Grow, 1995, *Asian Theatre Journal*, *12*(2). Reprinted with permission of the publisher (University of Hawaii Press).

"Using street theatre to increase awareness and reduce mercury pollution in the artisanal gold mining sector: A case from Zimbabwe" by Stephen Metcalfe & Marcello Veiga. *Journal of Cleaner Production*, *37*, 2012.

"Peter Weiss and documentary theatre: Song of a scarecrow" by Irmeli Niemi. (*Modern Drama*, *16*(1), 1973. Used with kind permission.

"Truth in translation" by Elizabeth Redden (pp. 17-23) and "Chaotic harmony" by Karen Birdsall (p. 20). *Swarthmore College Bulletin*, December 2006. Reprinted with permission.

"'That's who I'd be if I could sing': Reflections on a verbatim project with mothers of sexually abused children" by Amanda Stuart Fisher. *Studies in Theatre and Performance*, *31*:2, 2011. Reprinted with kind permission of Intellect Ltd.

"To witness mimesis: The politics, ethics, and aesthetics of testimonial theatre in Through the Wire" by Caroline Wake. *Modern Drama*, 56(1), 2013. Used with kind permission.

"Indigo" by the Dukes TIE Company. *SCYPT Journal* 26 (1993). By kind permission of the Dukes TIE Company: Ian Yeoman (Director), Danie Croft, Helen Clugston, Deb Williamson, Daley Donnelley, Lewis Frost and Chris Cooper (Actor-teachers).

"A journey of change with a Big Blue Whale: A theatre in education (TIE) programme on disability and dilemmas in the inclusive classroom in Korea" by Byoung-Joo Kim, *RIDE: The Journal of Applied Theatre and Performance*, 14(1), 2009. Reprinted with permission of the publisher (Taylor & Francis, Ltd, www.informaworld.com).

"Tapestry and the aesthetics of theatre in education as dialogic encounter and civil exchange" by Joe Winston and Steve Strand. *RIDE: The Journal of Applied Theatre and Performance*, 18(1), 2013. Reprinted with permission of the publisher (Taylor & Francis, Ltd, www.informaworld.com).

"Making the everyday extraordinary: A theatre-in-education project to prevent child abuse, neglect and family violence" by Peter O'Connor, Briar O'Connor and Marlane Welsh-Morris, *Research in Drama Education* 11(2), 2006. Reprinted with permission of the publisher (Taylor & Francis, Ltd, www.informaworld.com).

"INTERVIEW: Augusto Boal, City Councillor: Legislative Theatre and the Chamber in the Streets" by Richard Schechner and Sudipto Chatterjee, *TDR/The Drama Review*, 42(4) (T160-Winter, 1998), pp. 75–90. © 1998. Reprinted with permission of the publisher (by New York University and the Massachusetts Institute of Technology).

"Making bodies talk in Forum Theatre" by Paul Dwyer, *Research in Drama Education* 9(2), 2004. Reprinted with permission of the publisher (Taylor & Francis, Ltd, www.informaworld.com).

"Theatre of the Commons: A theatrical inquiry into the democratic engagement of former refugee families in Canadian public high school communities" by J. Alysha Sloane & Dawn Wallin, *Educational Research*, 55(4), 2013. Reprinted by permission of the publisher (Taylor & Francis, Ltd, www.informaworld.com).

"Theatre of the Oppressed in medical humanities education: The road less travelled" by Setu Gupta, Abhinav Agrawal, Satendra Singh and Navjeevan Singh. *Indian Journal of Medical Ethics*, 10(3), 2013. Reprinted with kind permission.

"Icons and metaphors in African theatre against HIV/AIDS" by Victor S. Dugga. *NJ: Drama Australia Journal*, 26(2). Reprinted with permission of the publisher (By kind permission of Drama Australia and *NJ*).

"Inside 'Inside View': Reflections on stimulating debate and engagement through a multimedia live theatre production on the dilemmas and issues of pre-natal screening policy and practice" by Gillian L. Hundt, Claudette Bryanston, Pam Lowe, Saul Cross, Jane Sandall & Kevin Spencer. *Health Expectations*, 14(1) pp. 1–9, 2010. Reprinted with permission of the publisher (John Wiley & Sons, Inc).

"Operating theatre: A theatre devising project with fourth-year medical students" by Max Hafler. *Journal of Applied Arts & Health*, 3(3), (2012). Reprinted with kind permission of Intellect Ltd.

"Social theatre in Bangladesh" by Nasmul Ahsan, *TDR/The Drama Review*, 48(3) (Fall 2004), pp. 50–58. © 2004. Reprinted with permission of the publisher (New York University and the Massachusetts Institute of Technology).

"A theatrical approach to the making of a national constitution: The case of Uganda" by Patrick Mangeni wa'Ndeda. *NJ: Drama Australia Journal*, 24(1), 2000. Reprinted with permission of the publisher (By kind permission of Drama Australia and *NJ*).

"Fitting the bill: Commissioned theatre projects of human rights in Pakistan: The work of Karachi-based theatre group Tehrik e Niswan" by Asma Mundrawala, *Research in Drama Education*, 12(2), 2007. Reprinted with permission of the publisher (Taylor & Francis, Ltd, www.informaworld.com).

"TFD, Environmental degradation and health issues" by Emem Obonguko. *Creative Artist: A Journal of Theatre and Media Studies*, 4:1, pp. 53–68, 2010. Reprinted by kind permission.

"Prose and cons: Theatrical encounters with students and prisoners in Ma'asiyahu, Israel" by Sonja Kuftinec & Chen Alon, *Research in Drama Education*, 12(3), 2007. Reprinted with permission of the publisher (Taylor & Francis, Ltd, www.informaworld.com).

"Notes from the inside: Forum Theater in maximum security" by Tim Mitchell in *Theater*, Volume 31, no. 3, 2001, pp. 55–61. Copyright, 2001, Yale School of Drama/Yale Repertory Theatre. All rights reserved. Republished with permission of the copyrightholder and the present publisher, Duke University Press. www.dukepress.edu.

"The subversive practices of reminiscence theatre in Taiwan" by Wan-Jung Wang, *Research in Drama Education, 11*(1), 2006. Reprinted with permission of the publisher (Taylor & Francis, Ltd, www.informaworld.com).

"The process and impact of intergenerational theatre making" by Jonathan Petherbridge and David Kendall. Reprinted with permission from Emerald Group Publishing, originally published in *Quality in Ageing and Older Adults, 13*(4), © Emerald Group Publishing Limited, 2012.

"Translating research findings into community based theatre: More than a dead man's wife" by Susan Feldman, Alan Hopgood and Marissa Dickins. *Journal of Aging Studies, 27*, 2013. Used with kind permission.

We dedicate this book to the memory of Augusto Boal. A giant in the field of applied theatre, he has left a legacy of practice that puts all practitioners, facilitators and applied theatre theorists in his debt.

It is not the place of the theatre to show the correct path
but only to offer the means by which all paths must be examined.

– Augusto Boal, 1985

November 2015
Victoria, British Columbia

PREFACE
WHAT IS THIS BOOK ABOUT?

In the seven years since we published the first edition of this text, applied theatre has continued to grow. A significant compilation of case studies and reflective theory about this artistic work appear in an extraordinarily wide variety of journals across disciplines such as theatre studies, education, health care, law and others. There is also a growing body of texts that addresses this discipline (Hartley, 2012; Kuppers & Robertson, 2007; Nicholson, 2005; Prentki & Preston, 2009; Taylor, 2003; Thompson, 2003, 2005, 2009; van Erven, 2001). Most recently, we are pleased to see a book series dedicated to applied theatre that takes up key concepts in contemporary research (Balfour et al., 2015; O'Connor & Anderson, 2015; Prentki, 2015; White, 2015). The second edition of this text continues to provide an international overview for students and practitioners anxious to acquire a basic understanding of what applied theatre is and how it works.

Since the publication of the first edition we have seen many shifts in practice that we reflect here in this edition. Chapter Three is a new chapter on story and storytelling in applied theatre. We felt that this chapter was needed for students and practitioners, as story is an essential component of theatre and theatre-making that was not directly discussed in the first edition. Chapter Five is a new chapter in *Part Two: The Landscape of Applied Theatre*. It emerged from our awareness of the growth of documentary theatre approaches in the field. We have refreshed the case study excerpts throughout the book and have included a total of 17 more recent examples from many locations. Our Further Reading lists have been expanded and updated and this edition offers Web Resources of projects and companies at the end of each chapter.

Part One offers three chapters that provide a brief historical and theoretical overview and a general analysis of the roots, contexts and contents of practice. They serve as a background against which readers may place their own experiences as well as their reading of the case studies that illustrate the ten categories of applied theatre that this text addresses. Following the introductory chapters, Part Two maps four core practices of applied theatre that we believe to be seminal to one's understanding of the field and presents case studies in Popular Theatre, Documentary Theatre, Theatre in Education and Theatre of the Oppressed. The chapters in Part Three identify genres that evolved from the core practices identified in Part Two and are defined in part by their intention: to heal, to raise sociopolitical awareness and to celebrate community through history and memory. In delineating these categories of practice, we recognize overlapping boundaries that can themselves serve as points of discussion reflecting the ongoing development of this collaborative art form. Each chapter includes a brief contextual overview followed by excerpted examples of case studies of applied theatre projects. Drawing on these, we offer sources for further reading and raise issues for examination and further investigation through questions for discussion. Each chapter concludes with suggestions for practical activities and Internet resources.

In assembling this text, we have selected from the diversity of applied theatre practices so that those new to the field or seeking examples of experience may gain a broader and deeper understanding of the potential challenges and rewards of working with communities – often non-experienced communities – through theatre. A number of readers may wonder why we have left out certain practices that some may consider to be applied theatre, such as drama therapy, simulations and employment skill training (e.g. with police, military, medical personnel and business people). Our decision is based on the recognition of *applied drama* as a process-based practice that does not generally involve a theatrical performance to an audience; this is the focus of our companion volume to this text (Prendergast & Saxton, 2013). While much of applied theatre begins as process, working in similar ways to applied drama, the word "theatre" (*theatron*: "seeing-place") means that a public or semi-public performance is a necessary component of the work (King, 1981, pp. 6–11).

The final chapters of Part Four address contemporary issues about which there is continuing discussion and upon which rests the success or failure of applied theatre work. These challenges of practice involve participation, ethics, aesthetics, assessment and reflection. The text provides an overview of examples of applied theatre work in order to open up the reader's appreciation for the breadth and depth of practice, and the final chapter and afterword begin to examine the properties that are indicative of effective facilitation and presentation.

Our selection process is focused on what we see as exemplary practices and draws on projects that have not previously appeared in book form; it is our intention to direct students of applied theatre to key journals in the field. The 38 case studies represent applied theatre practices on five continents and in 23 countries. This international scope points to the extraordinary power of theatre to engage and illuminate.

Invent [your] own path . . . Find your own way according to your particular personal needs, preferences, curiosities or desires.

Augusto Boal, 1998, p. ix

We have made every effort to keep words and punctuation as they appear in the original, but punctuation such as dashes, spacing and quotation marks have been standardized for ease of reading. Within the case studies, we use an ellipsis in brackets, […], to indicate a significant cut, a regular ellipsis, …, to indicate a small excision, and a spaced ellipsis, . . . , denotes the author's own punctuation. Each of the case studies we have selected is surrounded by a rich context of theory, other examples of practice and valuable insights that we could not include. We urge you to seek out the original articles and, following Augusto Boal's (1998) advice, invite you to choose those of interest and not necessarily to read them in the order in which they appear in the text.

While there are exceptional descriptions of the work in other languages, this text is limited to studies that have appeared in English or in English translations. The majority of these case studies have appeared in academic journals and are authored by scholars who may or may not be applied theatre practitioners themselves. We note with pleasure that in the intervening years between editions there is an increasing documentation by local practitioners and participants in their own voices.

The range of applied theatre practice is vast; it happens all over the world as part of a grass-roots arts-based movement committed to community reflection and social change. Wherever it happens, applied theatre offers a seeing-place where people can gather to share their stories; a doing-place to enact new possibilities of what-is, not-yet…

PART ONE

Theories, History and Practices of Applied Theatre

1.1 Where do we find applied theatre?

Popular Theatre: *Fashionable Immigration* is a University of Exeter popular theatre project that "attempt[s] to address the many misperceptions about immigration" (Price, 2011, p. 85). The play deals with a Polish girl named Anya who moves to Britain in search of work. She is exploited by an employer who confiscates her passport and forces her to work long hours under threat of being deported. Two laid-off local workers come to Anya's aid and help to rescue her from this situation. This show is performed in three different ways: as seventeenth-century *commedia dell'arte*, as a puppet show with giant 12-foot-high puppets and as a musical. Each of these popular theatre versions is assessed for its impact on audiences (Price, 2011).

Documentary Theatre: A South African community-based documentary theatre project, *Soil & Ash*, gathers stories from those affected by a proposed coal mine being built in their community (Dennill, 2014). The mine owners are allegedly conducting bribes and other tactics that are fracturing the community's sense of solidarity. The theatre project retells actual lived experiences and verbatim accounts of how the mine is affecting people, and how they feel it may effect them in the future. To do this, we cannot rely on the traditional theatre process in which stories are imagined or interpreted by a few separate people outside of the situation, and then merely dramatised on stage (Dennill, 2014, n.p.).

After each performance – held in community centres, local schools, churches and also at sports events – audiences engage with performers in a facilitated dialogue in which the actors may stay in character or speak as themselves.

Theatre in Education (TIE): Cardboard Citizen theatre company presents a TIE production in schools called *Home and Away* that addresses "an issue that has been thrust to the top of the political agenda in Britain in recent years, that of refugees and asylum seekers" (Jackson, 2005, p. 114). The play weaves together a traditional Ethiopian folk tale with the story of a young Ethiopian refugee living in England. The narrator, Teri, moves from ignorance to understanding as she encounters this young man and his culture; however, her empathy comes too late and he commits suicide. Following the performance, the audience is split into four groups, each actor working with a group to seek more positive endings. The company then moves into a forum theatre session where the actors and volunteer students test these "endings" out as the scenes are re-interpreted.

Theatre of the Oppressed (TO): Vancouver's Theatre for Living (formerly Headlines Theatre) creates a play in 2013 about mental health with six actors, one of whom is a former psychiatrist, and based on stories gathered widely from the community. The play, *Maladjusted: The Mental Health System. The People. The Play.*, presents the stories of a young girl struggling with depression and self-harm and a young man who is homeless and dealing with mental illness and addiction. The play examines the Canadian health system, which is viewed as mechanized in favour of the system over its clients. Audiences are challenged to change the play's outcomes to offer a more humanized health care system that places patients at the centre of care. Following the 30-minute play, scenes are re-played and stopped by audience members who replace actors and improvise in-role to try to alter the outcome (www.headlinestheatre.com).

Theatre for Health Education (THE): Health Action Theatre by Seniors, or HATS, is an applied theatre programme featuring senior volunteers who perform mimed scenarios on health topics for a diverse ethnic community. One production, "A Visit to the Doctor," has three scenes in which senior patients check-in and wait at a doctor's office, go through an appointment with the doctor and go for lunch at a cafeteria next door where one of them falls ill. Each scene involves frustrations, miscommunications and other challenges often experienced by senior immigrants trying to navigate the Canadian health care system. After the show, audience members are invited to stop the action as it is re-played to offer some solutions to the situations. HATS programs have successfully reached many senior immigrants in the lower income community of Parkdale, Toronto, in collaboration with St. Christopher House, a local community centre (www.hatstheatre.org).

Theatre for Development (TfD): A play entitled *Dukhini (Suffering Woman)* by Pakistan's Ajoka Theatre group exposes and explores:

> [...] the trafficking of women who are smuggled from poverty-stricken Bangladesh across India and into Pakistan under the false promise of a "better life," only to find themselves sold into prostitution to the highest

bidder. Under such an ideology, it is never the rapist/buyer of sex who is blamed but the woman who is raped or forced into prostitution – she has to bear the burden of having "dishonoured" her family, who will never accept her back because of the "shame" she has brought them. (Afzal-Khan, 2001, p. 67)

There are no happy endings for the women characters portrayed; they dream of returning home to their families but are trapped into slavery and prostitution by pimps who keep the women powerless and without hope. Ajoka Theatre, a 30-year-old company based in Lahore, continues to create and perform plays about development and peace issues and tours extensively (www.ajoka.org.pk).

Prison Theatre: *Journey Woman* is a week-long programme of theatre and drama-based work facilitated by England's Geese Theatre Company for female offenders and their caretakers. The week begins with a performance that follows the story of Ellie, a woman who has broken out of the cycle of hardship, offending and prison. Looking back on her life, Ellie revisits key episodes and moments of change: leaving home for the first time, her first involvement with offending, becoming a mother and her first prison sentence. Throughout the piece, the audience is invited to consider the different masks she has worn throughout her life, the different roles she has played and her different life stories. The audience members are enrolled as experts in Ellie's life, analysing the crucial moments, exploring her inner feelings and emotions and contemplating how moments from her past have impacted on her present and future. Geese Theatre, based in Birmingham, carries out its mask-based work in prisons, youth detention centres and with those on probation (www.geese.co.uk).

Community-based Theatre: Vancouver Moving Theatre (VMT) has carried out many community-based projects since 1983 in the Downtown Eastside neighbourhood, an area too well known for its high rates of drug addiction, crime, prostitution and poverty. *Storyweaver* is a project addressing Aboriginal community members' histories, struggles and resiliencies:

A cast of aboriginal artists, elders, dancers and Downtown Eastside community members help an old man – The Old One – open up to his life's journey, his regrets and hopes, through the teachings of the medicine wheel. His journey home gives voice to experiences of the urban aboriginal community, to voices not heard, to lives left behind.

VMT productions most often have dozens of cast members of many ages and cultural backgrounds (www.vancouvermovingtheatre.com).

Museum Theatre: At Washington's Smithsonian Institute in the summer of 2006, as part of an exhibit on transportation, a pretty young blonde girl dressed in 1950s fashion is found among the cars, buses and trucks of the period. She notices an audience gathering and tells them how excited she is because her boyfriend is coming and she hopes he is going to purchase a car. The boyfriend arrives and we discover that it is his parents who are buying the car and that they are already in the manager's office signing the papers. While the two young people are waiting, their conversation gives us a picture of how transportation played a major part of life in small-town America in the 1950s. Following this historical interpretation performance, the actors come out of role and engage the audience, many of whom are anxious to share their own experiences from that period, in a talkback discussion (Saxton, 2006).

Reminiscence Theatre: Toronto's Mixed Theatre Company performs *Old Age Ain't for Sissies* in 2013. Based on consultations with over 150 seniors in the Toronto area, playwright Rex Deverell's play takes place at a retirement party:

> For some the party heralds a glorious new era of freedom and adventure. For others it sounds a peal of doom. The drama is punctuated with songs resonating with the determination of seniors who want neither to be dismissed nor forgotten. … The production stars older actors with an array of backgrounds and experiences. … This interactive play invites the audience to come on stage, take on the role of one of the characters and explore possible options to the issues presented.

Mixed Theatre has been operating in Toronto for over 30 years and is committed to theatre as a tool for positive social change (www.mixedcompanytheatre.com).

1.2 What is applied theatre?

In our view, this "very capacious portmanteau term" (Giesekam, 2006, p. 91) is inclusive and does not carry any limiting fixed agendas. Instead, "the applied theatre label [is] a useful umbrella term . . . for finding links and connections for all of us committed to the power of theatre in making a difference in the human life span" (Taylor, 2006, p. 93). All of the above thumbnail narratives offer examples of a web of performance practices (Schechner, 1988/2003, pp. xvi–xix) that fall outside mainstream theatre performance and take place "in non-traditional settings and/or with marginalized communities" (Thompson & Jackson, 2006, p. 92). That is to say, these approaches to theatre most often are played in indoor and outdoor spaces that are not usually defined as theatre venues, with participants who may or may not be skilled in theatre arts and to audiences who have a vested interest in the issue taken up by the performance or are members

Applied theatre defies any one definition and includes a multitude of intentions, aesthetic processes and transactions with its participants.

Tim Prentki & Sheila Preston, 2009, p. 11

of the community addressed by the performance. Alternative theatre practices, including those described above, have historically been labelled with a number of diverse terms, such as grassroots theatre, social theatre, political theatre, radical theatre and many other variations. However, since 2000, "applied theatre" is the term that has emerged as the umbrella under which all of these prior terms and practices are embraced.

One example of how applied theatre can be different lies in the area of scripting. Whereas traditional mainstream theatre is most often centred in the interpretation of a pre-written script, applied theatre, in contrast, involves both the generation and the interpretation of a theatre piece that in performance may or may not be scripted in the traditional manner. In those cases where an applied theatre performance takes the form of a polished improvisation, a formally written script may never be recorded. There are very few complete examples of scripts, although the case studies that follow will often quote excerpts. As you read through these case studies, you will note the many ways in which applied theatre differs from "theatre" as most people would think of it.

1.3 Why applied theatre? How did it emerge?

Theatre has had an historic role in society as providing a relatively safe way of talking back to power. Across many cultures and traditions over time, we can trace patterns and instances of groups of people using the stage as a space and place to share their stories and their lives. This aesthetic and emotional outlet allows for potential *catharsis*, a safe way for citizens to express their concerns, criticisms and frustration to each other and to society at large. And often that opportunity has been enough. Some examples of this kind of theatrical expression are to be found around the world in the social dramas of rituals such as carnivals, Feast of Fools, initiation rites and through trickster figures in myths and legends – the servant figure in drama traditionally has had more power in the world of a play than his or her masters. The roots of Greek chorus, *commedia dell'arte*, Molière, Shakespeare and, closer to our own time, the comedies of George Bernard Shaw and Noël Coward, for example, have always been fed by this power reversal that is sanctioned and accepted within the protected space of the fictional world of the stage.

Catharsis (*katharsis*: purgation) is a Greek medical term that Aristotle uses to argue that tragedy does not encourage the passions but in fact rids (or purges) the spectator of them. Catharsis is a "beneficial, uplifting experience whether psychological, moral, intellectual or some combination of these."

Marvin Carlson, 1993, pp. 18–19

In modern western theatre history, playwrights such as Shaw, Henrik Ibsen and Bertolt Brecht offer a theatre of social criticism, debate and, in Brecht's case, potential revolutionary action. More contemporary playwrights, such as Caryl Churchill, Dario Fo, Wole Soyinka, Ariel Dorfman, Tony Kushner, Sarah Kane and many others, have focused much of their theatre on exposing and exploring social and political issues in their plays. Applied theatre is informed by these plays and playwrights to the extent that they offer clear models of how effective theatre can tackle a range of topical provocations and provide an aesthetic site for their considered examination.

Applied theatre works overtly either to reassert or to undermine sociopolitical norms, as its intent is to reveal more clearly the way the world is working. For example, reminiscence theatre, community-based theatre and museum theatre are most often reassertions and celebrations of memory and history. On the other hand, Theatre of the Oppressed, Popular Theatre, Theatre in Education, Theatre for Health Education and Theatre for Development are most often focused on undermining the status quo in order to promote positive social change. Prison Theatre and Documentary Theatre may fall within either depending on intention or context. Reassertions or undermining intentions are both ways by which we can re-examine the world to discover how it works and our place in it; they hold within them the potential to be educational, reflective and/or rehabilitative.

> All drama is…a political event: it either reasserts or undermines the code of conduct of a given society.
>
> Martin Esslin, 1976, p. 29

Marvin Carlson pointed out in 1993 that "[t]he continuing point of debate in modern theatre theory has been over whether the theatre should be viewed primarily as an engaged social phenomenon or as a politically indifferent aesthetic artefact" (p. 454). That debate continues. Herbert Blau criticizes theatre as aesthetic artefact (isolated and elitist), "a stronghold of non-ideas" (1965, p. 7). Theatre for Blau is a public art and one that should function at the "dead center of community" (p. 309). Like Brecht before him, Blau sees that the function of theatre lies with waking up the audience to its obligations and responsibilities through its collective imagination.

Using Bertolt Brecht's *lehrstücke* (short, severe and instructive works performed for audiences of students, workers and children [see Eyre & Wright, 2001, p. 204]) as the first indication in the twentieth century of a "new aesthetic" for theatre, we can begin to trace the threads of change through the work of Michael Kirby (1965) and Jerzy Grotowski (1968). Kirby wanted to rid theatre of the constraints of its conventional structure of plot (rising action, climax and dénouement) and replace it with something he called "compartmental structure" akin to collage (Carlson, 1993, p. 457). Compartmental structure

> To like the theatre you have to like its transience and its immediacy: it happens in the present tense and it's fallible. There's a sense of occasion in any theatre performance and of participation in a communal act: you go into a theatre as an individual and you emerge as an audience.
>
> Richard Eyre & Nicholas Wright, 2001, p. 11

As Carole Tarlington and Wendy Michaels (1995) explain, an applied theatre piece can be "linked logically, rather than temporally, to those [scenes] before and after it" (p. 20) foreshadows the often episodic nature of applied theatre presentations where scenes are linked by theme rather than plot development. Grotowski sought to create "archetypical images and actions that would force the spectator into an emotional involvement" (p. 455). He was interested in his highly trained actors addressing the needs of a small group of individuals in a totally open way (p. 457). Even such a theatrical anchor as intention or purpose was questioned by French theorist practitioners such as Fernando Arrabal (1973). Arrabal and his circle prefigured chaos theory by their abandonment of structure and the invitation to include "the widest possible elements" that embraced such opposites as "the sacred and the profane, executions and celebrations of life, the sordid and the sublime" (Arrabal, 1973, p. 98).

Richard Kostelanetz in 1968 drew attention to other significant shifts, of which two are important for our study here. "Staged performances" were much like traditional theatre but without the reliance on words. They were strongly movement-oriented and the actors performed without masks as themselves or as a kind of "neutral sign," the emphasis being on the experience itself and the *process of creation* rather than the *product of creative acts* (Carlson, 1993, p. 461, italics ours). Audiences, too, began to be recognized by theatre makers as integral to the wholeness of a performance. But after a couple of centuries of being quiet and in the dark, audiences did not always take kindly to this new attention; even today, being "recognized by the stage" can make people embarrassed or uneasy. The playwright Peter Handke attempted to revitalize the audience by making them conscious that "they are there, that they exist" (cited in Carlson, 1993, p. 462). Richard Foreman (1976) took this idea further by creating theatre pieces that were deliberately intended to lead the audience to become more self-aware and self-reflexive. Many of these "new" ideas came together in the work of Peter Brook (1968), whose theatre-making was designed to join spectators, actors and performance in a "communal celebration of experience" (Carlson, 1993, p. 464).

The relationship between the actor and the audience is the only theatre reality.

Peter Brook in Croyden, 2003, p. 28

It was clear by the middle of the twentieth century, notable for the dazzling pace of its change, that the relationship between actors, audiences and performance structures was undergoing significant shifts in aesthetic understanding. Indeed, 1968 has become for theatre historians, theorists and practitioners the dividing line between the traditional and the new theatre. The Avignon Manifesto, an open letter from young theatre radicals inspired by the student and worker uprising in Paris in 1968, makes the shift clear. It called for a theatre of "'collective creation' with no schism between artistic activities and 'political, social, and everyday events,' a theatre of 'political and psychological liberation' of 'direct rather than represented action,' which would place the spectator no longer in an 'alienated and underdeveloped situation'" (Copferman, 1972, cited in Carlson, 1993, p. 471).

There are three writers whose theory and practice are of particular interest as we explore the antecedents of applied theatre: Armand Gatti, John O'Toole and Augusto Boal. French director Armand Gatti, like Kirby, was intent on freeing theatre from its reliance on sequential time: theatrical action for Gatti was most generative when it allowed spectators/ participants to see the same thing from a number of different viewpoints, where endings remained open and available to questions. He was a forerunner of the popular theatre movement – a people's theatre, a theatre engaged with the popular culture of post-World War II society and belonging to it (Prentki & Selman, 2000). For this revolutionary theatre artist, the function of theatre was to enable "the disinherited classes" to create a theatre that reflected their concerns – not through performances *for* them but *with* them. He did this through a series of what he called *mini-pièces* – short scenes encouraging reflection, which might lead later to further action that could perhaps alleviate those concerns to some degree. Gatti saw himself not as a playwright but as a "catalyst of the creative powers of the people of the community" (Knowles, 1989, p. 202), and he saw the theatre as the means of giving language to those who lacked the words to describe their social situations.

The second practitioner/theorist was John O'Toole, whose 1976 text, *Theatre in education: New objectives for theatre – new techniques for education*, describes and analyses a number of UK-based case studies of school performances. In this seminal text, O'Toole lays the foundations that resulted in a vigorous two decades of TIE practice in England that still informs effective applied theatre practice today. In Chapter 5, "The perils and pleasure of participation," O'Toole draws our attention to a number of strategies and techniques used by various teams of actors to engage the audiences through what he calls "integral" participation in which the audience "acts as well as being acted upon" (p. 88). One of the most effective ways, he notes, is when:

> [O]ne or two brave teams have taken [the technique of hot seating] further and stopped the action for the children to discuss the situation with the characters, who then carried on the play according to the advice the children gave them. (p. 97)

This is, he suggests, a "technique worth exploring in more depth and more frequently" (p. 97).

This responsive, improvisatory strategy was taken up by Brazilian director Augusto Boal – founder of Theatre of the Oppressed – and became a key concept in his Forum Theatre. Boal himself was deeply influenced by Paolo Freire's *Pedagogy of the Oppressed* (1970/2000) that aims to empower learners as active agents in their own education. Similarly, Boal empowered theatre spectators to step into the action and change the outcome of a dramatic situation related to their lives. He called this process "rehearsal for the revolution" (Boal, 1979, p. 122). Indeed, the practice of engaging the audience interactively with the performance (before, during or after the performance – and sometimes all three), as seen in the work of Gatti, O'Toole and Boal, is a consistent characteristic of all forms of applied theatre.

This brief historical overview enables us to identify the strands that are integral to the fabric of applied theatre as an engaged, social, artistic phenomenon, and some of the characteristics of its practices:

- focus on multiple perspectives
- disregard for sequence as fundamental to effective structure
- endings that remain open for questioning
- less reliance on words; more exploration of movement and image as theatre language
- greater reliance on polished improvisation
- theatre as a close, direct reflection of actual life with an overt political intent to raise awareness and to generate change
- a collective approach to creating theatre pieces in which the makers themselves become aware and capable of change
- issues of local importance that may or may not be transferable to other communities
- audience as an important and active participant in the creation of understanding and, often, of the action

All of these shifts occurred inside a wider sociopolitical and economic context. The last half of the twentieth century boiled with new thought and was influenced by such things as the fall of the Berlin Wall, feminism, globalism, the Space Race, chaos and complexity theory, and the rise of the individual ready to question authority and ask "Who holds the power?" and "By what right?" In recent years, theories on *postdramatic theatre* (Lehmann, 2006) – that is theatre forms that are less driven by traditional models of character and plot development – have had an influence on theatre practices worldwide. Applied theatre, like all art, both reflected this new awareness and had foretold it in the practice and theory of earlier playwrights, actors and directors who were already laying the foundations for a more public art that truly functions at the living centre of its communities.

1.4 What is the purpose of applied theatre?

Theatre artists have always turned to their art form as a means of finding their way through crises and challenges: for example, Jean Anouilh's subversive adaptation of *Antigone* (1942/1951) was performed in Paris under the Nazi regime; Tony Kushner's *Angels in America* (1993) challenged audiences to address the reality of HIV/AIDS. This is theatre as activism, enfolded in the "safety" of entertainment, which rises "spontaneously from within situations of war, insurgency, political and civil crisis" and has long been a part of theatre tradition (McDonnell, 2006, p. 2). Another impetus for applied theatre involves "self-conscious attempts to influence political reality" (p. 2), using theatre as a facilitated intervention from the outside with communities for whom theatricality is not intrinsic. This interventionist theatre is the primary focus of this text.

James Thompson (2003) writes about the nature of intervention in applied theatre:

> Much applied theatre in its 'intentional' form creates a practice that seeks to debate vital issues and see those concerns transformed into new stories or within unfamiliar settings. . . . [It is a way] to provide people with a means to work their way through difficult transitory periods [as an] aid in seeing them safely into a new place or time.
>
> (pp. 200–202)

Interventionist theatre may be generated in a number of ways:

- An outside organization, generally a theatre group or individual facilitator, is aware of or is invited into a site that is struggling with sociopolitical issues. The needs expressed by the community become the themes explored through theatre processes and presented back to the community as a theatre piece.
- An outside agency commissions a theatre production for (or with) a target group to tackle a specific topic or issue for various purposes, most often educational.
- A facilitator or theatre company instigates a community-based theatre project that aims to celebrate or memorialize some aspect of the community for the psychological/emotional health of that group.

What is most helpful in guiding our understanding of these interventionist models is the distinction between *presentational* and *representational* forms of theatre. *Representational* theatre has as its organizing principle the creation of another fictional and hypothetical onstage world performed by actors who are intentionally hidden behind the mask of character from those who sit and observe in the audience. This theatre form represents people, times and places that are similar to or different from our contemporary reality but is clearly fictional and functions under the rubric of "the willing suspension of disbelief" (Coleridge, 1817). *Presentational* theatre, in contrast, is more interested in presenting non-fictional material within thinly disguised fictions of authentic contemporary reality. The actor in presentational theatre is less hidden behind the mask of character and is closer to being him or herself – although still protected by the safety of the role – thus enabling the actor to present

In believed-in performances people are who they perform, playing their social and/or personal identities: judges, accused, rabbis, lawyers, teachers, activists, bus drivers, lovers, whoever.

Richard Schechner, 1998, p. 77

12

a character who lives in the world of the audience as well as the world of the play. It is this latter presentational form that most often manifests in applied theatre practice. Bernard Beckerman (1990) summarizes the difference between representational and presentational theatre:

> What is normally called dramatic presentation is actually a form of *direct* presentation. The performer acknowledges the presence of the audience and presents the show making that acknowledgement explicit. This type of playing differs from the *indirect* form of presentation where the performer supposedly does not "admit" the presence of the audience and acts as though the activity performed has an autonomous existence. (pp. 110–111)

Whereas in representational theatre a fourth wall is in place much of the time, in presentational theatre the fourth wall is permeable, transparent and often breached by audience members who directly participate in the action of the play.

Applied theatre is not only local in its attention to the everyday world. It is also contemporaneously concerned with the greater issues of active citizenship and democratic practice (Nicholson, 2005) framed in the aesthetic structures of theatre, the most social of art forms. It is the negotiation of the aesthetic with the everyday through the medium of theatre that results in the variety of forms of applied theatre.

Summary

We hope that this overview of the history and aspects of theatre theory that are applicable will stand as useful background for the applied theatre practices that we now begin to examine. Remember that most contemporary theatre strategies and techniques you will read about in the case studies are based on the experiences of people whose own practice served as the playing space from which their theoretical understandings grew. As you develop your own practice, we urge you to write about it in ways that will enable those who follow you to learn from your experiences. Applied theatre is a multifaceted field and all of us who work in it (and on it) have a responsibility not just to those who come after us but also to those with whom – and for whom – we create the work. You will note that there would be little for you to read without the commitment and contributions of theatre practitioners and, especially, of applied theatre participants.

Simon Shepherd and Mick Wallis discuss presentation and representation from a theoretical perspective in their book *Drama/Theatre/Performance* (2004, pp. 225–235).

Further Reading

Ackroyd, J. (2000). Applied theatre: Problems and possibilities. *Applied Theatre Researcher*, *1*(1), unpaginated. Retrieved from http://www.griffith.edu.au/__data/assets/pdf_file/0004/81796/Ackroyd.pdf. Ackroyd raises some important questions and concerns for anyone interested in applied theatre to consider. You might also be interested in Ackroyd, J. (2007). Applied theatre: An exclusionary discourse? *Applied Theatre Researcher/IDEA Journal*, *8* (unpaginated) in which she revisits her earlier comments in terms of later developments. Retrieved from http://www.griffith.edu.au/__data/assets/pdf_file/0005/52889/01-ackroyd-final.pdf.

Balfour, M. & Somers, J. (Eds.). (2006). *Drama as social intervention*. Concord, ON: Captus. This is a collection of keynote speeches, papers and abstracts from the Research in Drama Education triennial conference of 2005.

Prentki, T. & Preston, S. (Eds.). (2008). *The applied theatre reader*. London, UK: Routledge. This text provides an indispensable collection of writings by theorists and practitioners that will deepen your knowledge of the field.

Preston, S. & Balfour, M. (Eds.). (2015). *Applied theatre* [Book series]. London, UK: Bloomsbury. This series of books from key theorists and practitioners is a welcome addition to the growing library in the field. The first four books in the series are on Aesthetics, Development, Research and Resettlement.

Taylor, P. (2003). *Applied theatre: Creating transformative encounters in the community*. Portsmouth, NH: Heinemann. This is a good introduction that employs theory in practice and practice in theory as Taylor reflects on his own and other applied theatre practitioners' work.

Thompson, J. (2003). *Applied theatre: Bewilderment and beyond*. New York, NY: Peter Lang.

Thompson, J. (2005). *Digging up stories: Applied theatre, performance and war*. Manchester: Manchester University Press.

Thompson, J. (2009). *Performance affects: Applied theatre and the end of effect*. New York, NY: Palgrave Macmillan. Thompson writes a wide-ranging analysis and description of work and practice in the United Kingdom and other countries. He interrogates many of the ethical and practical issues that arise in applied theatre.

Questions for Reflection and Discussion

1. In what ways might any theatre experiences you have had, either as artist or audience, resonate with any of the examples given in this introduction?

2. What can we learn from the history of applied theatre? How could we use this knowledge in our practice?

Suggested Activities

1. How would you describe applied theatre to someone who has not read this introduction or experienced applied theatre in other ways? Working with a partner or a group of three, take turns role-playing this conversation.

2. Reread the thumbnail descriptions of applied theatre practices (pp. 1–6). Which of these types of applied theatre most draws your interest? What is it that attracts you to this particular form? Write a reflection that begins with, "I could see myself working in this particular area of applied theatre because…."

CHAPTER TWO
PRACTICES OF APPLIED THEATRE

2.1 How do we make applied theatre?

Facilitation

As in so much of applied theatre, there are a number of terms for those who work in theatre with communities – teaching artist, director, co-creator, artistic assistant, Joker (Boal's term) and so on – but "facilitator" seems to be the most common and, in terms of its original meaning (to make easy), the most appropriate. The applied theatre facilitator is a multidisciplinarian who must know about theatre and how it works, as well as have an understanding of teaching and learning. It is this knowledge and these skills that make the work easier for those for whom theatre is unknown territory. In addition, a facilitator should be familiar with the social structures and community contexts within which he or she may be working. There are all-too-common instances of applied theatre projects being led by facilitators with insufficient knowledge and experience that result in experiences of little impact or value for anyone, either for those involved or those attending. Sullivan (2004), in delineating the skills of the Joker in Forum Theatre, describes the skills that all effective facilitators need as they function as the "conductor of the energies, intentions and desires released" (p. 23) during the devising and rehearsal process as well as (when appropriate) during performances:

> [The facilitator]…must be able to sense and serve the needs of the audience, and create a safe container for individual self-expression as well as manage the segues among performance of scenes, spect-actor interventions, processing the results of dramatic ideas from the audience, and direct communication with the audience. Effective [facilitators] must combine the skill of dramaturg, director, improvisational actor, drama therapist, political philosopher, rhetorician, talk show host and stand-up comic. (p. 23)

We see applied theatre facilitation as essentially grounded in drama and theatre and in education strategies and techniques, having close kinship with good pedagogical praxis. That is to say, a facilitator knows how to do something, why it is appropriate, when it needs to be done and how to do it in the most effective way. These are skills that require training and experience. In addition, participants benefit from a facilitator who is a communicator and a listener, and possesses both social and empathic intelligence (Arnold, 2005; Goleman, 1995, 2006) in order to work with people in groups and help them arrive at decisions. Facilitation requires skills of diplomacy as this kind of work is fraught with difficulties around what is left in and what is taken out and how an aesthetic product is shaped out of dramatic process. Also key to applied theatre facilitation is the recognition that the community participants – both actors and spectators – hold the knowledge of the subject under investigation, whereas the facilitator holds the aesthetic knowledge of the theatre form.

Scripting

An applied theatre process is a collaborative and negotiated dance choreographed between people for whom the content is significant and applied theatre facilitators, dramaturgs and/or playwrights who have both competencies and experience. In certain models of applied theatre practice, a playwright will be commissioned to write a play based on research, interviews and other primary sources. The playwright will often be involved in the rehearsal process to rewrite and restructure the play. In the case of a dramaturg, it is the participants who are doing the interviewing, retelling their stories, improvising and researching. Those contributions are then assembled and shaped by the dramaturg, who is involved in an ongoing way in the process.

A dramaturg is "the literary adviser associated with a theatre company" who may carry out documentary research, adapt the text, determine how meanings are linked, identify ambiguities, put forth possible inter- pretations and integrate the perspective and reception of the spectator.

Patrice Pavis, 1998, pp. 122–123

The facilitator, in many cases, may take on the role of dramaturg because he or she knows the discipline and theory of aesthetic strategies and understands how to use them within a pedagogy of practice. Most often, however, performances in applied theatre are playbuilt.

Playbuilding

Playbuilding is the root theatre activity of applied theatre practice and is a constant process of negotiated meaning-making. Playbuilding is also called "collective creation" or "devising." Collective creation emerges from late twentieth-century theatre practice and describes the creation of an original play based on documents or living research by a group of skilled performers often working with a director and/or dramaturg. Some examples in a Canadian context are *The Farm Show* (Theatre Passe Muraille) and *Paper Wheat* (25th Street Theatre), both created by urban professional theatre companies interested in exploring

For an interview with Peter Cheeseman, an exemplar of early documentary theatre, see Giannachi and Luckhurst's *On directing* (1999, pp. 13–20).

rural issues of farming in sociopolitical contexts (see Filewod, 1987). Devising is a British/European term referring to the gestation phase of the theatre-making process; the first of a number of stages leading to some kind of performance outcome. Alison Oddey (1996) describes devising as:

> [A] process of making theatre that enables a group of performers to be physically and practically creative in the sharing and shaping of an original product that directly emanates from assembling, editing, and re-shaping individuals' contradictory experiences of the world. . . . Devising is about thinking, conceiving, and forming ideas, being imaginative and spontaneous, as well as planning. It is about inventing, adapting, and creating what you do as a group. (p. 1)

When we talk about a piece of theatre that has been devised, it suggests that the work was originally created through democratic processes of exploration utilizing many forms of improvisation. Recently the term "ensemble theatre" has emerged that describes the work of theatre companies and artists dedicated to creating and performing their own collective works (Bonczek & Storck, 2013; Britton, 2013). We choose to use the term "playbuilding," a name that implies not just the process of building through devising/collective creation, but also the intended outcome – that is, the development of some kind of theatre performance. These performances are generally not "plays" in the traditional sense but rather a more postdramatic form that involves a variety of genres built around a particular theme. Errol Bray (1991) writes that the ensemble work of playbuilding:

> ...enables a participant to come to grips with the pleasures and problems of every aspect of drama and theatre; to be playwright, performer, director, composer, technician, designer, critic. It introduces participants to the creative discipline and co-operation required in theatre . . . . The process involves rehearsing the play as it is created, thus developing a strong presentation that comes to belong to the group in a very personal and committed way. (p. 1)

In applied theatre, the presentation then becomes the stimulus for engagement with a larger community (the audience) about the issues and themes under investigation. This conversation itself leads to the broader possibility of sociopolitical revelation and/or change. Even an applied theatre project intended primarily as a community celebration holds within its presentation the possibility of communal reflection and fresh envisioning.

2.2 Who are the performers of applied theatre?

Performance is always a component of applied theatre. There are different kinds of performers in applied theatre projects, ranging from highly skilled professionals to community participants with little or no experience. For professional actors who choose to work in applied theatre, there are particular skills required. Professional actors are, of course, used to touring and are adaptable to ever-changing conditions. They should also be able to both sing and dance (skills very important in performances for children and senior citizens) and be comfortable working in non-theatre spaces where there is no fourth wall. The ability of performers to engage directly with audiences – before, during and after a performance – is key.

When non-professional actors form a company, it is essential that the facilitator pays attention to the social and emotional health of the group in addition to teaching necessary performance skills. In a community-based model, facilitation involves enabling unskilled participants to function collaboratively within a dramatic process and to develop the skills that will allow them to move confidently out of the process into presentation. Often one of the goals will be to enable participants to continue the work of development and facilitation after the facilitator has left. This highlights the importance of time spent in rehearsal on the development of acting skills through improvisation, role play, characterization, movement and voice. The most important process in group development focuses on trust and safety so that unskilled performers become comfortable in risking themselves in performance. The job of the facilitator is to then negotiate, post-performance, between the performers and the audience as they reflect together upon issues that have been raised. There are, however, some circumstances where the facilitation may be undertaken by the actors or mediated by a non-theatre professional. For example, Somers and Roberts (2006) discuss a play on schizophrenia in which the post-performance discussion was led by an experienced psychiatric nurse (p. 32).

> [A] devising group working creatively under pressure is a particularly delicate species, with a fragile and volatile membership. It needs to be nurtured.
>
> Gil Lamden, 2000, p. 88

2.3 Who is applied theatre for?

Inherent within these models of applied theatre is the participatory element that carries forward from the rehearsal process into the performance and beyond through the interaction between performers, audience and facilitators. Simply put, like all good theatre, applied theatre is for an audience. In mainstream theatre performances, the interaction between audiences and performers is in most cases minimal and limited

Integral participation occurs when "individual or small group contributions [are] registered, considered and…acted upon."

John O'Toole, 1976, p. 104

to reactions within the performance that do not alter the outcome. In applied theatre, the opposite is true. Audiences are invited to engage both verbally and, in some cases, physically with the performance and their presence may be acknowledged by the performers before, during and/or afterwards. O'Toole (1976) calls this kind of audience participation "integral" in that this participation has the power to effect changes to the performance itself in a number of ways (p. 104). At the very least, an applied theatre piece will generally include a carefully facilitated post-show discussion that gives spectators the space needed to process and respond to what they have seen – what O'Toole calls "extrinsic" participation (p. 88). In other cases, a pre-show interaction with the audience may be necessary, especially when an audience is relatively inexperienced in spectatorship. This preparatory interaction invites the audience into the dramatic process and gives them guidelines as to their role in the performance. At other times, the audiences may be invited to a follow-up workshop in skills exhibited in the performance or used in making the performance. But, for O'Toole, this "peripheral" participation gives the audiences little power because whatever they may do or say, the structure of the play is unalterable (p. 88). Integral audience participation is directly opposite as it can involve speaking directly to characters as they engage with problems that need to be addressed, calling out suggestions for possible improvised responses to dramatic situations or, as in Boal's Theatre of the Oppressed, actually taking the place of a character and performing alternative solutions to a dilemma. An applied theatre facilitator needs to be very sensitive to the particular culture of the community for which the applied theatre piece is to be played, as there are many culturally diverse practices of audience response.

2.4 What are the interactions between actors, spectators and facilitators in applied theatre?

Play, games, sports and sacred and secular rituals are all forms of performance (Schechner, 1988/2003, 2002; Schechner & Delamont, 2013). In all of these, the audience is expected and encouraged to participate, either verbally, physically or both. In his analysis of these performance forms, Richard Schechner distinguishes between an *integral* and an *accidental* audience:

> An accidental audience is a group of people who, individually or in small clusters, go to the theater – the performances are publicly advertised and open to all. On opening nights of commercial shows, the attendance of the critics and friends constitutes an integral rather than an accidental

audience. An integral audience is one where people come because they have to or because the event is of special significance to them. Integral audiences include the relatives of the bride and groom at a wedding, the tribe assembled for initiation rites, dignitaries on the podium for an inauguration. (1988/2003, p. 220)

Schechner goes on to suggest that "an accidental audience comes 'to see the show' while the integral audience is 'necessary to accomplish the work of the show'" (p. 220).

We see four distinct models of actor/participant/spectator/facilitator interaction in applied theatre. An applied theatre project may draw upon one or more of these models, depending on its intentions. It is useful to note that the first two models below are generally engaged with integral audiences while the last two can move from integral to accidental audience engagement. In some applied theatre models, a script is generated with (and for) a particular community group but is then transferred to and performed by a troupe of skilled actors. This is seen most clearly in reminiscence theatre where interviews with seniors become the basis for making an applied theatre piece that is subsequently performed by professional actors for the seniors and their community. These models often involve the audience working after the performance with facilitators and actors (who may remain in role) and/or with drama-based activities to unpack the content of the performance. These four models, illustrated throughout the book, are:

In community conversations, "the focus is not on understanding theatrical craft or appreciating the skill of directors and designers, but rather on the potential for communities to express their own anxieties and hopes."

Anne Ellis, 2000, pp. 91–92

1. **Community-based model:** A piece of theatre is created for, with and by community participants primarily for an integral audience. This process is usually facilitated by one or more outside applied theatre facilitators. Their responsibilities carry beyond their facilitation of the process into the "community conversations" (Ellis, 2000, p. 91) that follow the presentations.

2. **Curriculum model:** A skilled group selects or is contracted to engage with a topical issue and generates a theatre piece for performance in the community, primarily for the purposes of education. As in the community-based model (above), the audience is generally integral.

3. **Transfer model:** A community-based applied theatre project and presentation to be performed for a more accidental audience is transferred to and adapted by a skilled acting troupe. For example, a local presentation may prove so successful that it is invited to tour outside the context of its origins.

4. **Interview model:** Interviews become the basis for an applied theatre piece that is subsequently performed for the interviewees and their community by a group of skilled actors. This model ideally involves inviting interviewees into the rehearsal process to evaluate the authenticity of the transcribed interviews into dramatic forms, as well as the usual post-show responses through community conversations.

Those who create and spectate in applied theatre have a concern for the issue or issues under consideration and are interested in collectively reflecting upon them. This process does not necessarily apply to mainstream theatre, where actors and audiences may have considerably less personal investment in the content of the play. The potential success of any applied theatre piece relies on the fact that the concerns, issues or ideas are available to an audience – that is, that the drama portrayed has relevance and resonance with the lives of those who witness it. Reflecting with an audience on how and why a performance works in terms of the meanings it makes, or fails to make, is a key component in gauging the impact of applied theatre.

2.5 How do we assess applied theatre?

Assessment depends upon which model of applied theatre is being evaluated. When external agencies are involved in the evaluative process, their interests will generally be around questions of efficiency and effectiveness. The financial commitment of an outside agency dictates that the measures of success will be primarily attached to the outcomes of the original purposes of the project. For example, in an applied theatre project intended to increase human organ donation, the number of organ donation cards signed by audience members became an indicator of success (Saxton & Miller, 2006, pp. 132–133). On the other hand, a presentation to raise audience awareness of patient issues with breast cancer did not have outcomes that could be assessed beyond the anecdotal or second-hand accounts (Gray & Sinding, 2002). In a third case, the question of what is to be valued and voiced publicly becomes even more complicated when the applied theatre company's purpose is to generate a community conversation on, for example, the societal challenges faced by lesbian, gay, bisexual and transgendered (LGBT) students (Freire, 2007). Assessment in cases such as this can be very "murky" as Paul Newman (2008) has pointed out.

> Drama cannot instruct. It confronts, perplexes and intrigues imagination into recreating reality.
>
> Edward Bond, 1996, p. xxxiv

A key question for any applied theatre company is: how do we balance privacy and protection with the need to prove worth? Outside agencies will likely employ evaluative language and terms concerned with efficiency and effectiveness that are not necessarily consonant with aesthetic performance practices. This is because they are interested, as performance theorist Jon McKenzie (2001) puts it, "in the bottom line: maximizing outputs and minimizing inputs" (p. 81).

Efficacy (*n*): Power to produce a desired affect or result.

Clarence Barnhart, 1965,
p. 264

To help us sort out these problems, McKenzie (2001) traces the use of the word *performance* in three distinct fields of contemporary society: culture, economics and technology. He suggests that cultural performance is centrally concerned with issues of *social efficacy*, or social justice – that is to say, how performance positively assists us in understanding ourselves, seeing ourselves, re-forming ourselves in relation to the culture that surrounds us and/or transforming the culture itself through performative actions (pp. 29–54). McKenzie sees the notion of *challenge* to be at the core of performance, however and wherever it may be used and found.

McKenzie's theory of performance as *social efficacy* allows us to limit assessment language in applied theatre to the realm of the efficacy of a process, not the efficiency and/or effectiveness of an intervention. Efficacy has the etymological root meaning "power" and is therefore an appropriate location for assessment rather than in realms of economic efficiency and technological effectiveness (pp. 55–81, 106–130).

One of the most appropriate assessment strategies, given this philosophical position in regard to social efficacy, is "contemplative assessment" (Morgan & Saxton, 1987, p. 198). "The nature of contemplative assessment is that it occurs outside the drama and thus outside the timeframe of drama ... [I]t cannot change the nature of the dramatic experience itself but is a result of it" (p. 198). This approach is concerned more with asking better questions than in finding the "right" answers (Morgan & Saxton, 1995/2006). Jackson and Lev-Aladgem (2004) follow this principle as they document audience involvement and responses and what is remembered over the long term of a theatre in education piece about teenage pregnancy (pp. 225–230). Prendergast (2008) offers a question series for audiences and performers to share as a guide for processing theatre experiences, among which are:

- What new questions has this performance generated in me?
- How do they shift my being in the world? (p. 143)

Assessment strategies in applied theatre should be context-driven and centrally concerned with giving voice to the participants: actors and spectators alike. Thus, assessment in applied theatre is primarily focused on "*what* is being interpreted rather than *how* it is being done [in the recognition that] it is not possible to prove the success of applied theatre performances quantitatively" (Saxton & Miller, 2006, pp. 134–135). Qualitative approaches to assessing move away from measuring how a presentation has succeeded or failed and towards considering its broader effect and affect on individuals and communities.

2.6 What are the key areas to effective applied theatre practice?

We invite you to consider keeping a self-reflective response journal as an extremely useful way to trace your journeys of discovery as you read. We also invite you to create an "operations manual" by logging those techniques and strategies in applied theatre practice that you find resonate with your own interests and learning experiences. In addition, you will find that many of the following case studies address four areas key to effective practice. The final chapter of this text examines these areas in more detail. We offer here some guiding questions in these four areas for you to consider as you reflect upon your reading of these case studies:

1. **Participation:** How key to effective practice are interactive collaborative processes that engage performers and their audiences with the material? How do we ensure that the quality of participation between facilitators and community players is as important a consideration as the quality of participation with audiences at the performance stage? How central are power relations to all participatory elements of an applied theatre process? How can these relations be made evident and kept in continuous negotiation?

2. **Aesthetics:** These are the qualities of an artistic work that we can identify and value. For example, how does a performance engage our multiple senses (hearing, sight, touch, smell and taste), exhibit moments of beauty, harmony, metaphor/symbol, recognition and surprise and use the elements of theatre (focus, tension, sight/sound, dark/light, movement/stillness [Wagner, 1976, pp. 148–158])? In what ways do the contexts of any given applied theatre project directly affect the aesthetic/artistic choices made by participants and the values generated from the work by audiences?

3. **Ethics/Safety:** Applied theatre takes as its first principle, "Do no harm." How can we better understand the cultural and sociopolitical boundaries through which we cross back and forth to do our work? How do we begin to generate our work in communities that do not know or care to know our work? How do we establish a way of working that helps communities or groups of individuals to create events that are self-determining and structured on principles agreed upon by the group? What is being left behind after an applied theatre intervention that allows for and generates further community thought and action?

4. **Assessment:** This is a huge problem for the arts and for applied theatre workers, as you may have gathered from your reading so far. How can we lay out a programme that is emergent in nature and cannot be predetermined? How can we guarantee a product? How can we measure the learning? What timelines can we realistically envision?

As you read through the examples in each chapter, you will become aware of the extraordinary range of strategies that promote the efficacy rather than the efficiency of an applied theatre project. You may also become aware of how much attention has been paid to the challenges presented by the four key areas we have outlined – particularly of assessment and exit strategies in applied theatre. Your reading and practice together should help you to begin to understand why and how you might address these issues.

Summary

This overview of applied theatre will have given you some understanding of the complexities and range of activities and approaches that make up the field. It is no doubt a challenging field within which to work, offering what Dorothy Heathcote calls a "treasure/burden" in the responsibilities to ethically care for and to artistically provoke community participants. In the last chapter of this introductory section, we address the significance of story and storytelling as fundamental tools of applied theatre.

> What it means to be a good citizen in pluralist societies is fraught with ambiguities and contradictions, requiring a revitalized political vocabulary and a renewed concept of radical citizenship.
>
> Helen Nicholson, 2005, p. 20

Further Reading

Bray, E. (1991). *Playbuilding: A guide for group creation of plays with young people.* Paddington, NSW: Currency. This is a seminal text on building plays from the bottom up. Full of examples of various types of playbuilt scripts.

Govan, E., Nicholson, H. & Normington, K. (2010). *Making a performance: Devising histories and contemporary practices.* London, UK: Routledge. A survey of twentieth- and twenty-first-century devising practices, mostly in the United Kingdom.

Graham, S. & Hoggett, S. (2014). *The Frantic Assembly book of devising theatre.* London, UK: Routledge. Frantic Assembly is a UK-based physical theatre company with over 20 years of devising works. This handbook outlines their collaborative processes.

Hartley, J.S. (2012). *Applied theatre in action: A journey.* Stoke-on-Trent, UK: Trentham. Hartley writes about her work in South America, the United States, Africa and the United Kingdom in always challenging settings. While her work is a blend of therapy and theatre that requires expertise, her projects are exemplary and she is an excellent storyteller.

Hoare, L. (2013). Challenging facilitation: Training facilitators for Theatre for Dialogue programmes. In A. Jackson & C. Vine (Eds.), *Learning through theatre: The changing face of theatre in education* (3rd ed., pp. 142-154). London, UK: Routledge. Good practical advice on how to best facilitate interactions that deal with sensitive issues.

Lamden, G. (2000). *Devising: A handbook for drama and theatre students.* Abingdon, UK: Hodder & Stoughton. A well-organized and accessible practical manual focused on the development of devising skills.

Neelands, J. & Dobson, W. (2008). *Advanced drama and theatre studies* (2nd ed.). London, UK: Hodder Education. This textbook for upper-level secondary students offers an excellent chapter on devising.

Rohd, M. (1998). *Theatre for community, conflict & dialogue: The Hope is Vital training manual.* Portsmouth, NH: Heinemann. An excellent manual for working with groups, particularly for building trust and generating story.

Weigler, W. (2001). *Strategies for playbuilding: Helping groups translate issues into theatre.* Portsmouth, NH: Heinemann. Full of ideas for working with groups based on Weigler's extensive practice in community-based theatre. Includes checklists and handouts to help facilitators guide participants in their decision-making processes.

Questions for Reflection and Discussion

1. In looking at your own community, where is applied theatre happening? Where might it happen and with whom? What community groups could benefit from an applied theatre project?

2. What experiences have you had in playbuilding or devising? What might have been some of the artistic or ethical challenges you remember occurring and how were they addressed if at all?

Suggested Activities

1. Choose a possible place in your community where you could imagine initiating an applied theatre project. Who would it serve? Who would participate? Who would make up the audience? What sort of awareness might be raised? In a paragraph, write a summary of the project including this information. Attach any relevant pamphlets, brochures, etc.

2. What sorts of knowledge and experience might best prepare an applied theatre practitioner? Examine a university or college calendar and list those courses that you (and your group) would consider to be essential or useful.

Chapter Three
Story, Storytelling and Applied Theatre

3.1 How is story related to applied theatre?

Story sits at the heart of applied theatre. The earliest theatre that we know were stories around the fire enacted through movement and sound, pre-dating language in the form of words. First Nations and other aboriginal communities worldwide maintain these ancient practices, adding in elements of mask and dance in highly sophisticated and complex narratives. Stories are teaching devices, and have always been effective ways for oral-based communities to pass on significant historical knowledge and cultural practices. A more western-oriented history of story reveals the development of drama as enacted versions of familiar tales from the Ancient Greek oral tradition, such as the epic tales of Homer.

> Through long practice I know how to tell a story, but I'm not sure what a story is.
>
> Ursula Le Guin, 1989, p. 37

A story, most simply defined, is a sequence of events, real or imagined, set in a realm of space and time. All stories are narrative in nature, while not all narratives are stories (Randall, 1997, p. 85). Stories are always about things that have happened whereas narratives are ongoing. The element of plot differentiates narrative – a sequence of events that may read on the page much like a list (as in annals or a chronicle) – from story. "A story consists basically of someone *telling about* somebody doing something" (p. 86). A plot with a beginning, middle and end enables humans to hive off a self-contained event from the unfolding narratives of our lives and this becomes a story.

Stories can be literal, almost journalistic, descriptions of something that actually happened; we call this type of story "non-fiction." With elements of humour, exaggeration, point of view and effective storytelling, non-fiction can be very engaging. Often when we are telling a literal or "real" story, we rearrange the elements of that story, highlighting parts, shaping the story to engage the interest of the listener. Retelling stories of our lives can help us as narrators to understand better what has happened, and the rearrangement and retelling to diverse listeners can assist a storyteller, for example, in coming to grips with a serious illness or loss. Conditions surrounding our exchange of stories, whether we are seated or standing, rushed or relaxed, on the street or around a dining table, shift a story as well. When we hear stories of someone's life we make an assumption that this person is telling the "truth." The facts of the story may continually shift according to circumstances, and we all know

Narratives are simply systems of stories... stories are pieces that can come and go, change, and morph, but the narrative remains.

Jeffry Halverson, 2011, n.p

storytellers who like to embellish the facts for effect. But the question always is, has that embellishment altered the truth of the story? These are significant matters when we use story to make theatre.

This leads us directly into fictional stories, which are "made-up" (i.e., imagined) yet can very often be rooted in facts and at their best point to a deeper truth about the human condition. How did fictional stories develop? Myths, fables, fairy tales, folk tales and parables arose as a means of explanation for mysterious events such as weather, seasonal change, birth and death. Creation myths provided imaginative explanations in the form of stories for early humans to structure their understanding of how the world operates. "[Stories] become the maps that allow us to understand the stream of events that make up our lives" (Yashinsky, 2005, p. 95). *How the Raven Stole the Sun*, for example, is a mythical story that allowed First Peoples in northern places to explain why and how the sun returns each spring after a long dark winter (Williams, 2000). Many early fictions had a pedagogical function, to instruct the listener about how to behave, what was right and wrong and so on. Teaching remains a strong underpinning of fictional stories. The inherently engaging nature of stories – our human attraction to hearing and/or seeing a satisfyingly shaped sequence of unfolding events – makes stories effective ways to pass significant knowledge on to others.

In applied theatre, theatre is a vehicle for entertainment and education and has an inherent attachment to the local and participatory. It is not surprising then that we get a blend of fact and fiction in many forms of applied theatre, on a continuum that can move from more factual to more fictional, depending on circumstances and choices made by facilitators and participants. In this way, what French philosopher Jean-Francois Lyotard (1979/1984) identified as "metanarratives" or "master narratives," which are used by power structures to get and maintain sociopolitical control, can be effectively countered by "local narratives":

> Local narratives ground master narratives in contemporary events and define a place where individuals can cast themselves in roles, aligning their personal narratives.... The real power of narrative lies in the *connections between stories*. ...[T]he connections can create a powerful

persuasive package that relates events at broad social and cultural scales, to what is happening now, and in turn to how we should think and behave. (Corman, 2013, n.p.)

Applied theatre can work very productively across this continuum within which a fictional traditional tale might serve as a catalyst or jumping-off point for more local non-fictional stories and storytelling.

3.2 What kinds of stories inform applied theatre?

Storytelling in the twenty-first century is quite different from the grand narratives of the past. We are subjected to so many types of stories on a daily basis, in the form of news reports, dramas and even advertisements. Within this flood of mostly mediatized stories and storytelling that can often feel overwhelming and undifferentiated, telling stories in applied theatre provides an opportunity to engage in a more local and communal way. Applied theatre functions in relationship with its audience and the shared stories, though central, are part of a larger process. This process gives equal weight to how a community comes together and how it also works collectively to make meaning throughout and following a performance. Thus, an applied theatre project has a beginning, middle and end in its design and delivery, just like a story. Paradoxically, the end of an applied theatre performance also holds within it the possibility of the beginning of new stories, or actions to be taken that can generate new stories. Whatever happens next, the follow-up to the applied theatre experience belongs to the community and is a shared responsibility.

> To engage our imagination from beginning to end, [a story] must rely on nuances and hints, subplots un-wrapped-up, loose ends left untied. The better or more artistic the story, then the more open it remains, the more loose-ended it is left.
>
> William L. Randall, 1997, p. 346

As you read on in this text about the many kinds of applied theatre, you will become aware of the equally diverse kinds of stories that inform applied theatre-making. There is a difference between stories of the here and now versus stories of the there and then. In the latter, for example, a reminiscence or museum theatre project will often draw on participant's, family members' and community memories. These are stories about things that have happened and while they may be questioned, the events can never be changed. Having said that, the characteristic of stories is that they continue to undergo change as they are shared and retold. In popular theatre, documentary theatre and theatre of the oppressed, stories can be personal but are also linked clearly to a larger social or political issue. Theatre in education, theatre in health education and theatre for development most often have an overt purpose to transmit a message through story. This purpose may serve a hegemonic agenda that facilitators and participants need to recognize in order to resist. Almost all of these stories within applied theatre forms may be structured to offer a beginning and middle but remain in process, and therefore are more narrative in nature. This open-endedness requires audiences to craft, through imaginative engagement and post-show conversation, what happens next.

What emerges in this brief survey is yet another continuum of practice that extends from personal story to political story. An applied theatre project may contain a mix of both these types of story, having more or less of one or the other, again dependent on context. Overall, no matter what story forms are prominent in any given project, the invitation for audiences to respond is integral. All of these dramatized stories are conversation starters; a call to remember, to think, to become aware, to take responsibility and to provoke the possibilities of change. The best audience for that kind of response is committed, engaged and most often deeply connected to what is occurring on the stage.

3.3 What is effective storytelling?

To tell a story well the listeners must be involved. This is an art of conversation more than a monologue. The host [facilitator], teller, and listeners are all complicit in the mission of keeping the stories alive.

Dan Yashinsky, 2005, p. 57

When we think of a good storyteller, we think of someone who is capable of telling a story that is engaging, entertaining and possibly enlightening. A good story happens in a space that feels intimate, to an audience that is prepared to listen. What story or stories are told depends upon the relationship of the storyteller and listeners; the living skein of attention between storytellers and listeners is imperative. Traditional storytelling practice is informal, spoken by one storyteller at a time and is dependent on the voice. The storyteller's job is to draw the listeners into the imagined world without disappearing himself or herself (Croyden, 2003, p. 214). The connection between the story, applied theatre performers and their audience is closer to a storytelling model. Storytellers and actors train in very different ways, as actors are charged with the challenges of disappearing into a character, so performing in applied theatre is distinct from traditional acting practice and often feels more like being in conversation. As Michael Harvey (2010) puts it, the storytellers "appear as a version of themselves rather than characters whose existence is limited to the actions portrayed on stage" (n.p.).

The storyteller's job is to serve the story not the performance.

Michael Wilson, 2006, p. 84

Drawing on this close relationship with storytelling, we offer here some strategies that support effective storytelling in applied theatre:

1. **Engaging**: As in storytelling, the space in which an applied theatre project occurs is often very informal. We might call these "found spaces" such as community

halls, meeting rooms, libraries, museums and so on. Harvey describes these kinds of spaces as "porous" in that surrounding sounds are often audible with "skilful performers weaving real-world intrusions into the performance" (n.p.). This skill is allied with improvisational skills (the ability to adjust and adapt from moment to moment) that are very useful for participants in applied theatre. Unlike the traditional fourth wall of the theatre, this work asks performers not to screen out audience response, but rather to weave it in. Often the lighting in these found spaces keeps the audience and performers visible to each other. In other words, the audience sees the performer looking at them and the performer in turn is able to read the responses of the audience; there is a direct and immediate engagement. How a performance is opened and the relationship between performers and audience is established is key in this regard. The invitation to enter into the event (gathering) and the means by which it concludes (dispersal) is as important as the event itself (performance) (see Schechner, 1988/2003, Chapter 5).

2. **Shaping:** Stories are the way we shape our experience, and a satisfying story has a satisfying shape with a clear beginning, middle and end. Unlike storytelling, which is usually told by a single individual storyteller, applied theatre is performed by a collective. Thus, stories told in the latter model require careful shaping. As lived experiences are often the raw material of an applied theatre project, the devising and rehearsal process focuses on cooking participants' experiences down into collective stories within a collective narrative. How to shape an experience into a "good" story – and from there into equally satisfying theatre – is crucial and sits at the heart of effective facilitation.

> Experiences are intensely complicated and hard to recount...because I know too much about my personal history, and lack the necessary distance for simplicity.
>
> Robert Fulford, 1999, p. 4

Finding the right aesthetic distance for both a story and its storyteller is part of the shaping process (see Prendergast & Saxton, 2013, pp. 16-17).

3. **Tension:** Part of effective engagement with, and shaping of, stories and storytelling lies in the creation of dramatic tension. "Storytelling is a dance between suspense and revelation" (Yashinsky, 2005, p. 153), and as Yashinsky reminds us, we all know how a good story leaves us anticipating the response to "What happens next?" Using the game of "peek-a-boo," Yashinsky tells us that we need to think about the moment of maximum suspense: "You can't build suspense in your telling unless you know when you're *peeking* and when you're *booing*" (p. 153). Unexpected twists and turns, unusual plot elements or character choices, or how a listener may be surprised are all tactics used to create tension. Finding the right balance here is important. Creativity theorist Mihalyi Csikszentmihalyi (1975) reminds us that all creative acts require a sustained tension between boredom and

anxiety. If a story feels too familiar, it lacks tension and audiences may tune out, disengaging themselves. Alternately, if a story is too strange, or troubling, or even too provocative, the anxiety it causes may push audiences to separate themselves from the event. Good tension is taut but not tight, and should never be slack.

4. **Voice:** Who is telling the story? A story can be told in first person in a couple of different ways. A storyteller can tell a story "as if" they were the protagonist of the story (This happened to me…). Or, a story can be told from a witnessing perspective, with the storyteller having seen what happened but from more of a reporting position (Let me tell what I saw the other day…). A storyteller can be a part of the story in a supporting role, or can simply report on what he or she saw and heard. Third person storytelling is the more traditional tale-telling form such as "Once long ago…" as an omniscient narrator. Variations could involve the judicious use of second person (*You* walk into the cave and sense the dragon…), or a story may be told from an unexpected point of view, as the wall, or the tree, or the cup of coffee that is present in the midst of a story and can tell it from a unique narrator position. In applied theatre, the storyteller appears to be very much himself or herself, but can also move towards a middle ground of active presence that involves taking on a role or multiple roles. Collective storytelling in applied theatre makes creative use of differing voices or actions to tell a story from several perspectives. The points of view, and the various attitudes taken towards a story, are more important than characterization; "acting" the story in a traditional theatrical sense. A committed storyteller generally has no trouble being heard and understood, although a facilitator should pay attention to the kind of space within which stories will be shared (acoustics, porosity, etc.). Sometimes it may be helpful to support participants with exercises that develop articulation and projection to ensure their voices and stories will be heard.

> As soon as one element is amplified there is a danger of creating an incoherent aural world if the other elements are not also amplified.
>
> Michael Harvey, 2010, n.p.

5. **Gesture:** A storyteller works most often within physical constraints, either sitting or standing; however, upper body movement, facial expression and vocal shifts offer many opportunities to draw an audience into the imagined world of the story. But, this limited movement palette should change in the collective storytelling of applied theatre that invites a more theatrical approach. In moving towards theatre, participants can take on and shed roles and make use of creative movement, props, costumes, light and sound to elevate the storytelling. As a facilitator, asking "What is it we need to help our audience see the story better?" is an effective way to bring in theatrical elements such as gesture, or movement, or a prop or sound effect. Helping audiences see, hear and understand is at the heart

of the rehearsal and devising process, and the choices made will often alter as the work progresses, becoming more refined or changed entirely because something "better" is found.

These five storytelling strategies support effective practice to establish a positive relationship with an audience and to build a greater sense of community as a result.

3.4 How does storytelling change in applied theatre?

In the shift from single person to collective storytelling, there is also a move from individual to group ownership of a story or stories. We see this as the most radical aspect of applied theatre practice, in its insistence on collectivity in a highly individualized world. "My Story," with its consonant risks of privilege and preciosity (untouchable and unchangeable), becomes transmuted into "Our Story," a collective story that gains the qualities of fluidity and malleability in both telling and receiving. Many of the stories that we use in applied theatre come out of our shared history and are already in the public domain. This is often the case with museum theatre, documentary theatre, community-based theatre and TIE. But many stories originate as private and are shared within a group's devising process. This is more common in reminiscence theatre, prison theatre, TO and popular theatre in which public and private stories are woven together. In these latter forms, a personal story is told and given over to a group willingly by a participant with the clear mutual understanding that it is open to change. While personal stories can be powerful examples, they need to be opened up in ways that allow participants and audiences a sense of agency and alternative possibilities. Then the opportunity for action becomes present, and that is the whole purpose of applied theatre.

We are wired to each other socially because we recognize the other as us.

Hannah Wojciehowski &
Vittorio Gallese, 2011,
pp. 12–13

We see this necessary move from "My Story" to "Our Story" as also a move from non-fiction to fiction. Applied theatre may take a range of stances, from "This is the way things are (or were)" as factual and essentially unchangeable, to "If we know more we may be able to change the way things are," to the possibilities of utopia: "This is how things are and how they can and should be changed." In all of these cases, no matter what intention underpins a project, we see it as essential to transfer stories from being visibly non-fictional – as told by a storyteller who lived the experience being told – towards a collective story, the narration of which is shared and the nature of which can then become open to interpretation and response. Fictionalizing through collective role allows for the necessary aesthetic distance for audiences to feel comfortable engaging in a meaningful post-performance dialogue with participants. Fictionalizing and collectivizing "My Stories" into "Our Stories" gives the freedom to shift and shape these personal events and opens up space for the imagining of better outcomes, better worlds (see Prendergast & Saxton, 2013, pp. 48-58; 2015).

The action of applied theatre is to give people a sense of agency and voice, whether they are participants or audiences. When a participant directly tells his or her own story there are ethical questions about exposing the teller to possible negative repercussions. An "owned story" makes it impossible for the audience to suggest changes such as alternative actions because the story has already happened, and is therefore fixed and frozen. The need to be seen and have one's story heard may feel very important to participants, and rightly so. But to present stories in an entirely non-fictional mode diminishes the possibility for envisioning alternative outcomes that fictionalizing allows (Djikic et al., 2009). Anonymity is a key ethical construct in research, and we see it as equally important in applied theatre.

3.5 What are the issues around the uses of story in applied theatre?

Stories are powerful, for better and for worse. Even when cloaked in fiction and metaphor, stories shared, rehearsed and performed in applied theatre draw in large part on personal experiences. Ethical practice reminds facilitators to regularly check-in with participants around their comfort level with how material is being shaped and framed. The co-creation and maintenance of a safe space is paramount. Yet, on the other hand, there is an equally important need to encourage the group to be playful and to approach stories as clay to be moulded, not cut glass to be protected. Finding this balance between care for the wellness of the group and the necessary messiness of creative process is one of the challenges of applied theatre facilitation. Creativity demands freedom from scrutiny and judgment, both of which are part of watching and listening. In an applied theatre process, a storyteller should be protected from being over-scrutinized or from feeling judged (or even worse, shamed) by both the facilitator and the group. As we lay out in a sequential set of workshops in *Applied Drama* (Prendergast & Saxton, 2013), a group is best served by taking all the time necessary to develop as a dramatic ensemble before stepping into the telling of personal stories as performance material.

> The storyteller cannot be the healer, diagnosing and treating all manner of complaints by "dispensing the right story." The story may heal. The storyteller is not a healer.
>
> Michael Wilson, 2006, p. 104

One of the problems when working with relatively unskilled participants in non-theatrical spaces is the lack of theatricality. Applied theatre in our view is not a "stand and deliver" model of a set of face-front monologues. Theatricality, the vocabulary of theatre-making, involves all the aspects of effective storytelling we outlined in Section 3.3. A facilitator should also take stock of his or her own sense of what makes "good" theatre. It is often what we call the "juicy bits" offered by participants that we respond to as theatre makers. The thrill or *frisson* we may feel in response to a story tells us "This

In general, if the outside story is what happens to me, then the inside story is what I make of what happens to me and what I tell to myself.

William L. Randall, 1997, p. 57

is going to be effective on stage," and of course we must trust these intuitions. That said, in order to avoid exploitation, an ethical facilitator should check in with him or herself about how a story is to be changed and used, as well as with the storyteller and the group.

As facilitators we invite participants to reflect on their lives and circumstances and to tell stories for the purposes of theatrical translation. This process is most often beneficial, but we must remain vigilant and mindful about potentially negative repercussions. The reinscribing of trauma through dramatic enactment has been critiqued by Thompson (2009) as culturally inappropriate in certain contexts; many cultures do not practice psychoanalysis and thus may not value the retelling of an event as therapeutic. Stories of victimhood, for example, may be dramatically compelling. These kinds of difficult stories need to be reframed as past events with which it is possible to come to terms, so as to empower both participants and audience to socially imagine their way towards a world in which these events no longer occur (Taylor, 2004).

What if a group of immigrant women from a culture in which women are still seeking equality with men chooses to perform their stories of resistance to patriarchy? How does a facilitator protect this group from an audience that may contain community members who are hostile to this project? An effective use of metaphor might provide one workable solution. Interweaving traditional stories from a particular culture with stories of lived experience may provide the necessary protection required in this case. Traditional tales featuring strong female protagonists (such as Scheherazade in *A Thousand and One Nights*) create spaces for participants to cloak their personal stories in mythic attire. Tales of resistance may also be drawn from history (Joan of Arc, the Suffragette Movement, Rosa Parks), or popular culture (Wonder Woman, Oprah Winfrey) to provide metaphoric settings for local stories. Working through metaphor allows participants to express their ideas through genres that reach far beyond the naturalistic scenes of daily life. Inviting participants to play their stories through dramatic genres (such as soap opera, science fiction, fantasy, talk show, trial, shadow plays or puppetry, and so on) offers distance and often may illuminate aspects of stories that have been hidden or ignored (see Cahill, 2010). Playing with personal stories in these ways, participants become aware of possible narrative approaches, dramatic frames for a performance, or of signifiers or symbols that can emerge. *The Red Violin*, for example, is a 1998 Canadian film that follows a red-coloured violin across three centuries and multiple owners (Fichman & Girard, 1998). In similar ways, a symbolic object may become a unifying metaphoric device that holds a collection of stories together in a satisfying dramatic way.

I can only answer the question, "What am I to do?" if I can answer the prior question, "Of what story or stories do I find myself a part?"

Alisdair MacIntyre, 1981/2007, p. 216

To return to the ethical context of this section, all the advice offered here is a way to ensure that participants see themselves as owners of the work. The protocol of using other peoples' stories through the granting of permission must be established and followed by the facilitator, and this includes stories gathered by the group from the community. The value of stories lies in the fact that once they are told they are out in the world and so can change, shapeshift and adapt in a constant process of mutability. How an audience receives the theatrical versions of participants' personal and other selected stories is one thing; what they will *do* with them is another. Whatever story is being told, either as storyteller or as applied theatre performer, it should carry the seed of the future within it (Yashinsky, 2005, p. 53).

Stories only reveal their truth when they are questioned.

Michael Wilson, 2006, p. 37

Summary

This chapter sets out to explore the relationship between story and theatre in general, and between storytelling and applied theatre in particular. Our shared familiarity with stories makes them ideal means by which performers extend an invitation for an audience to engage and respond. Telling a story well involves practice and we offer a number of effective approaches, many drawn from writing by professional storytellers. We trace the importance of creating safety for both audiences and participants by creating fictionalized versions of non-fictional story sources. The vocabulary of theatre and how it is employed by facilitator and participants creates the necessary aesthetic distance required in applied theatre. Stories shared in these ways become available for an audience to envision alternative outcomes, in order to address social issues in a communal way. All of these points of consideration support effective storytelling and are echoed in Yashinsky's (2005) reminder that "[t]he human race has never found a better way to convey its cumulative wisdom, dreams and sense of community than through the arts and activity of storytelling" (p. 4). The "how" of this means of conveyance is what we are trying to unpack here as potentially useful for applied theatre practitioners.

The truth about stories is that that's all we are.

Thomas King, 2003, p. 2

Further Reading

Harvey, M. (2010). *Staging the story*. Retrieved from http://storytelling.research. southwales.ac.uk/media/files/documents/2010-03-01/Staging_the_Story_Final_ version.pdf. Harvey's focus is on what happens to stories and storytellers when they move from less formal to more formal performance spaces, with useful points applicable to applied theatre.

Kelin, D.A. (2005). *To feel as our ancestors did: Collecting and performing oral histories.* Portsmouth, NH: Heinemann. A useful guide to using gathered oral histories as sources for drama and playbuilding.

Mellon, N. (1992). *Storytelling & the art of imagination.* Rockport, MA: Element Books. A how-to on storytelling practice that supports and extends the strategies offered in this chapter.

Sawyer, R. (1965). *The way of the storyteller.* New York, NY: Viking. A seminal storytelling text that remains a classic.

Sturm, B. The enchanted imagination: Storytelling's power to entrance listeners. *School Library Media Research,* 2, [online] Retrieved from http://www.ala.org/ aasl/aaslpubsandjournals/slmrb/slmrcontents/volume21999/vol2sturm. Sturm examines what happens to people when they listen to stories, what he calls "the storytelling trance." The article goes on to define what assists attentive listening in storytelling practice.

Weigler, W. (2011). *Engaging the power of the theatrical event.* Unpublished dissertation. University of Victoria, BC. Retrieved from https://dspace.library.uvic.ca:8443// handle/1828/3575. Weigler has created a research-based system using cards that illustrate effective theatrical approaches for community-based groups to use as prompts and vocabulary.

Questions for Reflection and Discussion

1. How might you create a good ambience or atmosphere for storytelling? What things do you see as most important? How might a simple ritual such as the lighting of a candle assist you in this way?

2. How might you deal with someone who uses story as a time-waster or whose story is inappropriate or offensive?

3. What might be the ethical issues around adaptation and appropriation when taking "true" stories, or even fictional stories from other cultures, and shaping them into theatrical forms?

4. What kinds of circumstances may make the telling of an experience hard to recount? How might you support a participant in telling a difficult story?

5. Stories are part of every facilitator's luggage. What kinds or genres of stories appeal to you? How might your attraction or aversion to certain types of stories inform your practice?

Suggested Activities

1. Questions for prompting a story:

    - Have you ever known a true-life hero?
    - What kinds of trouble did you get into as a child?
    - If you ever moved to a new home, what surprised you? What did you miss from your old home?
    - What stories can you tell about unusual animals you have encountered or known?
    - Have you ever had a supernatural experience? What was your response to that event?
    - What were you famous for as a baby?
    - Were you ever lost? How were you found?
    - Which of your ancestors do you think of the most? What keeps this person in your memory?
    - What is the story behind your name and/or the name of your family?
    - Every family has its own unique sayings and expressions. What may be some of the proverbs or sayings that you grew up with? (drawn from Yashinsky, 2005, p. 97)

2. Select a myth, fairy or folk tale that might be useful to illustrate the work of an organization in which you are interested. How might you tell it within the organization and what do you see to be the moral? How might you have your listeners decide for themselves? (Drawn from Yashinsky, 2005, pp. 46-47)

3. List the roles you play in life. Attach a story to each of these roles. How are they different? How do they form the narrative of your life? What are the emerging local and historical narratives that guide the personal narrative?

PART TWO

The Landscape of Applied Theatre

CHAPTER FOUR
POPULAR THEATRE

Introduction

Popular theatre has a long history and because it was created to address the concerns and lives of ordinary people, is often referred to as grass-roots theatre. Popular theatre draws on mythologies and folk tales and flourishes in many parts of the world; for example, *pongsan t'alch'um* are masked dramas still performed today in South Korea. In the western world, its roots are clearly traceable to the Dionysian rituals of Ancient Greece. In these rituals, as in all popular theatre, social norms were subverted, and it became possible for performers to satirize the all-powerful religious and political leaders of the day.

> Art is not merely contemplation, it is also action, and all action changes the world, at least a little.
>
> Tony Kushner, 2001, p. 62

Regarded by those in authority as a sanctioned way for "the masses" to "let off steam," in popular theatre there has always been the question of risk and boundaries: What happens if a theatre performance goes too far? What price is there to be paid in talking back to power? These questions are as politically and socially appropriate today as they ever were.

Over time, popular theatre has never lost that early impulse towards socially conscious theatre that takes on indigenous and accessible forms such as song and dance, circus and sideshow acts, puppetry, mask and mime – entertainment forms that clothe subversion with wonderment at the skills and delights of high theatricality. Examples of popular theatre forms that emerged include Italian *commedia dell'arte* with its stock characters of clever servants who triumph over their foolish masters; the circus and sideshow traditions along with their grotesque, comic and dexterous elements; animal acts such as bear-baiting and bullfighting; and the worldwide traditions of spectacle, pageants and parades. Joel Schechter (2003) defines contemporary popular theatre as a "democratic, proletarian and politically progressive theatre" (p. 3), and borrowing from Peter Schumann's definition of puppet theatre (p. 6), Schechter also calls it "illegitimate." Placing this "illegitimate theatre" up against the "legitimate theatre" – mainstream literary theatre that is usually performed in purpose-built spaces – sets up popular theatre as a theatre of subversion and celebration, and one that is highly participatory in nature.

Prentki and Selman (2000) place the roots of contemporary popular theatre with Paolo Freire's principles of education that embrace "the notions of exchange, participant ownership, reflection and action" (p. 8). Following Freire's notion of "conscientization" (p. 39), popular theatre aims to raise the critical consciousness of its participants and audiences towards the taking of action. In this way, the intentions of popular theatre begin to mesh with Bertolt Brecht's political theatre and later Augusto Boal's Theatre of the Oppressed in offering performers and spectators a language that can lead to transformation. The name "popular theatre" has now become an umbrella term for this kind of politically and collaboratively created theatre.

> For Brecht (1938) "popular" was writing that is "intelligible to the broad masses, taking over their forms of expression and enriching them/ adopting and consolidating their standpoint/representing the most progressive section of the people...."
>
> John Willett, 1964, p. 108

"Popular theatre [is a] creative approach to analyzing, naming, and acting on problems and working creatively with conflict," write Butterwick and Selman in 2003 (p. 8). While this definition could apply to all applied theatre practices, it is the sociopolitical element that helps us to distinguish the purposes and practices of popular theatre. To be considered truly "popular," there is an implication that the project is free of outside influence (e.g., free of curriculum in theatre in education or funding agencies in theatre for development) and that the community holds the ownership of the piece. The reality, however, can be very different as economic or political agendas may mean that popular applied theatre projects may be *for* "the people" but not necessarily be *by* them, or *of* them. Even though the carnivalesque frames of the early popular theatre have almost disappeared, popular performance forms such as music, dance, song and mythic figures (as in Bread and Puppet theatre) are still being used within the popular theatre-making process (see Price, 2011).

The tension between authorship and ownership throughout the history of popular theatre is one that allows us to see how popular theatre has developed towards more collaborative forms over the past decades. While there are still playwrights who write politically and in sometimes popular forms (as with Dario Fo and Tony Kushner), true popular theatre privileges improvisation over the written text. In this context, we are more interested in the collective authorship and ownership of popular theatre processes that clearly belong to the world of applied theatre.

> Whilst some popular-political theatre troupes still perform today, the kinds of activism associated with their practices, and the ability of their work to generate the kind of response that might contribute to a resolution of the issues they perform, appears to have faded.
>
> Jason Price, 2011, p. 76

Although today it is less common to find a popular theatre project that involves the use of puppets, mask, mime and/or spectacle, it is our intention to focus the case studies we have selected on the more traditional and historic roots of this genre.

> *The first case study takes us back to the 1970s when alternative theatre practices were flourishing all over the world. Welfare State was a leading popular theatre company in England and this case study describes the political work company members did and the ways in which they worked. Next, an Australian case study documents one part of a larger statewide education project, Risky Business, on anti-bullying. Here, puppets are used as a "way of looking at the dark underbelly of things" and as a means of connecting with students' aboriginal culture. So too with the third case study, in which cultural traditions are woven into a satirical performance by a comedy troupe that plays in the bars and massage parlors of Bangkok. The final example blends popular theatre and theatre for health education in a project that illustrates the difficulties of working in politically unstable environments, in this case Zimbabwe.*

4.1 Popular theatre as spectacle
from *The Welfare State Theatre*
Theodore Shank. (1977). *TDR: The Drama Review*, 21(1), 3–16.

There are revolutionary socialist theatre groups, often comprised of Marxists, who play almost exclusively for trade Union members at meetings and workingmen's clubs, attempting to raise political awareness with respect to the worker in a capitalist society and to stimulate discussion about political problems. And there are theatre groups that do not consider their work overtly political who make plays dealing with the problems of certain constituencies such as teachers, children, old people, prisoners, women or gays, sometimes involving them in theatrical activities as a kind of therapy.

In 1976–77 the largest Arts Council subsidy received by a "fringe" or "experimental" group went to the Welfare State Theatre, which refuses to be placed in any of these categories. …They refuse to condescend or patronize by adapting their work to specific audiences. They present the same work for children and adults, for well-educated artistic sophisticates at art festivals, often on the continent, and for those in small towns and the ghettos of large cities with little education who may never have attended live theatre or an art gallery. The reactions of their spectators range from adulation to stoning.

John Fox [artistic director] considers much of what is done by groups with "social" aims as "baby minding, to keep children off the streets, but it has nothing to do with art or theatre or poetry." [...]

Welfare State has made two kinds of performances. They have made large outdoor environmental spectacles incorporating regional mythology and invented myth-like images for audiences of 3,000 or more, and they have presented small performances intended for no more than forty spectators. […]

The great majority of Welfare State performances are for people who live in small towns or in the ghettos of large cities – people who have had little, i[f] any, experience with the arts. Often the performances are sponsored by local community centers, and under these circumstances most of those who attend the performances are of school age. The attitude of these children at the outset is often aggressive and sometimes violent. […]

In September 1976, performances of plays from *The Island of the Lost World* cycle were sponsored by a community center in Halewood, a town of about 25,000 in the north of England where a Ford factory is the principal employer. On Tuesday (September 7)[,] Welfare State set up the white canvas enclosure in an open area of the town and were immediately troubled by children. The first performance was scheduled for Wednesday evening, but on Wednesday morning rocks were already being thrown and there was danger the canvas would be ripped and children hurt. They took down the enclosure and decided to do only processions in the streets, beginning at 5:00 that afternoon. By the time they had done three processions with breaks between them, the children were becoming dangerous. Rock[-]throwing became more frequent, they were clinging to the back of moving vehicles, there was an attempt to steal a Welfare State bicycle, one of the children was hit by a frustrated member of Welfare State and an argument ensued with the child's mother. It was decided that processions were not a good idea as they were raising energy and giving the kids expectations that would not be fulfilled by performances. So they decided to perform away from Halewood and bring the children to the performances by bus, sixty at a time.

On Thursday it was beginning to rain. The group dispersed to find a new site.

Near Burtonwood, ten miles away, they discovered a nearly deserted U.S. Army base, where they set up the white canvas enclosure inside a warehouse. Their first performance took place on Friday evening, and three more were given on Saturday afternoon and evening.

Welfare State audiences are always greeted in some fashion at the entrance to the area. For some productions, the Welfare State band, including most of the company, meets the arriving spectators at the entrance gate. At the U.S. Army base, the bus loads of spectators from Halewood were met outside the warehouse by a member of the group dressed in a seedy old-fashioned black tuxedo. The audiences consisted predominately of children between the ages of six and fourteen, but there were also some babies and adults. They were led into the warehouse where a labyrinth had been set up leading into the white space.

A Guide, with a craggy green-and-white face that looks as if the makeup had been applied with a palette knife, gestures silently with his bamboo hand for the spectators to follow him through the labyrinth. In the semidarkness, they are confronted by a series of grotesque figures and sculptures. Later a four-year-old girl was asked what she thought of the experience. She replied, "It was lovely. There was a man with a funny hand." When asked i[f] she had been frightened, she said, "Oh no. It was lovely, he was all gooey in the face. He told me where to come." A three-year-old, holding tightly to her mother's neck, sobbed quietly during most of the first play, looking only briefly at the performance. A woman, sitting some distance from one of her charges, called instructions to him throughout the performance. In one performance, a man of about thirty-five who was there for the second time felt compelled to share his pre-knowledge with his friends, telling them what was about to happen, warning them and making jokes.

From the time the spectators enter the labyrinth they hear live music being played on saxophone and strung piano frames that have been removed from their cases. When the audience is seated, a woman dressed as a mythological bird appears in the window-like opening in the canvas wall and sings the song that is used at the beginning and end of the performances:

As the wind ties skeins
In the heart of a tree
So the wind
Blows seeds in the air

As the wind fold petals
In the Lattice of bone
So the wind
Blows men to the stars

As the wind drives smoke
To the edge of a field
So the wind
Finds fire in the sky.

The purpose of the song, says the director, is to charge the space, to define it with music at the beginning of the performance and, at the end, to defuse the space and return it to what it was.

In each of the forty-minute Halewood performances, the song was followed by the same three plays from the cycle, separated only by the entrance of a "Blue Priest" wearing a cowl, who set up or removed props. The first two plays, *King of the Ditches I* and *II*, are based on Ghelderode, but the story probably goes back to the Middle Ages. In the first, the King of the Ditches with white face, skull cap, costume of coarse brown material, and feet wrapped in rags, enters carrying a two-foot wooden boat in which there are three pilgrim dolls made of brown burlap. The entire play is a monolog by the King of the Ditches, who also speaks for the Pilgrims who are on their way to Rome. The King taunts them and tortures them with a knife, making them sing and dance. He pulls them around on their boat and finally makes "a miracle" by burning one of them at a stake. A five-year-old in the audience, sitting on the lap of a man, kept asking, rather calmly, "Is he going to cut us with the knife?" A thirteen-year-old relieved his fear by making a joke about buying a pair of "shoes" like the King's.

In *King of the Ditches II*, all of the characters are played by human performers. Two blind pilgrims enter, clinging to each other. Their costumes seem to have been collected from medieval castoffs and their makeup is grotesque. The brightly costumed King of the Ditches (John Fox), with bones and feathers for a headdress and a dried beet root for a nose, gives them advice. None of the roads leads to Rome; they are in the ditch country not having left their native land. He offers them shelter, but the pilgrims mistrust him, first thinking he is an echo[,] then, thinking he intends to harm them, they swing at him blindly with their sticks, hitting each other. Finally, the pilgrims step in a hoop representing a ditch.

> *I can do nothing*
> *The ditches are deep.*
> *The blind will not sing*
> *They have come to the end of the road.* [...]

At the conclusion of the final play at each performance [t]he strings of the piano frames are plucked several times; then the song that opened the entire performance is sung off[-]stage.

When the song is finished, music from the Welfare State band is heard coming from the entrance to the warehouse, and the spectators get up from their seats and go toward it. The band, playing, leads them out of the warehouse to the bus that brought them. The band continues to play as the bus departs for Halewood. As the bus drove away following one of the performances, a twelve-year-old boy shouted, "Rubbish!" [...]

The esthetic objectives of Welfare State precede their social objectives. They are not making plays in order to accomplish a social end. However, having made the best work they can, they are determined to perform it not only for those who are already predisposed to their kind of work but for people who have little or no experience with the arts. They are not taking culture to the provinces, they live in the provinces; and they do not condescend to their audiences by thinking that Halewood will accept work that is inferior to that acceptable in London. They do not have an intentional political objective, but a political attitude is implicit in their work.

> ***John Fox:*** *If you choose to read it as such, there is a very clear political statement in the energy of our performances, the fact that we show ourselves open in making them, and that we are committed to our art and our lives being together. We are showing that although we are intellectuals, we work with our hands and discover that every moment of the day is different from every moment of the previous day, so we are learning and growing all the time. That is an enormously important political message in a death culture. But we do not use the techniques*

of a death culture, which are to make a lecture or a didactic statement about something, canonizing and fossilizing it. Instead, we are actually doing it.

4.2 Puppetry with at-risk youth
from *Walking in both worlds: Snuff Puppets at Barak Indigenous College*
Kate Donelan & Angela O'Brien. (2006). *Applied Theatre Researcher, 7*(2), 1–14.

This paper focuses on the Snuff Puppets case study, a performing arts project conducted at Barak College, a residential secondary school for [i]ndigenous students ([n]ote: pseudonyms have been used for both the name of the college and for the students). The Snuff Puppet artists worked intensively with the young people for two weeks, writing a story, designing and building giant puppets, developing music and dance, and creating a performance. The participants performed *Singing the Land* at a community event at the conclusion of the project. The following account of this performance project, in its unique, culturally complex site, explores the serendipitous application of theatre involving giant puppets. It highlights the challenges of engaging the young [i]ndigenous people and negotiating cultural differences.

Although it was not the intention of either the Snuff Puppets or the Risky Business team, the focus on giant puppets in performance process and product exemplified Edward Gordon Craig's theory that theatre is more inspirational when it rejects "impersonation and the reproduction of nature" in favour of representing the spiritual: "beautiful things from the imaginary world...strange, fierce and solemn figures... impelled to some wondrous harmony of movement" (Craig, 1911, p. 74). Craig argues that the human actor should be replaced by "god-like" puppets, Ubermarionettes (p. 81) . In the Snuff Puppet project, the involvement of the huge animal puppets not only illustrated Craig's theory that the use of Ubermarionettes can offer a transformative theatre experience, it also supported Barak's cultural curriculum and allowed the young people to create a liminal theatre space which connected them to their Aboriginal Dreaming and the mythical Land that existed before human time. [...]

Phase one: Meeting the puppets
On the first day of the project, the Snuff Puppets artists met with the students in the conference centre, a beautiful building overlooking the valley and housing the school's collection of Aboriginal paintings and art[i]facts. This space, used only for "special occasions," contrasted with the old and poorly maintained portable buildings normally used for classes. The artists laid out two large puppets from their "Nyet-Nyet" project. One of the students, Scott, was drawn to the giant blue-green Bunyip puppet with its pendulous breasts and huge webbed feet. With the support of puppeteer Nick, he climbed inside it and worked out how to manipulate its outsize limbs.

As researchers, we watched from the window as the Bunyip lumbered across the basketball courts where boys who had ignored the bell were still playing. He continued onwards through the school grounds and emerged from the side of the portable classrooms like a giant Pied Piper with 20 students trailing behind. A female student manoeuvred herself into the other huge "Nyet-Nyet" puppet and joined the Bunyip in gambolling around the space. The first session could now begin.

Andy, the puppet designer, explained the project to the 24 young people:

> We're going to make a performance together by the end of the two weeks. We're going to build puppets like these two after we've got together some stories from you guys. We're looking for people who are into dancing and singing and performance-making. Today we'll play some theatre games together, get thinking about some ideas for stories, and do some drawings and designs for the puppet.

The session of theatre games, led by Sarah, the artistic director, began awkwardly when the deputy principal intervened to remove a thick rope that had been laid out in the space. She explained to us: "Rope has bad associations for one of our kids." After three games, many students drifted away. The task was to create the story of the play, but discussion with the remaining students was stilted and unproductive.

Tony Briggs worked with a group of boys who covered a large whiteboard with lurid drawings. They talked about how logging was destroying native flora and fauna and began to develop some characters. Their ideas were constructed into the plot outline of the performance:

> Bush animals are living in harmony. A logging truck crashes in the bush, killing a kangaroo but not its Joey. Poisonous oil is spilt into the environment. Creatures emerge from the poisoned lagoon. Eagle watches the disaster from above. Orphaned Joey appeals for help and Eagle transforms into a young woman who eventually sings the land back to health. (artistic director's notes)

Phase two: Building the puppets

> We use cane and bamboo and fabric and hot glues to hold them together. We use a range of materials that are often about how puppets move and operate. But the most basic one is making three-dimensional cane shapes, a sphere a head a body or starting from a backpack frame which means you carry the puppet on your back, which means you can have a long frame above your head, or it's like making humans or animals from the bones up. (Andy, puppet designer)

...Students were expected to participate in the process of building the puppets alongside the puppeteers. However, by the second day it became clear that the involvement by most of the young people was sporadic and many seemed reluctant to persist at the technical tasks despite the encouragement of adults. [...]

> *By 11.30 only one student, Brodie, is still in the hall working alongside the puppeteers. The other kids are scattered around the school grounds, kicking footballs or hanging around the residential houses. Sarah rounds up a group and, with the assistance of Tony Briggs, they set to work cutting out the fabric for the eagle's wings, gluing with the glue gun and pushing in the stuffing. In half an hour they are all gone again, leaving their tools, the glue and bits of puppet in a tumbled heap. Brodie remains. He has worked out a way of opening and closing the emu puppet's mouth and he demonstrates this to Nick. Tony Briggs comments approvingly on the huge size of the evolving emu puppet and explains: "[T]his is the size of animals before men came." Brodie turns to us and says: "That's true, that's a fact!"* (field notes, day five)

Phase three: Creating dance and music

Dance was an important component of the preparation period and the final performance. Sarah discovered that dance provided opportunities for expression that were not otherwise available for the girls. . . . For Tony Briggs, the students' affinity with dance was not surprising:

> *There was nothing special in working on the dance with the boys: it's something they have all been a part of at some stage or another during their stay at Barak. It's their culture. This was one of the main reasons the school was started in the first place, to preserve our culture. Dance and storytelling are fundamental to this.*

The young people engaged with the music activities more readily than with designing and building puppets. Many of the young people demonstrated considerable ability with drums and guitars. A small group of boys, including the boys from the remote community, were proficient with [i]ndigenous instruments and played clap sticks and the didgeridoo for the traditional dances. A small group worked intensively with James, the musician, on the creation of a digitalised soundtrack.

Phase four: The performance of Singing the Land

The performance took place on a sunny Saturday morning in the grounds of Barak College, in a natural outdoor meeting place between the school buildings and the main road. Sarah had selected the performance space in front of and around a large tree-trunk painted with Aboriginal symbols. [...]

> *The artists and the students are still working on a last dress rehearsal even as the audience is arriving. There are families and friends with children and babies, and older non-[i]ndigenous people who are "friends" of the college. There is palpable excitement, even amongst the young people who are not involved in the performance. Behind the audience, under trees, the two mothers from the Northern Territory have set up a table with their bark paintings and shell necklaces.*

> *The performance begins about half an hour after the scheduled time as Sarah, the director, introduces the play: "The students have designed and helped build the puppets. They have written the story and composed the music and written the lyrics." To one side, a small group of young artists with drum kit, synthesiser, guitars and traditional instruments are warming up.*

> *Four girls enter and perform their version of a traditional dance. It is a subdued performance – the girls move forward with repetitive movements, waving branches of gum leaves; their heads are bowed. They perform to clap sticks and didgeridoo, played by the musicians. This is followed by a more confident and vigorous dance by three of the boys, representing kangaroos and emus. The music speeds up and Scott ends the dance with a showy leg-kick.*

> *At this point, the music changes to a simple digitalised piano piece on loop. The Emu enters slowly; his movements are deliberate as he leans forward to simulate eating. The effect is quite powerful and we are surprised the young person inside the puppet is managing so well, although he is having problems with the huge feet. Wombat enters from behind the audience. A young female student is manipulating this puppet; again, the movements are slow and theatrically powerful. The Kangaroo enters from behind the tree, the largest of the puppets at around ten feet. The animals meet and commune.*

> *There is a dramatic change in the music from the simple piano to a raucous rap song, "My Big Black Truck." Five boys enter running from the road, carrying giant logs to represent a logging truck. The "truck" crashes into the Kangaroo.*

> *Tony Briggs begins his narration of the story, explaining the accident and the consequence: "The Joey, finding himself alone, searched through the*

bush looking for his mother." The youngest boy from the Northern Territory emerges as the orphaned kangaroo and moves around the performance space. A tall blue Creature appears, somewhat like a misshapen man but faceless and spotted as though with a terrible disease. Tony explains how the petrol has poisoned the lagoon and the Swamp Creature has been disturbed. The Joey asks the creature how the land might be repaired. A huge Eagle appears, the most spectacular of the Ubermarionettes. The performer moves across the space, displaying the great bird – a significant symbol for the school – with its wings outstretched. The narrator explains how the Eagle transforms into a beautiful young girl (who emerges from behind the tree). The Joey asks her if she will sing the country back to life. At first she refuses, too ashamed to sing by herself. After the Joey begs her to sing, the girl agrees and as she sings the animals return to the land and the play ends.

It has been quite a spectacular and moving performance, despite the lack of rehearsals. . . . (field notes, performance day) [...]

Outcomes for the students

In spite of what we perceived as disengagement from the project by many of the young people, senior staff at the school were extremely positive in their responses. They argued that the impact of the project for the school community and for many of the young people had been significant.

The deputy principal spoke passionately about the impact of the project beyond the immediate school community. . . . Another senior staff member recognised the benefits for young people who became involved. . . . One of the themes that emerged from the data was the importance of the mentoring relationships that developed between the artists and some of the young people as they engaged in the puppetry construction, music and dance workshops, performance-making and rehearsals. [...]

The deputy principal of the college outlined the positive effects on many individual young people with histories of family breakdown, violence, substance abuse and depression. [...]

Tony Briggs identified considerable personal achievements for the young people:

I think the entire group of students who participated managed to discover more about what they are capable of when they step out of their comfort zone. I saw a visible change in attitude and demeanour with some of the students after the event; they seemed to carry themselves with a little more pride.

4.3 Comic performance in Bangkok
from *Duen Phen: Joker performance in the nightclubs of Bangkok*
Mary L. Grow. (1995). *Asian Theatre Journal, 12*(2), 326–352.

The Joker Performance
   The joker performance is a form of urban entertainment popular in Bangkok Clubs frequented by the working class. The genre derives its inspiration from traditional and popular Thai culture, and its routines rely heavily on comic improvisation and audience interaction. Scenarios typically feature familiar folktales composed of seemingly incongruous and surprising elements that subvert the audience's expectations. In an evening's entertainment comedians portray Thai mythic heroes tethering their elephants to pursue villains on a Kawasaki[,] or Han Solo rescuing a princess from the Chao Phraya River moments after she is seduced and betrayed by Mohamar Kadaffi. By lacing scenarios with current events and situations – and, moreover, by encouraging audience members to participate – comedians explore new ways of performing stories that have been a part of Thai cultural heritage for centuries.
   Like most forms of improvised comedy, the joker performance is at the forefront of popular Thai culture. The genre's very survival demands that comedians keep pace with the moment. . . . Comedians who play the Thai joker performance skil[l]fully combine themes and images belonging to both the emergent and the residual culture, and they often juxtapose one against the other, thereby creating ridiculous and imaginative scenarios. This style of nightclub comedy not only provides insight into those structures of thought and belief that remain constant through time, but it also highlights change in the Thai sociocultural system. […]
   I was continually impressed by Duen Phen's creative attempt to reflect upon and ridicule social, economic, and political issues in Thailand and the international community. During the two years I accompanied the troupe in and out of clubs like the Gold Sweet Café, the Can Can Palace, and the Tick Toc Shop, I watched them cultivate a loyal following among audience members and club owners. Their fans repeatedly told me that Duen Phen's comic material gave voice to their everyday concerns. Their comedy often involved issues of class conflict, broken love, economic hardship, and the hope for something better to come. I realized that here in the nightlife of Bangkok was an emergent social commentary inspired and framed by the traditional performance genres I had observed in the countryside, yet it was also shaped and reshaped by the influences of an ever-changing and increasingly global urban lifestyle characteristic of Bangkok. […]

"Saiyasaat": A Typical Routine
   The routine known as "Saiyasaat" was performed at the Phop Suk (Meet Happiness) Café on November 4, 1987. It featured four characters: an Announcer, a Spirit Medium, a Country Bumpkin, and a Child, each played by members of Duen Phen. A drummer

and *ranat* player provided musical accompaniment.

The action begins when the Spirit Medium, costumed in a flowing cape, enters through the audience and joins the Announcer onstage. The Medium then begins to speak, rattling off an impressive list of his accomplishments, including levitation, fire eating, and mental telepathy. Accompanying this monologue Duen Phen's musicians play melodies that suggest the arrival of an Indian snake charmer. The Medium is soon visited by a Country Bumpkin who wants to win the lottery. This new character wears a checkered *phakhaoma* and a pair of rubber thongs, typical attire of an upcountry peasant. His bare chest appears hollow as the performer sucks in his breath and hunches his shoulders. In an effort to impress this client, the Medium chants mantras of gibberish while grandly striding to and fro. Finally he turns to the audience and shouts:

> I am a great master, a practiced ascetic, an indestructible force in the universe. All people love me, all people venerate me, all people come to me for advice. Stop your drinking! Stop your romancing! Watch my powers unfold.

Several of the audience members respond with applause, while others jeer and hiss.

The Medium then challenges everyone to witness his skill in mental telepathy, adding that his expertise far surpasses the monetary fee humbly offered by his ignorant client. He selects a Child seated in the audience to assist in his demonstration. After fussing a bit, the Child is dragged to center stage by the Announcer, where he stands staring blankly at the audience and picking his nose. Finally he steals a fearful glance at the Medium and begins to whine. The Medium orders the boy to stop, pushes him into a chair, and then drapes an enormous cloth over him. Muffled sniffles and sighs can be heard as the Child resigns himself to the task at [h]and.

The Medium then walks among the audience members and stops at a patron's table. He selects a glass of beer, holds it up for everyone to see, and asks the Child to identify the object. Onstage the Child, still covered by the cloth, responds with the correct answer. Overwhelmed by the Medium's impressive display of power, the Country Bumpkin falls to his knees and gestures with a *wai*. Triumphantly the Medium moves to several other tables where the "miracle" is successfully repeated with a variety of items. Audience members who initially expressed scepticism at the Medium's skill now shout words of praise. Turning to the Announcer, the Country Bumpkin remarks:

> This man is a great master! He has great power. With his help I am sure to win the lottery. I will stake my entire life savings on whatever number he selects.

Gloating with pride over his success, the Medium continues the demonstration, but this time he capitalizes on his fame and solicits money from converted audience members. Suddenly the room is filled with people waving banknotes and urging the Medium to come to their tables. Calculating the situation, he goes to a group offering a large reward. The Medium quickly selects an item from their table, holds it up, and asks the Child onstage to identify it. After a few moments of silence the Child blurts out a response. It is incorrect. Grabbing another item, the Medium demands a repeat. But again the Child's response is wrong. The Country Bumpkin, now suspicious of a scam, quickly runs to the chair and snatches away the cloth covering the Child – exposing the Medium's planted accomplice, the Child, who is puzzling over a sheet of paper that apparently does not list the last items held by the Medium. Realizing the jig is up, the Medium dashes for an exit. A drum roll accents the punchline and the show is over.

Behind all these shenanigans lies trenchant social commentary directed at Thai spirit mediums. In October 1987 the State Lottery Bureau faced a serious crisis of credibility when it was discovered that six of the seven wheels used in the previous month's drawing were rigged. . . . As this scandal hit the Thai news media it created an uproar throughout the country, for many people had invested fortunes in the lottery hoping to beat the odds with a lucky number. Not only was the nation's confidence in the State Lottery Bureau shaken; so too was the reputation of spirit mediums who claimed to assist their patrons in selecting winning numbers. [...]

While members of Duen Phen jokingly refer to the lottery as "Thailand's national pastime," they too are eager to purchase lottery tickets in hopes of winning substantial cash. They are sceptical of spirit mediums who claim supernatural powers, however, and openly resent those who extort money from the poor and naive. Kii Simakok of Duen Phen explains: "Spirit mediums are only playing a clever performance. They often take advantage of people in desperate circumstances by taking money from those who need answers to their problems. Our performance demonstrates how cunning these practitioners are."

Duen Phen's role as critic and social commentator is best understood in relation to audience members seeking this form of comic entertainment. The joker performance is popular in the notorious nightlife sector of Bangkok, where it is enjoyed by a variety of people, primarily Thai, who work [h]ard for a daily wage yet are never quite able to improve their standard of living. Construction workers, taxi drivers, blue-collar employees, hustlers, and call girls typically frequent the joker performance. Many audience members, as well as the comedians themselves, have come to the urban center of Bangkok from the rural countryside in search of new economic opportunities. Compared to the low wages or even underemployment of the rural areas, most workers have in fact increased their financial earnings. At the same time, however, these people are also compelled to spend most of their wages just to keep pace with the high cost of urban living. Moreover, some of them are seduced by the consumerism that is now part of Bangkok life and gamble or spend their meager earnings on a wide variety of luxury goods. [...]

Thus comic inspiration for Duen Phen's "Saiyasaat" performance was drawn from current events – in particular, the scandal that shook conventional faith in the legitimacy of the lottery and the relationship between spirit mediums and their clients. Furthermore, the comedians explored the struggle between existing and emerging value systems, as well as the vulnerability of people experiencing social, economic, and political change. In "Saiyasaat" Duen Phen exposes the internal conflicts of Thai society for its themes and social commentary. Events that shape and reflect a dynamic Thai worldview are the target of comedic exposé.

4.4 Street theatre for safer practices
from *Using street theatre to increase awareness and reduce mercury pollution in the artisanal gold mining sector: A case from Zimbabwe.*
Stephen Metcalfe & Marcello Veiga. (2012). *Journal of Cleaner Production*, 37, 179-184.

[In Zimbabwe] a travelling play, Nakai, was developed to increase awareness in mining communities about the dangers of mercury intoxication in the villages of the project area. The idea was to use the play to draw the attention of the miners and the public to mercury vapour exposure and environmental pollution. Street theatre was used as a way to interest miners and [the] public in the training program.

Nakai: using theatre to raise awareness about mercury hazards
Travelling didactic theatre like Nakai has a long history in Africa. Early colonial mission schools exploited traditional drama when they mounted plays to foster European values amongst indigenous students, and by the 1930s, travelling street plays were used throughout Africa to communicate development messages intended to engender conformity to new social, economic and agricultural practices.... [...]

The decision of UNIDO's [The United Nation's Industrial Development Ogranization] Global Mercury Project (GMP) to use street theatre as an awareness strategy in Zimbabwe grew from sponsorship negotiations with the Amakhozi Theatre Productions, the producer of "Amakorokoza," a Zimbabwean television series popular among artisanal miners which contrasts the lives of poor miners with a rich, well-connected mining family. The GMP had hoped to embed its mercury safety messages in Amakorokoza's storyline, but because sponsorship fees exceeded GMP resources, Amakhoza proposed an alternative in which local miners and their family members would perform a scripted play introducing awareness of the hazards of mercury use in the villages where the GMP practical training would take place. This strategy divided the project area into 5 km "walking radius" zones in order to ensure that everyone could easily attend the performance and trainings. Development of the play storyline was to be based on concerns identified at a stakeholder colloquium involving the Ministries of Health, Mines and the Environment and national miners associations and unions.

"[T]ransportable demonstration unit" (TDU), a trailer containing low cost, more efficient and cleaner gold concentration equipment and a portable classroom.

Stephen Metcalfe & Marcello
Veiga, 2012, p. 180

Unfortunately, the logistics of the colloquium and mining community involvement proved too costly and the idea of a strong participatory approach with mining communities was dropped in favor of a scripting workshop with the local community[-]based group, the Zimbabwe Panners Association. The play was performed by a travelling troupe of semi-professional actors and traditional dancers. The GMP opted for this scenario, in which traditional drumming and dancing would draw crowds to view a didactic play. After the play, the Zimbabwe Panner's Association would demonstrate mercury vapour collecting retorts and efficient gold recovery sluice carpets as an introduction to the TDU training.

The scripting workshop sketched out a storyline where the son of an environmentally careless mining family falls in love with the daughter of a more established and environmentally responsible farming family, exacerbating an old interfamily conflict, but also leading to an eventual resolution. Amakhosi's professional scriptwriters then fleshed out the storyline of Nakai, which follows the blossoming love of two young people, Nakai and her artisanal miner boyfriend Aringo. The play's Shona title, Nakai, means "precious little thing" and refers equally to the gold amalgam that artisanal miners recover and burn, and to the wife and unborn child of Aringo, who both become intoxicated by exposure to mercury vapour. Nakai's father (Tabengwa) was a farmer whose land has been invaded by gold panners, and Aringo's father (Ndebvucaewaya) was a successful artisanal gold dealer. At the beginning of the play, Tabwenga unsuccessfully tries to drive the artisanal miners from his farm. Soon, Nakai realizes that she is pregnant, but an attempt to secure her father's blessing for her marriage with Aringo fails. Nakai then leaves her father's home and moves in with Aringo, who later suffers dementia and impotence from exposure to mercury vapors during amalgam burning. Nakai also becomes sick and nearly loses their baby during delivery. Tabengwa regrets his harsh treatment of his daughter and after Ndebvudzewaya begins to improve the environmental practices at his mines, he blesses the marriage between their two children.

Challenges and limitations of the approach

The tense political environment in Zimbabwe from 2006 to 2008 greatly impacted the delivery of the GMP training program. Amakhozi's director was arrested for producing a satirical political play that ridiculed President Mugabe, GMP training was closely watched by Zimbabwe's secret police, and "Operation Chicoracoza Chapera," a police action aimed at curbing the runaway sale of gold in the black market, led to the arrest of over 30,000 miners. GMP field activities were scaled back because the artisanal miners in the project area would not risk attending classes. Rather than introducing the training in each village as planned, Nakai was presented as a stand-alone play at locations selected for maximum audience draw.

As noted, the overall effectiveness of the early didactic theatre programs was considered poor, and recent findings suggest that the ability of travelling didactic plays like Nakai to generate behavioral change remains limited…. Nakai was entertaining and successful in terms of audience size (8800 people or about 5% of the project area's population), but its impact on miners' mercury use behavior was probably limited to the increased use of retorts in the region. The public, in particular women who are the main affected parties to mercury pollution, appreciated the initiative and the recommendations given by the GMP trainers at the end of the plays were spread from mouth to mouth.

Nakai was born from budget-driven compromises, and was never intended to be a stand-alone travelling play, but rather complementary to a structured training and awareness campaign. Even though Nakai's storyline was developed by a local miners' association familiar with mining communities and their needs, scripting participants did not actually live in the mining villages. This was a limitation since it is important for the local community to identify familiar faces and situations in the play. […]

The theatre play was only a door to open discussions about social issues and practical technical alternatives simultaneously. Unfortunately, while miners found Nakai entertaining, they rarely stayed for post-performance discussions with the local miners association and not all attended the series of courses and equipment demonstrations at the TDU. About 700 miners had been trained in lectures given by the trainers. […]

Under adverse political and economic conditions, however, the vulnerability of the least powerful is an important limiting factor in participatory initiatives. […]

"Participation," in and of itself, has its shortcomings. It has long been an "article of faith" in the development milieu that when project beneficiaries participate in program planning, management, and evaluation, the likelihood of effective implementation increases substantially. However in practice, national and local elites can easily consolidate power and direct project benefits to themselves by dominating participatory processes and community[-]based organizations. In addition, when vulnerable community members speak out, they can expose themselves to the rancor of those whose interests are challenged. Furthermore, despite official rhetoric, donor agencies can be ambivalent toward politically troublesome, open community dialog….

That said, successes were achieved. Specifically, Nakai brought awareness that mercury use is dangerous and can be used more safely to nearly 9000 people, and some 700 miners were introduced to safer mercury use and more efficient gold recovery methods. […]

The behavioral change approach recognizes that empowerment of the target audience is essential to achieve change. Empowerment opens the door to new choices, but it does not ensure that new behaviors will be adopted, as significant cultural and economic forces (such as Zimbabwe's exploitive mineral processing centers) often stand in the way.

Real engagement of the beneficiaries of international organization and industry funded development projects is essential for successful program implementation. Community involvement in planning, for example, can disclose who has power and where the program structural limitations might lie, and generate achievable community-designed success indicators. The openness and transparency of "drama-discussion" or "start–stop" theatre for development can be a powerful tool to draw beneficiaries into the planning process and to help ensure that local elites are unable to capture the project's benefits during implementation. In regions such as Africa where there has been a history of community drama, exploring solutions to community needs through informal plays is a form of dialog that resonates well with traditional cultures.

Further Reading

Bates, R.A. (1996). Popular theatre: A useful process for adult educators. *Adult Education Quarterly, 46*(4), 224–236. From an adult education perspective, Bates outlines both terms and processes for popular theatre.

Butterwick, S. & Selman, J. (2003). Deep listening in a feminist popular theatre project: Upsetting the position of audience in participatory education. *Adult Education Quarterly, 54*(1), 7–22. This essay looks at facilitation skills needed when working with challenging material and promotes the notion of "deep listening" as part of the reflective process.

Coult, T. & Kershaw, B. (Eds.). (1983). *Engineers of the imagination: The Welfare State handbook.* London, UK: Methuen. More reading about the UK company Welfare State.

Haseman, B., Baldwin, A. & Linthwaite, H. (2014). Folk opera: Stories crossing borders in Papua New Guinea. *RIDE: The Journal of Applied Theatre and Performance, 19*(1), 98-109. The Life Drama project (www.lifedrama.net) "is a drama-based sexual health promotion project" (p. 98) in Papua New Guinea aiming to prevent the spread of sexually transmitted diseases. The use of indigenous folk opera forms is presented as a key strategy in the project.

Prentki, T. & Selman, J. (2000). *Popular theatre in political culture: Britain and Canada in focus.* Bristol, UK: Intellect Books. This text has an excellent collection of case studies with particular emphasis on process and facilitation.

Price, J. (2011). To teach and delight? Examining the efficacy of popular theatre forms in radical theatre practice. *Studies in Theatre and Performance, 31*(1), 75-93. Price considers the aesthetics and benefits of popular theatre forms in the twenty-first century as explored through student projects he has facilitated.

Salverson, J. (2001). Questioning an aesthetic of injury: Notes from the development of *BOOM*. *CTR: Canadian Theatre Review, 106,* 66–69. Salverson was commissioned by the Canadian Red Cross to develop a play on land mines and made use of clowning in its inception. This issue of CTR also includes the script of *BOOM*.

Questions for Reflection and Discussion

1. Who are the audience members for each of the case studies in this chapter? What do they hold in common and how are they different?

2. Looking at your own theatre experience, where have you seen the use of mask, puppet, music and/or spectacle? How are those experiences of that kind of performance different from other kinds of theatre you have seen?

3. Popular theatre uses practices that are often outside of our traditional understanding of theatre. What criteria might we use to assess its effectiveness?

4. What is the difference between *popular* and *populist* theatre?

Suggested Activities

1. Identify an audience, location and locally relevant topic that you would like to explore through theatre. Invite a skilled practitioner of mask, puppetry or circus techniques to offer a workshop. How might you incorporate some of these new performance skills into the project?

2. "Comedy makes the subversion of the existing state of affairs possible." – Dario Fo (n.d.). Nobel prize-winning actor, director and playwright Dario Fo has drawn on clown traditions throughout his distinguished career to create highly political and activist theatre in Italy and around the world. In small groups, create and perform a clown-based piece of theatre that has a satirical and subversive intent.

3. Create a short piece of politically based theatre that tackles an issue of shared concern. Recreate the piece using puppets you have built, bought or borrowed. These puppets could be as simple as children's toys or dolls, even kitchen utensils endowed with character. How does the use of puppets change or shift the meanings within the piece?

4. Choose a political issue in your community. Write a song in any style with the intention of moving people to take action.

Web Resources

Bread and Puppet Theater, Glover, VT http://breadandpuppet.org/

Jumblies Theatre, Toronto, ON http://www.jumbliestheatre.org/

Runaway Moon Theatre, Enderby, BC http://www.runawaymoon.org/

San Francisco Mime Troupe, San Francisco, CA http://www.sfmt.org/index.php

Teatr Grodski, Bielsko-Biala, Poland http://www.teatrgrodzki.pl/en

Welfare State International Archive, Bristol, UK http://www.welfare-state.org/

Chapter Five
Documentary Theatre

Introduction

Documentary theatre is a genre that arose in the twentieth century for sociopolitical purposes and in resistance to mass media. The intention of this genre was to inform audiences and to provoke community discussion or action on a wide range of issues. Our research on documentary theatre shows most of the work occurring in what we would define as mainstream theatre settings rather than as community-based applied practice. However, we see within the field of applied theatre the roots of documentary theatre approaches; those roots are apparent in popular theatre, theatre-in-education and in theatre of the oppressed to varying degrees. In recent years, applied theatre practitioners have been drawing more extensively on documentary theatre approaches as are seen in the case studies that follow.

> In its attempt to illustrate man's (sic) condition and the world of our time the theatre has two alternatives. It can create on the stage a reality of its own where the laws of the world outside the theater are only partly valid. The other alternative is to approximate to the world outside and to start with the social and historical facts.
>
> Irmeli Niemi, 1973, p. 29

The didactic purpose of documentary theatre was and continues to be to offer materials about real-world events to audiences in an accessible form. Using previously published documents such as newspaper stories, government reports, statistics, tables, trial transcripts and so on, documentary theatre makers present authentic material that is edited but unaltered in content. These sources and events are generally well known by an audience but in the juxtaposition of points of view and alternative perspectives there is the possibility of dramatic tension. The interest generated by the clashing of viewpoints can make this type of theatre very effective in performance. As Taylor (2011) suggests,

> In the context of contemporary distrust of grand narratives, fact-based dramas about the failures and corruption of institutions can generate emotional enlistment and channel it towards a demand for the reform of institutions and the public sphere. This may not be the politics of revolution but it is the politics of reform, which might be as much as we can ask for at present. (pp. 233-234)

The varied techniques used in documentary theatre offer many possible and fruitful adaptations within applied theatre practice as a way to place participants' local and personal issues within larger global and critical systemic contexts. Verbatim theatre, for example, makes use of participants' or witnesses' testimony on an event or shared experience rather than retrieved material such as official reports or published transcripts. In this way, verbatim theatre (also called theatre of witness or testimony theatre) "tends to acquire its authority more from its use of word for word accounts than its use of concrete, retrieved and verifiable 'evidence'" (Stuart Fisher, 2011, p. 196).

The history of documentary theatre can be traced back to the Russian Revolution (1917 on) in the east and the Great Depression (1929 on) in the west. These dramatic historical events led directly to the rise of this new theatre form in which propagandist or counter-propagandist intentions gave artists and audiences opportunities to reflect together on what was happening around them. The Living Newspaper, for example, was developed in Russia in the 1920s. Around five thousand Blue Blouse theatre troupes toured to factories and communities nationwide to perform in this style to largely illiterate audiences on the issues and events of the day. The shows drew heavily on popular forms such as melodrama, pageants, processions, variety shows and music hall revues so that the performances "involved a 'parade' of headlines, intricate dance and choreography... song, skits, pantomimes, masks, and puppetry" (Favorini, 2013, p. 99). The purpose of this large-scale project was known as "agitprop," arising as it did from the Department of Agitation and Propaganda in the Soviet government. Agitprop documentary theatre had an explicitly political agenda to present the government's position on national and world events. These largely black and white depictions involved heroic portrayals of the communist Soviet Union and demonization of the capitalist West.

After the stock market collapse of 1929 and the severe economic repercussions in the 1930s, the American government under President Franklin Roosevelt funded the Federal Theatre Project. From 1935 to 1939, this project hired out-of-work writers, actors and directors to create topical plays performed across the country on issues such as social housing, disease prevention and government corruption. These documentary plays included Living Newspapers that took a similar left-wing perspective as the Soviet model, although tempered somewhat in the western context of (supposed) democracy and individual freedom. Reaction against some of these productions from members of the US Congress and others in positions of power led to the end of the Federal Theatre Project after only four years.

Documentary theatre seems inevitable in an age dominated by scientific investigation and technological invention. But it also seems part of our passion for getting down to the truth, seeing behind the scenes.

Peter Cheeseman, 1970, p. vii

Documentary theatre practice fell away somewhat in the 1940s and 1950s but reappeared as a form through the 1960s in England and Germany. In England, progressive director Joan Littlewood's company Theatre Workshop mounted an important production in 1965 called *Oh What a Lovely War!*, a satirical musical play about World War I that proved very popular with audiences. Another UK director, Peter Cheeseman, was inspired by Littlewood's work to begin creating documentary plays on local and historical events with his company Victoria Theatre at Stoke-on-Trent. Cheeseman and his collaborators developed a method that involved a months-long research period during which documents were gathered and oral history interviews were carried out with community members and government or industry officials. Cheeseman's innovation was in the use of interviews and their transcripts as source materials. These materials were then transformed by the acting company into a collective creation incorporating only direct documentary evidence, the rule being that nothing extraneous or fictional was included (Cheeseman, 1970). At the same time as Cheeseman's company began in the mid-1960s, the German writer and playwright Peter Weiss premiered a play in 1965 called *The Investigation* based on his attendance at the Frankfurt Auschwitz trials. Weiss' contributions to the development of documentary theatre include using the trial format and in taking some dramatic license in creating collective characters who represent the testimony of many witnesses, perpetrators and survivors (Niemi, 1973). Both of these approaches have evolved into more contemporary documentary theatre forms including the popular "tribunal theatre."

Moving towards the present, we can chart the growth of documentary theatre in many countries and under many labels or terms: "theatre of the real includes documentary theatre, verbatim theatre, reality-based theatre, theatre-of-fact, theatre of witness, tribunal theatre, nonfiction theatre, restored village performances, war and battle reenactments, and autobiographical theatre" (Martin, 2013, p. 18). We note that Forsyth and Megson (2009) describe documentary theatre as "a burgeoning field of theatre practice, focusing on…relationship with the archive, its potential resistance to hegemonic structures of power, and its contribution within the public sphere" (pp. 1-2). Contemporary documentary theatre has arisen with force over the 20-year period that coincides with the Internet revolution. The unfiltered and immediate access to information provided by the Internet (for many but far from all people) has radically shifted many aspects of human existence, including the practices of theatre-making.

The following case studies demonstrate this twenty-first century shift away from official documents as the only source for documentary theatre-making and towards capturing and presenting, in as authentic a way as possible, the stories of people who have been involved in and/or directly affected by an event or situation.

Our first case study is historic and presents an overview of one of documentary theatre founders Peter Weiss' project, "The Song of a Scarecrow" from 1967. This play exemplifies early documentary theatre approaches in the use of characters who represent different political and economic groups or attitudes, verbatim material from various official documents, use of a dramatic chorus and the setting of a trial. "Truth in Translation" was a play created from interviews and workshops with translators who worked for the Truth and Reconciliation Commission in South Africa following the fall of apartheid. "That's Who I Could be if I Could Sing" is a British project based on interviews with mothers whose children were victims of sexual abuse. The author and playwright provides us with the best example we have found of a verbatim theatre project that also functions effectively as applied theatre. The last case study addresses the ongoing political issue in Australia of refugee detainment in camps while the federal government determines their status. "Through the Wire" was developed from interviews with four detainees, one of whom later was cast in the production alongside other professional actors. The repercussions of this project included the government withholding touring funds, a nervous response by those in power that reminds us of the potential this kind of theatre has to question, inform and disrupt.

5.1 Fight for freedom
from *Peter Weiss and documentary theatre: Song of a scarecrow*
Irmeli Niemi. (1973). *Modern Drama*, 16(1), 29–34.

Song of a Scarecrow is built according to a clear trisection, resembling the defendant-witness-court arrangement of *Die Ermittlung* [*The Investigation*]. The characters are now disposed in groups of oppressors, victims of oppression, and sympathetic onlookers. The oppressors are clear-cut types: a general, a bishop, a gentleman, a lady, a scarecrow. The Africans, on the other hand, are represented by a chorus and four speakers who also act as narrators and present short, sharp scenes about the lives of the natives. The oppressors speak mostly in grandiloquent poetic prose, the African speakers in rough and unpolished rhyming verse, familiar from [Weiss'] *Marat Sade*. The lines of the chorus contain lyrical, sentimental passages based on African folklore.

The scarecrow of the title is a big metal structure which stands on the stage throughout and symbolizes the power of the oppressors. It is deliberately and concretely inhuman. Its size and appearance are related to its effectiveness and its falsehood: the unholy alliance between the church and capitalism has raised it. Weiss'criticism, however, is directed not only towards these traditional institutions, but also towards the more recent continuers of oppression and exploitation, especially NATO and the gigantic foreign industrial corporations. By rising above the characters on the stage the scarecrow represents the highest authority, well-established and unreachable. Its nucleus is known to be of waste, trash, and manure, but although this is known, nobody can remove the lustrous marks of external glory: the medals, the ribbons, the jewelled cross. Furthermore, the resisting of knowledge is the most effective of the scarecrow's weapons and is used by the power group behind it to maintain its prominent positions:

> Above all such a gentleman must maintain
> Or even increase ignorance.
> Because most of them cannot read or write,
> It does not matter if they get angry and make a noise.
> Even keeping body and soul together is hard for them,
> In vain they try to dig themselves out of the manure.
>
> (p. 205)

Society is ruled by those who have knowledge and money, the generals and bankers of Portugal, the white immigrants in Angola. In the course of eleven thematic "songs" the gulf between different groups of people is revealed in various miniature scenes. Economic struggle is the driving force behind the racial prejudices. There are clear contrasts between the views and aims of different groups: the difficulties of the victims of oppression in their fruitless attempts to obtain justice are confronted with the excuses to which powerful people have recourse. [...]

In the distribution of power the contrast is most striking: everything operates through the colonial authorities; the Africans cannot participate in making decisions, nor have they the right to own land or forests. The victims of oppression cannot choose what work they will do, and the work they are given is often so hard that they cannot find the time to learn to read and write. It is only after a strict interrogation that a native can have the rights of an "assimilado":

> I have not been punished before
> I can read and write Portuguese fluently
> I am familiar with the glorious history of Portugal
> I have given the pledge of loyalty
> I have two testimonials to my character
> I have a health certificate
> I have a permanent job
> I have always paid my taxes conscientiously
> I go to church regularly
> I have reached the necessary level
> Of education and morals.
>
> (p. 218)

Monologue is here used in a way characteristic of the political play. The "I" who speaks is only the representative of a small group, but he is completely identified with his group. There is nothing individual or different about him. Each line discloses the prevailing situation and simultaneously criticizes it with a disguised, satirical shaft. What is presented as "the glorious history of Portugal" and "the necessary level of education and morals" is not unambiguous. [...]

The play makes a sharp distinction between that violence which is a part of systematic oppression and the smoldering hatred within the mind of the oppressed. Individual human fates are of no importance to the system. This is most clearly shown in the small scene about the life of a native woman called Ana. It is only here that the play approaches the distress of an individual human being and the little things of every day:

> That is the box on which we eat
> That is the pan
> That is the jug
> There are flies at the mouth of the jug
> The flies fly out of the jug
> At the children
> The flies creep into the children's eyes
> One of the children has a fever.

(p. 232) [...]

The beginning of the play discloses and analyzes different manifestations of power and oppression. It is not until Part VIII that active sympathy for the victims of oppression begins to change into a call for rebellion. The speaker who earlier behaved like a cool lecturer now turns directly to address "peasants, convicts, prisoners." A radical attitude is also reflected in the alteration that Weiss has made in the chorus text: the originally distant and impersonal lines "the land must belong to those who cultivate land/ people who build the houses must live in those houses" have been changed to "The land that we cultivate must belong to us/ we must have a right to live in the houses we build." An "agitation poem" resembling an incantation or a ritual, bound to a tense, suggestive rhythm, repeats the refrain "Crush his power." The views of the three groups become increasingly clear-cut; sometimes it is "I," more often "we" or "they"; as a result the attempted rebellion is suppressed by the unity of the capitalist power.

Weiss' optimism is seen as the play nears its end, but it is not undisturbed. The scarecrow is knocked down, but the class distinctions, the lines between the visible and the concealed, remain and even become more prominent. Information spreads into the cells of political prisoners through secret channels; the contrast between the prisoners' experiences of torture and the ever-growing reputation of Portugal as a tourist country is made to seem grotesque. The last words of the chorus, spoken by the victims of oppression, are distressfully broken and sparse: "a sound of hatred" smoulders in them and they do not conceal the price to be paid for freedom.

Song of a Scarecrow takes a direct and sharp political stand. It contains a strong protest against prevailing conditions and those who profit from these conditions. It detaches the protagonists from the chaotic basic material and exposes the reality in them through strong simplifications, by juxtaposing the big and the small, the individual and the group, by utilizing antitheses and repetitions as well as rapid changes of situation. The play has, like documentary theater in general, been blamed for its lack of objectivity, but Weiss objects to this criticism. He regards objectivity as a concept used by those in power to defend their actions; "a call for patience and order always comes from those with whom everything is well and who do not want to lose their interests."

According to Weiss the documentary theater cannot be compared to authentic, political expressions of opinion. Even when it seems to be formed in a moment and to function without preparation, it is, however, a work of art; if it were not, it would not, in Weiss's opinion, have a right to exist.

5.2 Translating testimony
from *Truth in translation*
Elizabeth Redden. (December 2006). *Swarthmore College Bulletin*, 17–23.
Including a performance review *Chaotic harmony*
Karen Birdsall. (December 2006). *Swarthmore College Bulletin*, 20.

For the translators who served South Africa's Truth and Reconciliation Commission (TRC), there was no turning away when Nodwzakazi Juqu described the compulsion to burn her dead son's bullet-ridden shirt – "I have never seen a shirt like that with so many holes as if rats were eating on it. I just had to burn it because I couldn't look at it for too long, it was really going to affect me mentally."

Nor could they block their ears when Michael Bolofo described touching his intestines in disbelief after he, at 17 and on his way home, fell under fire into a pool of his own blood.

In an unprecedented social experiment, the gross human rights violations that had been hidden beneath apartheid's bloody cloak gushed out of South Africa's busted gut for 2 years, beginning in 1996. In a public forum, the TRC sought testimonies from victims and perpetrators – who were promised amnesty if their crimes were found to be politically motivated. Every word was translated into the 11 languages spoken in South Africa so that no crime, no confession would go unheard.

The TRC translators relived the tales of violence as they interpreted them in first person. They embodied both the machinery of oppression and those who raged against it. They retold the bloody truths and relived story after story, but their own story has lingered untold – until now. [...]

Truth in Translation, a theatrical production conceived and directed by [Michael] Lessac, tells the story of the translators who acted as vessels through which testimony from the TRC flowed. As the temporary repositories of a nation's memory, the translators became the living intermediaries between South Africa's past and present, translating the past in real time to help the country forgive and forge a future. The unique experience of becoming a chattering witness is what now brings these translators to center stage.

Truth in Translation premiered this summer in Kigali, Rwanda, with four lights and a microphone, in theaters that weren't really theaters. Each day, about 50 children attended the rehearsals, pulling up chairs to watch the cast prepare, recalls Jackie Lessac, Michael's wife and executive producer for the project. During night-time performances, audience members would translate the translators' stories for one another, silence welling into sound and settling back to silence, languages slipping over one another as the play progressed. After each production, conversations with the audience would last for hours, as the play opened a space for citizens to confront their own country's past and present: the 1994 genocide and the people who still have to pick up the pieces.

"People were talking about things they normally don't talk about, normally keep back," Michael Lessac says. Things like... "How is it possible for mothers to kill their own children? For fathers to kill their own children? For fathers to kill their wives? "

"What is the difference between killing your nephew from killing your child from killing your fourth cousin from killing your 10th cousin?"

Following the Rwanda visit, the play made its South African debut at The Market Theatre in Johannesburg for a 1-month run in September. [...]

Truth in Translation is more than a play. The project seeks to address the consequences of genocide and civil strife around the world. Final rehearsals before its Johannesburg premiere in September were held in Rwanda, where cast members...visited the sites of the genocide there.

Chaotic harmony: A review by Karen Birdsall

Truth in Translation is not an easy theater experience – it is what South Africans would call 'hectic.' The subject of the play is raw and brutal, and the material is delivered by the 11-person cast at a frenzied, relentless pace that crowds out space for reflection. One is almost dizzied by the movement, the noise, the intensity of exchanges, and the multitude of languages.

Various elements are woven together in a way that is chaotic but, somehow, also harmonious. Above the stage, grainy video footage of the TRC hearings is projected against a screen made of T-shirts; below, the ensemble is in constant motion, all 11 cast members on stage at once, continuously reconfiguring the set comprised of modular metal units that serve alternatively as desks, billiard table, and bar. A small upstage contributes the musical glue.

Anyone who has spent time in South Africa recognizes the power of Hugh Masekela's music to capture this country's particular mix of joy, sorrow, humour, expectation, injustice, and resilience. The music – along with the play's occasional moments of humor and light-heartedness – [is] effective in gently bringing together the diverse members of the audience, before releasing each person to grapple individually with the play's subject matter. Today, 10 years after the TRC, a "new South Africa" may indeed be emerging, but for the racially mixed audience at the Market Theatre, the story being told on stage resonated very differently depending on one's own history in this country.

With so much to absorb, I found myself focusing intently on a few of the 11 characters.... Each character proceeds through an individual journey, from the naïve excitement of landing a job as a translator, through the realization of what the work will entail, to the coping methods needed to get through it. Many of the characters uncover a personal connection to a political past: What began as something abstract gradually takes on a very real meaning. Some lose themselves in drink. Some repress the emotion for as long as they can. Some knit furiously and silently.

The play contains a number of particularly charged moments – the "comforter's" wrenching song at the close of the first act, the re-enacted interrogation between a black and white interpreter, the cantankerous bartender throwing his son's ashes across the stage. Yet for me, the most intense and powerful moments came during the scenes that depicted the hearings themselves, when eight translators interpreted simultaneously – some speaking English, others isiZulu, Sesotho, isiXhosa, Afrikaans... There was no coherent story to follow, only a cacophony of overlapping phrases, translated sentences, painful accounts of torture, abuse, and loss, spit out like bullets in multiple languages all at once.

I was gripped by the expressions on the translators' faces. Anyone who has translated at length from one language to another knows the intense concentration required to perform the role, but few people have needed to translate as they did – speaking in first person, alternating between the words of accused and accuser, becoming a conduit for wretched stories and soulless excuses, speaking with a matter-of-factness that belied the gruesome testimony. The eight translators, with their hands cupped over imaginary earpieces, stared blankly into space, listening intently to the voices in their ears. Yet the horror was just below the surface, and it came spilling out when they switched off the interpreting devices, crumbling into themselves and sometimes into one another.

Although the Truth and Reconciliation Commission translators had a mandate to be impartial channels, inevitably they absorbed the stories of the perpetrators and victims of apartheid – truth and lies, healing and horror. They could not hide, and denial was not an option.

[Truth in Translation is] proffering hope and facilitating dialogue among people who crave what the TRC offered: a space to seek truth and, potentially, forgiveness. "They want to talk to us and are totally unthreatened by us, and they do talk," Lessac wrote in an August e-mail he titled "Notes from Rwanda."

"So we travel from genocide memorials and museums … to performing in a stadium for 10,000 cheering people (music and songs) … to talking with victims … and perps … and hearing stories about people who actually killed their children because they were afraid … to people who wouldn't talk about anything to people who had stories roiling inside them so that they came out like water from an unstopped faucet…."

5.3 Reciprocating roles
from *'That's who I'd be if I could sing': Reflections on a verbatim project with mothers of sexually abused children*
Amanda Stuart Fisher. (2011). *Studies in Theatre and Performance*, 31(2), 193–208.

Using verbatim to tell an individual's or a community's story engages the writer in an ethical contract with those offering up their life experiences. In this context the individual offering their story becomes the verbatim subject and as such should have some agency within the process. […]

The distinction between testimonial, factual and verifiable 'truth' takes on monumental emotional and legal significance when dealing with the issue of child abuse. It soon became clear from the experiences of the mothers we worked with that the process of providing verifiable evidence of sexual abuse to a court of law is extremely complex and disturbing for both the child and the parent(s) caring for them. […]

Yet despite the fact that most child sexual abuse is perpetrated either by a family member or by someone known to the child (and in the home), this form of abuse rarely comes to public attention and the story of the predatory paedophile is far more likely to be taken up by the popular press. Familial child sexual abuse then continues to be treated as a taboo or a secret that is difficult to talk about. This issue was raised early on in our verbatim project by many of those involved. It consequently shaped the development of our methodology and informed our decision to focus on verbatim theatre strategies rather than a documentary theatre approach. […]

The project that eventually became known as 'From the Mouths of Mothers' was a collaboration between myself (a senior lecturer in Applied Theatre at Central School of Speech and Drama), Big Fish Young People's Theatre Company (a company that, at that time, used theatre to address issues relating to social injustice and young people) and Mosac (a charity that provides support resources for non-abusing parents and carers of sexually abused children). It developed out of Big Fish's three-year lottery-funded project on unwanted sexual contact and enabled us to address the issue of sexual abuse in a fully supported and clearly defined context. By focusing on the narratives of mothers rather than the young people themselves, we were able to ensure that those participating in the project could receive emotional support by the services provided by Mosac.

Furthermore, all the mothers who participated in the project had been invited to do so by Denise Hubble, Mosac's counselling coordinator. This meant that Denise could identify particular individuals she felt were at an appropriate point in their emotional journey to participate in this kind of project. The interviews, which lasted between two and three hours each, were undertaken by two colleagues and me. They took place in the counselling room at Mosac, the location of the interviews was important for one of the objectives of the project was to ensure that the mothers felt comfortable and empowered by the process of creating the play. The values implicit to the project's methodology both informed the interview process itself and placed the empowerment and well-being of the mothers themselves at the heart of the project. Whilst the objective of creating a play of artistic integrity was of crucial importance, it was also hoped that the reciprocity with/ between the mothers would be an experience that in some way would be beneficial and positive. As the playwright, this of course impacted upon the artistic choices I made. The interviews produced seven enormously complex and emotionally powerful stories. Out of respect for the mothers who spoke to us, I chose to tell each of these stories in the play, rather than selecting the most poignant or the best told. By doing this I was conscious of not eradicating or silencing any of the women who had so generously offered up their stories to us.

It was from a desire to generate a supportive creative process that led us, at the start of the project, to ask the mothers directly about how they would like the interview process to operate and how they wanted their stories to be told…. From discussion with the mothers it became clear that whilst there were many differences in the way each woman narrated their experiences, there were also many similarities in the stories that were told (particularly in relation to the way the families had perpetually been let down by the legal system and social agencies of care), it was also clear that these mothers had already – too often – experienced the voices of 'others' either silencing them or contradicting their testimonies… Instead the play would seek to find a way of performing the mother's stories so they could be listened to and perhaps finally heard. …The result was a verbatim play that used only the material that was transcribed from our recordings of our interviews with the mothers we spoke to.

The process of editing this material together into a play was a complex and, at times, difficult process that began with the task of transcribing the fourteen hours of interviews we had recorded. As the playwright I then worked with the transcriptions, listened again to all the interviews and gradually worked together a structure that enabled me to tell each mother's unique story whilst also pulling together shared themes and moments of commonality. The danger of this approach was that I might have inadvertently sensationalized or manipulated the mother's stories in my endeavours to generate a coherent story and structure.

Adopting this kind of reflexive approach, which incorporates the participation of verbatim subjects themselves in the creative process, is certainly not a new approach to theatre making, and is one that is particularly familiar within applied theatre practices.

Yet, interestingly within a lot of the commentary around verbatim and documentary theatre there seems to be very few examples of playwrights evaluating their projects by consulting those whose stories generated it. [...]

Throughout the work on From the Mouths of Mothers, I became increasingly intrigued by the dynamics of the relationship that developed between the mothers who told their stories and the actors who performed them. ...From the initial dynamics that developed between the actors and the mothers at this reading, it became clear that this relationship – which seemed to be one of an intense identification – was a positive, even therapeutic aspect of the project. [...]

> The oddest part was hearing someone playing me [...] Superb actors.
> The singing was brilliant too.
>
> (Christine 13 September 2007)
>
> Yes! And everyone thinks I can sing now!
>
> (Saara 13 September 2007)
>
> No that's what you'd sound like if you could sing!
>
> (Anne 13 September 2007)

The final exchange between two of the mothers who, following the play – I refer to as 'Saara' and 'Anne' – is particularly interesting because it encapsulates some of the key questions I have about the relationship between the mothers and the actors. The singing that Saara refers to here is when 'her actor' sang a short child's rhyme at the start of each of the five movements of the play. This was not in the script, it was not sung 'in character' nor did it allude to any aspect of Saara's character. It was a moment of theatricality invented by the director as she was preparing the rehearsed reading. [...]

For the mothers then, their identification with the actors was a positive, empathetic experience that 'connected' them to each other and the whole process of the project itself.

5.4 Detaining asylum seekers in Australia

from *To witness mimesis: The politics, ethics, and aesthetics of testimonial theatre in Through the Wire*
Caroline Wake. (2013). *Modern Drama*, 56(1), 102–125.

The four asylum seekers in *Through the Wire* [by Ros Horin] come from a variety of places (Shahin, Farshid, and Mohsen are from different cities within Iran, and Rami is from Iraq) and a variety of religious backgrounds (Shahin, Farshid, and Mohsen do not mention religion, and Rami is described as Christian, specifically a Chaldean). They also work in a variety of professions (Shahin is an actor and playwright, Farshid a pathologist, Mohsen a court officer, and Rami a student of hospitality). Despite these differences, however, their stories start to sound remarkably similar. For instance, in scene six, Farshid tells of working in a pathology lab and conducting an unauthorized test on a urine sample believed to belong to an Ayatollah. Soon afterwards, both his co-conspirator and his father were arrested and tortured, and Farshid had to flee to a family farm, where he hid for almost a year. During this time, his collaborator was executed, and the clinic's technician and nurse "disappeared," prompting Farshid to leave Iran altogether. In the same scene, Mohsen tells his story of working in a corrupt Iranian court, where a notorious murderer had consistently and rather suspiciously avoided prosecution. When Mohsen raised concerns about this, he was promptly promoted far beyond his experience and abilities. Still concerned, he proceeded to publish his allegations in a journal, at which point the secret police issued a death warrant and went to his mother's house to destroy his files. Shahin tells a similar story: having been banned first from playwriting and then from acting, he nevertheless persevered with his theatrical activities, collaborating with a friend who was doing a doctorate in drama and wanted to stage one of Shahin's plays. When the secret police raided one of the rehearsals, they took the actors and director in for interrogation, leaving Shahin little choice but to flee. In short, these stories can be summarized as I crossed the authorities; I was warned; I crossed the authorities again; a collaborator was arrested and tortured; I had to escape.

Just as their stories of persecution start to resemble one another, so too do their stories of escape. Farshid paid money to a people smuggler, sneaked over the Iranian border into Pakistan, and then flew to Malaysia. Though he tried to get to England, the people smugglers told him that it was not possible at that point in time and suggested that he go to Australia. Similarly, Mohsen escaped over the border to Turkey, from where he flew to Malaysia and then to Perth (though he was told that he was flying to England). Shahin flew to Malaysia, tried to get to Germany but failed, and then went to Australia by boat. Like the persecution stories, these escape stories can be summarized as I escaped from Iran; I arrived in Malaysia; I tried to seek asylum elsewhere; I failed; I tried to seek asylum in Australia. In this way, the refugees' real stories are rendered not only repetitive but also repeatable and by implication scripted and performable.

While such patterning is a function of the play's structure, it is also likely to be a function of the refugee-determination process itself, whereby vastly different stories are all forced to fit into the same generic shape. In fact, the staging of this scene illustrates precisely this aspect of the refugee-determination process by performing the emergence of each story identically. One by one, the asylum seekers come downstage to sit on a chair and tell their stories while speaking into a microphone and looking into a video camera. This image, a shoulder-wide shot of the speaker, is then displayed, via a live feed, on a large screen at the back of the stage. Thus, while the scene's structure works to emphasize the stories' similarities, the staging works to emphasize their theatricality, in the sense of doubled and performed, spectacular and cinematic.

This interview scene is followed by another (scene seven), in which Farshid suddenly and forcefully announces: "But I couldn't tell my story like that to Immigration. No, not at all!" From here the scene slides into chaos, as the actors deliver the following lines loudly and rapidly, often speaking simultaneously:

MOHSEN, RAMI, FARSHID	I was in the small room at the airport.
ALL	I was frightened.
MOHSEN	I was cold.
RAMI AND FARSHID	I was hot.
ALL	I was shivering . . .
FARSHID	My mind was in panic.
ALL	I tried to answer his questions . . .
FARSHID	I was telling my story from one part to another and I'd try to make a link... it was all in my mind... but I couldn't manage my mind . . .
ALL	To just tell my story in order.
FARSHID	I mean the Immigration – they pick you up on . . .
DOREEN	You didn't say that part first . . .
GABY	Now you're saying this . . .
SUSAN	So you didn't mean that . . .
DOREEN	This is not adding up.
FARSHID	I mean they don't really realise how nervous are the people who just arrived.
DOREEN	When you come from that sort of intimated [sic] environment . . .
FARSHID	You don't know how much to say or not . . .
MOHSEN	We have never had trust in officials in our life . . .
RAMI	Maybe that man works for the secret police!

Even as this frantic scene undermines the reality of the prior scene, it also reinforces the reality claims of the play more broadly. Here, it becomes clear that the previous scene was not an imitation but an invention; the interview as the refugees would have had it, not as it was. In this way, the play stages a reversal: the real stories are revealed as theatrical fictions, and the theatrical stories are rendered real, in the sense that they are less structured, more scattered, and by implication less rehearsed and thus more authentic. [...]

If providing autobiographical information in the program worked to reduce the distance between theatre and reality, then casting Shahin Shafaei as himself collapsed it altogether. While the program notes and publicity alerted some spectators to the fact that Shafaei was playing himself, others did not realize until the final scene, when the lights dimmed and the seven actors stood in a line and turn their backs to the audience. ... When an image of Shahin appeared on screen and the actor playing him turned around to face the audience, the two were one and the same and there were audible gasps....[...]

Regardless of whether spectators knew in advance, the presence of Shafaei seems to have caused some confusion afterwards, leading some spectators to conflate every actor with his or her character, especially those playing asylum seekers.[...]

The revelation of Shafaei prompts me to reflect on other ways in which the traumatic [reveal] might reverberate throughout the play. I wonder how Shafaei feels about repeating his story onstage. I wonder how Farshid, Rami, and Mohsen feel about watching actors repeat their stories onstage. Moreover, I wonder how these stories emerged in the first place. Presumably, Horin had to interview the asylum seekers, but just how did she do so? For all its effort to reveal the interviewing methodology of the government, the play is strangely reticent about its own. Unlike other verbatim plays, where writers insert themselves into the text, *Through the Wire* shows no traces of the interviewing process or the interviewer.

Further Reading

Bottoms, S. (2006). Putting the document into documentary. *TDR: The Drama Review*, *50*(3), 56-68. Bottoms' essay provides a critical perspective on documentary theatre in which he questions whether theatre can ever recreate the real.

Cheeseman, P. (1970). Introduction: Documentary theatre at Stoke-on-Trent. In P. Cheeseman and the Victoria Theatre Company, *The knotty: A musical documentary* (pp. vi-xx). London, UK: Methuen. An invaluable historical document that captures this company's way of working from inception to production over a period of months.

Favorini, A. (2013). Collective creation in documentary theatre. In K. Mederos Syssoyeva & S. Proudfit (Eds.), *A history of collective creation* (pp. 97-112). New York, NY: Palgrave Macmillan. An excellent international survey of the many iterations of documentary theatre through the twentieth century.

Forsyth, A. & Megson, C. (Eds.). (2009). *Get real: Documentary theatre past and present.* New York, NY: Palgrave Macmillan. This scholarly collection includes case studies on documentary theatre projects and artists from the twentieth century and contemporary practices worldwide.

Holzapfel, T. (1976). *Pueblo rechazado*: Educating the public through reportage. *Latin American Theatre Review*, *10*(1), 15-21. A historical Mexican documentary theatre project from 1968 that includes useful definitions and characteristics and considers the political intentions of the work.

Jeffers, A. (2006). Refugee perspectives: The practice and ethics of verbatim theatre and refugee stories. *Platform*, *1*(1), 1-17. Retrieved from https://www.royalholloway. ac.uk/dramaandtheatre/platform/home.aspx. Jeffers provides a brief history of verbatim theatre and raises a number of important ethical questions around the use of refugee stories.

Martin, C. (2013). Theatre of the real: An overview. In C. Martin, *Theatre of the real* (pp. 1-21). New York, NY: Palgrave Macmillan. Martin surveys what she calls "theatre of the real" in the opening chapter of her book on this topic.

Nagel, E. (2007). An aesthetic of neighborliness: Possibilities for integrating community-based practices into documentary theatre. *Theatre Topics*, *17*(2), 153-168. Nagel offers her experience as facilitator and playwright working in a community-based project that challenged the use of professional actors performing local stories.

Questions for Reflection and Discussion

1. How might the place and time you choose to conduct an interview for a documentary theatre project affect the interview itself? What considerations and planning might you do to ensure your interviewee is able to best tell their story?

2. What is your response to the use of "traumatic reveal" in *Through the Wire* (Section 5.4) in which at the curtain call one of the actors is revealed to also have been the subject of an interview? What are the ethical implications of either concealing or revealing an actor who is also a participant telling his/her own story on stage?

3. Who determines the point of view or stance taken by any given documentary theatre project? In our research, it seems clear that in most cases a playwright organizes documents and/or interviews into a script representing his or her perspective on a topic or event. Yet in applied theatre practice, again in general, this is not the process because interviewees are also the co-creators and performers. What might be some of the ways in which a documentary theatre playwright could ensure that his or her control over the material may be mediated by those whose stories make up the content?

4. A number of critics and theorists have pointed out the importance of reminding an audience that what they are seeing is a construction of the real, not reality itself. Bottoms (2006) suggests that this use of metatheatricality "encourages spectators to think for themselves about the processes of representation involved [as] intertextual references" (pp. 66–67). What are the advantages and disadvantages of having a playwright character within a documentary play (as is often seen)? What aesthetic possibilities lie in using the construction of the play as part of the performance itself?

Suggested Activities

1. With a partner or in a small group, list the variety of research and creation strategies that are available when creating documentary theatre. What are some of the best practices you can locate that could bridge from documentary theatre to applied theatre in terms of shifting the role of informant to one of participant?

2. Gather as many news sources as possible around a particular event of shared interest and relevance.
    a) Create a theatre of reportage piece with the constraint that every word spoken or image used is derived from your sources (newspaper articles and television reports, letters to the editor, editorials, commentaries, blog posts, protests, trials and so on). Perform this as a workshop.
    b) As an extension, carry out some interviews with community members on your chosen event, seeking a range of perspectives, and weave excerpts from these interviews into your play. Perform this version.
    c) Finally, share your own responses to this event as monologues that are then swapped and rehearsed by someone else in the company.
    d) Consider and determine your intended audience for the project. What is it you want them to gain from seeing it? Perform for them. Facilitate a meaningful post-show conversation (see Prendergast & Saxton, 2013, pp. 180-181).
    e) Assess the project by reflecting on the variety and effectiveness of theatrical genres used, the perceived audience response in performance as well as the post-show comments and questions, and what each individual member of the ensemble and the ensemble itself gained from this experience.

Web Resources

8 the Play, Los Angeles, CA http://www.8theplay.com/ (see also http://www.youtube.com/watch?v=qlUG8F9uVgM)

Black Watch, Glasgow, SC www.nationaltheatrescotland.com/content/default.asp?page=
home_showBlackwatch. (see also www.youtube.com/watch?v=A4cIV-e1wcU)

Truth in Translation, Los Angeles, CA www.truthintranslation.org

Verbatim Theatre, London, UK http://www.nationaltheatre.org.uk/video/an-introduction-
to-verbatim-theatre

CHAPTER SIX
THEATRE IN EDUCATION (TIE)

Introduction

Theatre in Education (TIE) developed as a new theatre form in England in the 1960s. At that time, progressive government policies regarding funding for the arts meant that many theatre companies were able to create new programmes for community outreach. In fact, funding was tied to companies engaging in these kinds of community-based projects, and working with local schools was an obvious site for partnerships. These theatre companies were beginning to work in school settings (as opposed to schools coming to the theatre), so it was imperative that curriculum content became part of the challenge in creating theatre for these new audiences. For professional actors who were very often members of the resident company, the typical way of working in a traditional proscenium theatre was called into question because they were working in classrooms, with very little in the way of production support, and with audiences that were deliberately small in number. In addition, this close relationship with the student audience invited a higher level of participation and a different kind of audience participation than was in use in contemporary children's theatre, of which Brian Way's London Theatre Centre (established in 1953) was the most reputable example. Because they were dealing with audience participation *and* curriculum, the actors who worked at and toured the schools were required to gain an understanding of and ability to achieve effective teaching. The result of these developments was a new genre of theatre – theatre in education – and a new kind of actor, called an *actor-teacher*.

> TIE sits comfortably under the umbrella of applied theatre but at the same time can lay claim to playing a significant, if often unrecognized, part in shaping its various educational, social and political aspirations, its theoretical frameworks and its wide range of eclectic practices.
>
> Anthony Jackson & Chris Vine, 2013, p. 2

[The children] do not dispassionately watch, as they might a chemical experiment or a vaulting demon-stration; their emotions are actively engaged, willing and desiring and responding to the tensions and the humours of the action.

John O'Toole, 1976, p. 33

Conversely, for teachers in schools, this new practice became an opportunity for professional development and training in drama/theatre education. Teacher workshops, and the direct involvement of teachers in developing and implementing materials that prepared and followed-up each performance, became of central importance in delivering and assessing the success of TIE projects.

The scripts created by TIE companies were most often devised collaboratively by the members of the "team" with teacher input, and they often addressed issues of local relevance as well as curriculum content for specific age groups. The devising process demanded that actors also be capable of working collaboratively, researching and holding broad critical perspectives on sociopolitical and educational issues. Central to an effective process was the ability to keep the needs of the audience and the needs of the curriculum contained in an aesthetic framework. The resulting theatre performances, as best practiced, held intellectual and emotional resonances for their audiences. By universalizing the particular local and authentic references in performance, and through post-performance reflection, students were exposed to wider relevant aspects of the issues.

James Hennessy (1998) answers the question, "What is TIE?" in the following points (which he does not claim as absolute terms):

- TIE, like all forms of theatre, is a socially oriented activity usually taking place in a defined space and requiring the willing and tacit agreement of all involved to be bound by conventions necessary to sustain an awareness of fiction.
- TIE is performed before captive audiences; young people have no choice in attending a performance.
- TIE's prime intention is to teach; it is a mediated learning experience (usually) initiated by the actors through characters that are integral to the dramatic narrative.
- TIE, like other forms of theatre, is dependent on the physical, emotional and intellectual involvement of the participants.
- TIE's praxis has evolved through work in schools and colleges. Productions (usually) target age-specific, but mixed ability and gender, students from one class or group. [...]
- "Central to the (TIE) work ... are the twin convictions that human behaviour and institutions are formed through social activity and can therefore be changed, and that audiences, as potential agents of change, should be active participants in their own learning" (Vine, 1993, p. 109).
- The essential difference between TIE and conventional theatre is the quality of the relationship the actors share with the audience .... TIE directly engages its

audiences by encouraging them to participate within the art form; to be actively –
and interactively – responsive to and responsible for the dramatic narrative
(Hennessy, 1998, pp. 86–87).

In summary, what distinguishes TIE from traditional theatre is the devised nature of
the work and the high levels of engagement between actors and students.

In the 50 years since its inception, TIE companies have both flourished and declined
as the practice spread worldwide. As governmental policies in England became more
conservative in the 1980s, centralized funding for TIE companies – many of which
were openly critical of certain political stances and decisions – was threatened and
in a number of cases, withdrawn. Some TIE companies survived by maintaining
their educative thrust while adapting their programs to become more attractive to
local school boards. Other companies devised work that could be played to larger
audiences in bigger venues like gymnasia or auditoria; the principle of participation
was still central to the practice, but was necessarily – because of timetable strictures –
moved into preparatory and follow-up activities. The content of programs became
more general with a growing reliance on study guides rather than active partnerships
with teachers. Yet TIE companies did not vanish. More recently, an interest in TIE
has revived as part of the interventionist mandate of applied theatre in educational
contexts. Throughout this text you will note, as Jackson and Vine (2013) point out,
there are a number of case studies that "fly" under other names but are very much
rooted in the original intentions and practices of TIE: "learning through theatre
remains the governing theme" (p. 2).

*The first case study "Indigo" offers an example of a TIE project from England
that models the earlier approach of the genre as it was practiced in the 1960s
and 1970s and reflects the interest in and commitment to sociopolitical issues.
The Korean study "Big Blue Whale" presents a project on the challenging
topic of disability for elementary school children. Students encountered
disabled characters dealing with barriers to their inclusion in the classroom.
Next, "Tapestry," a recent British TIE project, tackles the timely yet delicate
topic of religious radicalization in a project for secondary school students.
The project was part of a larger government-funded initiative to prevent
violence based on religious extremism. Another major challenge today in
education and social work is the issue of domestic abuse in a variety of
forms. "Making the everyday extraordinary" is valuable because it looks
at an applied theatre programme developed on a national scale in New
Zealand in conjunction with government ministries, local social agencies
and schools.*

6.1 Human rights

from *Indigo*

Dukes TIE Company. (1993). *Standing Conference on Young Peoples Theatre [SCYPT] Journal, 26,* 21–26.

For much of the last year the television images of the devastation and suffering in the former Yugoslavia have been relentless. Have they been powerful? Perhaps we remember the news item which "exposed" the existence of the concentration camps: [p]erhaps we remember the broken and burned bodies of the entire population of the village carried from the cellars by the UN troops. We may look at the broken buildings in Sarajevo and remember a few short years ago the entire world's media gathered for the winter Olympics in one of Europe's most beautiful and cosmopolitan of cities. Perhaps initially we followed the development of this apparent madness quite closely. Remember the questions: Do we understand it? How can we come to understand it … this world seemingly gone mad?

In the end though, do we become inured; do the images continue to flash across our TV screens while we begin to accept that it is mad[?] There is no logic. Another small war rages.

The television reports are watched by our children. Are they powerful? Our children have an enormous capacity to understand. They have a vast capacity to empathise with the experience of their fellow human beings who struggle to survive in the midst of the hellish violence unleashed by neighbour on neighbour. Every fibre of their being[s] knows the suffering. They are not reliant on the television reports. As young people[,] they are intuitively so much closer than we are to the knowledge that civil war rages in every part of the world. As children, they are in its front line, and given the opportunity, will give powerful expression to their empathy and drive themselves tirelessly towards understanding.

Indigo is a Theatre in Education programme for lower secondary students which each day [seeks] to develop the collective understandings of all those taking part about the forces of nationalism. […]

We develop a fiction. A class of children become[s] a delegation from the International Council of Nations – ICON. Their task [is] to undertake a study of the social/economic situation, and to draw up a charter of human rights for the small nation of Borovia.

How this fictional context for our drama is made available to the children[,] how they meet it and what of themselves they bring to it, is crucial.

The actor-teacher framing the children has an extremely delicate job to do. She welcomes the children, allows them to "stare" briefly at the company and at the design elements that will assist the drama as it develops. She then poses a simple question:

"When I say the words 'Human Rights' what do you immediately think about?"

This question is placed as simply and as directly as possible. The actor places as little of herself as possible between the words and the children. There is usually a moment of silence before the first tentative responses are offered. This silence is allowed to sit as a natural and unthreatening silence. It is not often that we are asked such a question.

Very gently, and giving due weight and respect to each and every meaning offered[,] the actor moves the group toward sharing socially with those next to them and eventually into sharing their more developed responses with the whole group. At a given point another actor, unannounced, records what is offered[,] finding a simple and direct language and drawing the connections that are being established. The record is as true a reflection of the social understanding of the group as is possible. This opening to the work is concluded when the actor leading the session reads through (again, in [a] direct and uncluttered manner) our conclusions.

This process, of developing from an individual[']s courageous first response to a highly developed social statement[,] very often (for all involved[:] children, company and teachers) made available a profound and moving content.

> "Every Human Being has the right to live in peace; to have health care, education, a shelter and justice. People have the right to their own beliefs. Every Human Being has the right to have help, and the responsibility to give help. The right to love and be loved. Human Beings have the right to believe in whatever gods they wish to believe in. We have the right to move about freely without fear. Human Beings have the right to work, and holiday and celebrate. Every Human Being has the right to their own name."

This statement . . . is not in the moment regarded as fixed, complete, all embracing . . . it is an embodiment of what the enquiry is opening up for us. It is a trail.

As the actor facilitating begins to twilight the children into frame[,] they already have a strongly felt sense of the significance of their present enquiry; they know that the world they inhabit does not guarantee these rights. The contradiction is socially present in the room.

As the ICON Delegates, experts in the field of Human Rights, receive their official identification, Borovia stands in the centre of the school hall. The Nation is embodied in the form of a small Tailors workroom; there are no walls; there are portals[:]

A window
A door
A portrait frame: [e]mpty, full length
A full length mirror: [n]o glass, again only the frame

Each of these portals is connected, the whole room/nation girdled and embraced by rich swathes of brilliant Indigo cloth. This girdle denotes an interior and an exterior.

Inside, some simple workmanlike furniture, the tools of the tailoring trade, and a tailor's dummy upon which rests the recently completed ceremonial jacket with its brilliant Indigo Sash. In another corner a second tailor's dummy, holding work in progress. Outside nothing.

As the framing proceeds, the actors move into place and Borovia becomes peopled. The object of enquiry begins to live. The children are aware. It is an indeterminate beginning: things are sensed but not yet known.

An old tailor and his young apprentice enter the room and begin to cut and sew. Focussed and comfortable with each other. Outside the room in the "street," a man sits curled beneath the window; alone. Also outside, a woman sits on bulky bags of laundry.

The delegation is informed they have been invited to Borovia by The Prince: [h]e is recently returned from a life in exile, ready to grasp and weld the future of his beloved Borovia[,] a nation newly re-emerged into independence after the collapse of the "Old Empire." They learn that the Prince is the recognised leader of the emerging INDIGO party.

> "INDIGO the colour of my Nation's Flag, the colour of the very blood that runs in Borovian veins."

The Prince greets the delegation and invites them on an initial tour of his country. Other than those of the ICON Delegates, should they choose to ask questions, his is the only voice. He speaks warmly and sincerely of his fears, hopes and aspirations. He requests their help. Borovia needs the assistance and recognition of the international community. The delegation pauses by the window:

> "A window on my Nation. For so long the window has been boarded up. No light has spilled through to warm the hearts or guide the footsteps of my people. INDIGO will tear down the shutters…the light and air will enter Borovia again …."

The drama is now fully underway. The tailor's room, the five actors, and the delegates with the secretary/facilitator constitute the whole that is Borovia. Though highly selective and sparse, it is a complex whole, not easy to discern in its totality. Each of its parts offer the delegation fleeting and contradictory impressions.

Indigo is a fully participatory programme. As it develops[,] the delegation meet[s] and interact[s] with the roles: sensations registered during their first "tour" are shared in the hotel room; perceptions are developed. As each part of the whole is probed and becomes revealed to them, they develop a sense of the quality of Borovia. The portals begin to offer a way of seeing. Borovia is gradually discerned as a sum and unity of opposites:

The Tailor: A man who is highly skilled, and proud to make the jacket for the Prince. He came to Borovia many, many years ago. (The actor knows him to be Jewish and feels that in many ways the man's life embodies the history of our century.) He is overjoyed that once again there is independence for Borovia and has a vast optimism for the future. There is little cloth left in his shop. He awaits payment from the Prince.

The Apprentice: Young, Borovian. He loves his master and is a good pupil. He welcomes the return of the Prince and longs to learn the stories and the songs that for all his short life have been denied him. (The actor knows that the future direction of his developing ideas is necessarily uncertain. He embodies potential.)

The Laundry Woman: One of the mountain people; Borovian, but with a distinct ethnic identity. Her people came from the mountains long before the days of the Empire. She works hard. She does the laundry for the tailor and has done so for many years. There is an almost perceptible unease about her and she is loathe to enter discussion with the visitors from abroad. (The actor knows that for this woman the return of the Prince is an indeterminate beginning ... she senses its impact on the community.)

The man in the street: He has no work. Under the Empire he had work. The return of the Prince has had no material [e]ffect on the quality of life. (The actor knows he represents an entire disenfranchised layer.) Waiting. Through the window, he catches the eyes of the other young Borovian.

The Company [players] understand the economic position of the roles. In many senses[,] they are archetypes. They embody the joint and conflicting aspirations of the society. There is little pre-determined dialogue or action. The development of the action of the drama is very much dependent on what the children bring. The actors interact directly with the delegates and listen closely as they reflect "privately" in the hotel room. Each development in the analysis they are making of the situation provides the stimulus for the actors to intuitively develop the forms to drive the children closer to the essence of the Borovian predicament. At no point does life in Borovia cease to go on. As the children debate with each other, the signing is still on offer, confirming, contradicting, confounding.

The facilitator is the only member of the company operating overtly at the teacher end of the actor/teacher spectrum. She can stop the drama and use any of the available conventions to peel back the layers of appearance.

The children's sense of a society poised on the verge of communal violence grows. However, from within the stricture of the frame, they cannot intervene directly into the fabric of Borovian society and devise alternative narrative solutions to the developing economic and social problems.

On many occasions, attempting to explain to the Prince and/or the other protagonists the likely outcome of a position held or of a course of action, they would draw on their knowledge of the real world. ...Their knowledge of the world driving their meaning making within the drama[,] and the drama (their very real subjective relationship to the people) driving them ....

"Look, you have to understand...."

... to push that [a] bit further, by necessity, their grasp of events witnessed through the television news images.

As the situation inexorably builds, they struggle to create their charter for Human Rights. It cannot remain simply a statement of principle; it begins to have the quality of a programme of action. They are naming the phenomena they are witness and party to.

At the end of the programme, the actors hold the image the facilitator has chosen to arrest[:]

- The apprentice sings the Borovian National Anthem as the tailor stares confusedly at his image in the mirror.
- The man from the street is measured for a new suit, an Indigo tie with a new white collar.
- In the street, the Mountain Woman, "cleansed," lies face down in a pile of dirty laundry. In the room the tailor is covering the windows.

These are moments. Each performance of the programme would ideally "live" its own truthful development and would offer different aspects. The children, now twilighting back out of role, are invited to let the image work on them and then to place the charter they have made in it. They and the Company know that this is not a resolution. [...]

This has been an attempt to offer the objectives and intentions of *Indigo* as an example of work conceived and created for and with young people in this period. [...] The practice of the programme[,] our experience of the integrity of the children and their determination to remain truly human in the world, was a rich and enabling learning experience.

> He stands so proudly
> an image of darkness
> looking up
> into the future.
> A man of Borovia!
> A rabble of thoughts
> churn inside him,
> a strained weary expression
> on his face
> which is a diary of secrets.
> A Prince of Borovia,
> A Prince of thoughts.
> Borovia was his wife.
> He was father
> to the children of Borovia.
> He wanted to be Borovia.
> He tried to be Borovia.

> He murdered himself inside.
> His mad watchful eyes swerve towards me.
> > – Rowan Taylor, Yr. 6, Whalley C. E. Primary School

6.2 Disability and the inclusive classroom

from *A journey of change with a Big Blue Whale: A theatre-in-education (TIE) programme on disability and dilemmas in the inclusive classroom in Korea*
Byoung-Joo Kim. (2009). *RIDE: The Journal of Applied Theatre and Performance, 14*(1), 115–131.

In an emptied yet barely spacious school music room, a group of fifth graders are sitting on the floor, facing one side of the room, with subdued excitement and anticipation. Their eyes are busily navigating around the backdrops, small sets, and simple lighting equipment before them. 'Are we going to see a musical theatre? Or Peter Pan?', a boy yells out. As the lights dim, the enthusiastic applause roars. An actor greets the spectators, introduces herself as also a fifth grader and explains why she, Dasom, has invited them over to the music room: she needs their help and advice. … Dasom suggests that she show her story and the spectators give their opinions and advice.

The theatrical presentation begins with a newly transferred student, Chain, being introduced to the class, at times playfully including the spectators. The class immediately notices the new boy's peculiar traits – such as distinctively bigger size and older age, aimless stare, nose-picking and slapping without reasons, and inability to communicate with others – which the teacher vaguely explains as 'mentally handicapped' and 'autistic' symptoms. Not knowing exactly how to accept this unusual classmate, the fifth graders are asked to befriend him. A mature and dutiful girl, Bomi, is assigned by the teacher as a designated mate for Chain. Both the teacher and Chain's mother who respectively assert their expectations in a same phrase: 'I depend on you, Bomi'.

While Bomi and others try to stand by Chain in and out of the classroom, the ever-growing difficulties in living with a handicapped classmate gradually keep snowballing. Likewise, so do the classmates' mounting complaints: a smart, yet competitive boy, Myung-Suk turns against Chain; another girl, Dasom, grows indifferent to him; and Bomi's frustration increases while she shoulders the pressure of looking after Chain alone. One day, the classmates inadvertently provoke Chain's abrupt outburst that was triggered by his own traumatic childhood memory. And the perturbed autistic boy accidentally wounds Myung-Suk.

The performance ends with the teacher's call for a serious forum of the entire class – including the audience. How and why such incidents have happened? How do they perceive someone like Chain in the classroom, and how do they communicate with him? Why do they need to be with a classmate like him? Should they reject him or embrace him? And, what could they do to live together with someone like Chain?

The Background

The theatre-in-education (TIE) programme, *A Big Blue Whale's Dream*, is first devised and implemented by PRAXIS, a newly established group of young actor-teachers and theatre specialists in South Korea, in 2005. The programme is one of the first major TIE projects commissioned by South Korean governmental arts agencies. In a country where terms like 'educational drama/theatre' or 'applied theatre' praxis are not yet widely known and are still in the inception stage, the programme was a rarity in being a TIE project fully financed by both local and metropolitan cultural foundations. [...]

The title of *A Big Blue Whale's Dream* refers to the title of Chain's favourite picture book which, along with projected illustrations, opens and closes the drama. The lone Big Blue Whale travels a long way in search of friends – only to find himself being repeatedly rejected by others: for his freakishly huge body, for his strange skin colour, for his awkwardly muffled voice, and for his honest mistake that injured other fish. In the theatrical performance, the storybook ends as the Big Blue Whale embarks on yet another journey to make friends. How will the story of Chain's end? [...]

[T]he realities in the inclusive classroom on a daily basis often reveal stories that are far from the ideal: teachers, students, parents and administrators all voice their worries. Among various reasons, a vast majority of studies concur that general students' understanding and perception towards the disabled can be the crucial agenda in inclusion and that more diverse and effective educational programmes to enhance their perception are urgently needed.... [...]

Recognising the demographic and social concerns in the community, Goyang Cultural Foundation commissioned PRAXIS to create a new and engaging TIE programme for the general students in the inclusive classroom to enhance their awareness and perception towards the specially needed students. To secure the necessary budget and sustained support throughout the entire process of the project and beyond, Gyonggi Cultural Foundation of Metropolitan Gyonggi province joined to form a unique three-way partnership: a local arts organisation, a metropolitan arts organisation, and local drama/ TIE specialists.

The journey begins: the preparation

Members of PRAXIS began the research in the summer of 2005: we studied documents and resources on special and inclusive education; participated in related programmes such as an inclusive youth summer camp; conducted drama workshops for local special education teachers; and commenced field research for data collection by observing local classrooms and interviewing disabled students, non-disabled students, teachers, assistant teachers, and parents of the disabled students in the area. With the analysis of the collected data and the retrieved pre-questionnaires, it became more evident that the daily realities of the inclusive classroom were indeed not so roseate – at least not always – as we outsiders had cautiously presumed. [...]

Despite lectures and occasional disability awareness programmes by the special education teacher, there existed conflicts, hostility, indifference and uneasiness among the general students as much as sympathy and compassion. The general students were instructed to be 'good friends' with the special classmate no matter what; but without substantial understanding of *why* or any guidance as to *how*. [...]

Here comes the Big Blue Whale: the TIE programme implemented

Designed specifically for fifth or sixth graders in inclusive classes in Goyang City, *A Big Blue Whale's Dream* opened in December 2005. The first four performances were given at a theatre with the young audience seated on the stage around the acting area. The team then visited five local schools in the area, giving a total of 13 performances, reaching 1316 youngsters. In 2006, the programme received another grant from the Korea Arts and Culture Education Service (KACES) as part of the Arts Education for the Socially Marginalised Initiative, and *A Big Blue Whale's Dream* was again implemented in Goyang City for 10 performances, meeting 765 new young people in the area.

Each performance usually begins with a brief encounter with a character and is followed by a 40-minute theatrical presentation. The post-theatre workshop opens up with debriefing the drama and the issues addressed, then the Joker and the young audience together invite the three characters in the drama (except for Chain) for 'hotseating'. Questions posed by the young people range from simple ones such as about the actor-teachers' real ages or whether the Chain character was indeed a disabled person, to serious ones such as investigating the rationale of each character's behavioural and emotional change in the drama, and even denouncing the other two characters for not sharing Bomi's agony. Here we excluded Chain during the entire post-theatre forum because the final image of Chain in the drama was so emotionally powerful and effectively curious that his hotseating might disrupt the spectators' empathy and limit their imaginative interpretations of his persona. Also, there were concerns of potential distractions in having the presence of an actor who portrayed the disabled boy in the drama.

Gradually, the differing positions of each character towards Chain emerge: Bomi wants him to return as before; Myung-Suk opposes the idea, citing the difficulties and accidents; and Dasom is not sure.

For a more in-depth discussion, the audience is then divided into three small groups according to the character that most closely corresponds with their own viewpoints. While the 'unsure' group meets with the like-minded Dasom character, the 'favourable' students who support Bomi's position face opposite-minded Myung-Suk, who problematises the discussion and challenges their rationale. Likewise, the 'unfavourable' group sits with Bomi who listens to the students' stories, acknowledges their grievances, and yet gradually challenges their logic and perceptions. During the animated, at times heated discussion, the doors of the young people's perceptions swing open.

The 'unsure' group explores the enigma of Chain's mind through dramatic activities that lead to discussion of good: they discussed and created individual tableaux portraying their interpretations of the disabled character's feelings and desires; then sharing each tableau's inner voice using 'thought-tracking'; another series of individual and group tableaux and 'thought-tracking' that portrays a special mate in their real life; an enactment of short anecdotes of their experiences with the real-life Chain; and then discussing the benefits and difficulties of living with a disabled classmate. The 'favourable' group gradually convinces Myung-Suk through anecdotes learned from their real-life experiences with disabled friends. Then they teach him in practical ways how to handle problematic situations, based on their experiences, by using Boalian Image Theatre and intervention techniques. And the youngsters of the 'unfavourable' group articulate their arguments and vent their suppressed grievances in Bomi's sympathetic ear. After their emotional discharge, they become noticeably more lenient and attentive in discussing the special classmate and pondering options.

After sharing the small group discussion, the entire session ends with the audience writing letters, along with embedded post-questionnaires, to characters of their choice. A week later, PRAXIS concluded the programme by revisiting the schools and conducting in-depth interviews with participating students and teachers. [...]

A Big Blue Whale's Dream certainly is not a flawless TIE programme. Despite the largely favourable responses from the participants, we may never really know what lasting impact it truly had on those young people's perceptions. Nonetheless, we witnessed that it had a momentous significance on, at least, one student – by empowering him to speak his thoughts and by liberating him so that his voice could make the differences. Empowerment and liberation – what more could we ask for?

6.3 Countering radicalization

from *Tapestry and the aesthetics of theatre in education as dialogic encounter and civil exchange*
Joe Winston & Steve Strand. (2013). *RIDE: The Journal of Applied Theatre and Performance, 18*(1), 62–78.

Tapestry was a participatory Theatre in Education (TiE) programme dealing with issues relating to radicalisation and violent extremism that toured secondary schools in Birmingham and the Midlands, UK, in the autumn of 2009. Devised by the Birmingham-based company The Play House, it was funded by the UK PREVENT initiative, introduced by the then Labour government, a funding stream intended to help counter the radicalisation of young British nationals that might lead them to join extremist political groups and engage in acts of terrorism. [...]

Deborah Hull [artistic director of The Play House] was approached by the local PREVENT team in charge of school liaison and asked to devise a programme for local secondary school children in July, 2009. From the outset, she was determined to avoid any portrayal of political radicalisation as solely a problem for the Muslim community. … [T]wo aspects…that struck Deborah – the significance of gender issues in radicalisation and of humour as a means to counter its rhetoric – she saw as relevant beyond the parameters of radical Islam. In particular, the use of humour when approaching serious issues readily chimed with many previous programmes devised by The Play House, who have a tradition of using it as an integral part of their artistry. Before touring, the programme was trialled with different audiences of teachers, police officers, youth workers and members of the local Muslim community, including a group of Muslim women.

In its final version, *Tapestry* ran for about 90 minutes and consisted of two parts, with interactive elements between each and at the programme's conclusion. The play opens inside an abandoned shop to the sounds of a violent demonstration outside. Sheltering here is Nazia, a British Muslim girl of Pakistani origin, quickly joined by her brother-in-law, Jason, a white working-class British youth who has been on the demonstration, and by Hassan, a young Muslim of Nigerian descent, an acquaintance of hers who has been part of a counter demonstration. A fight ensues between the two young men which Nazia manages to break up. Outside the protest has now escalated into a riot, and so the three are trapped in the space together. Nazia strongly admonishes both young men for becoming involved in such a violent protest, and they each counter her challenges by laying out their opposing positions, recounting key incidents from their lives that have shaped their thinking and their attitudes. In doing this they press one another into service in order to act out the experiences that have led to their current extremist standpoints.

The theatrical device of casting one another as characters to play out their stories does much to lighten with humour the anger, hurt, confusion and resentment that these stories reveal. Hassan recalls a moment after the London tube bombings, being spat at while waiting for a bus and Jason counters with a typical moment from his experiences of unsuccessfully trying to find a job. The laughter provoked by the verbal interplay as the scenes build contrasts with and emphasises the shocking nature of the acts of aggression and rejection with which they conclude. Each of the boys then illustrates a typical moment from their unhappy home life, and they both recall meeting and listening to charismatic speakers: Peter Jeffrys from the extreme right-wing *Young Patriots* and Dr Farooq from the Islamist *Circle of Truth*. Both leaders seem to have answers to their grievances and propose action to remedy them. Nazia, however, challenges the boys with stories of the pressures she faces as a first-generation, British-born Muslim girl – again, there is much ironic humour in her account – and she forcefully asks them to reconsider where their current paths are leading them. Having attempted to reason to no noticeable effect, she runs out of the shop in anger and exasperation. Both Hassan and Jason try to call her back, but she is quickly injured, and this first part of the programme ends with them both rushing out to try and help her.

The young people in the audience are now given the chance to talk to Jason and Hassan in turn in order to try and find out what has happened to Nazia, to challenge them on their stand points and to make suggestions as to what they think each ought now to do. Here, too, the actors do not shy away from using humour to enliven the question and answering and to provoke animated verbal responses from the audience, who are then asked to discuss why Jason and Hassan have become involved in their respective organisations and what activities they might become involved in in the near future, if they remain associated with extremist groups.

The concluding short scene is quiet and non-confrontational as Jason and Hassan meet unawares in a hospital waiting room, both having decided to visit Nazia and both having ironically bought her the same present. It becomes evident through their cagey discussion that they have each been reflecting on the events of the previous week and have begun to question their association with the extremist groups they belong to. The play nonetheless ends on an inconclusive note and the audience is asked to suggest what positive actions Jason and Hassan can now take if they leave the extremist groups, but still want to change things.

The findings of the quantitative survey

[S]tatistics [gathered] underline the play's success in capturing the authentic voices of the two disenchanted young men. Significantly, they also suggest that those who found the play enjoyable, interesting and good at provoking discussion included some, at least, within the minority who had sympathy with one or other of the extremist positions as well as with the female character who constituted the moral centre of the play. The 58% who indicated that they felt differently than before is nonetheless a tantalising figure; we cannot be certain on how they felt differently and in what ways they felt differently, but the fact that they felt differently at all is arguably an educational achievement in itself. This is something that the qualitative data can throw some light upon, and will constitute part of our agenda in the ensuing sections of this article. [...]

[The play] engaged the vast majority of its diverse audiences through the perceived realism of its content and characterisation and through its lively use of humour; ... young people on the whole found it thought provoking and informative. [...]

The play's realism was something that many students commented upon in the qualitative data. 'It's showing a lot of reality', said one Muslim girl; 'The kind of stuff about life, racism and religion that is relevant', told another. 'The parties are actually quite real, they could actually be happening, like the BNP', a Muslim boy commented. 'The things the Muslim character said about religion, I could believe that's true', said a White British boy. The actual form of the play, however, was not at all realistic in any narrow sense of the term. The set, for example, was minimal, the most striking aspect being the large backcloth, featuring a union jack whose colours had been altered to include more than the usual red, white and blue. In particular, the fact that the boys enlisted one another to act out incidents from their own histories was highly unbelievable as something that might have really happened. None of this was commented upon, however; it was the actors and their acting that the interviewees found believable, even as they remained always aware, in the Brechtian sense, that it was acting that they were looking at. [...]

Conclusion

The participatory aspects of *Tapestry*, those moments which students saw as particularly important, when they were invited to have their voices heard in dialogue with the characters, took the form of a competitive exchange, with students challenging the views of both Hassan and Jason assertively, sometimes aggressively – as indeed the actors hoped they would. But, of course, these views were being *played* by the actors, however convincingly, and the students knew they were. The exchange was therefore inevitably lightened by this knowledge, and it was the cleverness and skill of the actors in playing the game that the students enjoyed and that encouraged them to play harder themselves. Such is the aesthetic achievement of good participatory TiE and its special contribution to democratic dialogue – its ability to create and sustain a spirit of lively and enjoyable exchange over sensitive and difficult issues and to leave the great majority of the participants with a spirit of goodwill and the strong feeling of an hour or so well spent when the exchange is finally over and the strangers – both actual and fictional – not only leave the school but also leave the ripples emanating from an intense encounter behind them.

6.4 Child abuse and family violence

from *Making the everyday extraordinary: A theatre in education project to prevent child abuse, neglect and family violence*
Peter O'Connor, Briar O'Connor, & Marlane Welsh-Morris. (2006). *RIDE: Research in Drama Education, 11*(2), 235–245.

In September 2003 the New Zealand Department of Child, Youth and Family approached Applied Theatre Consultants Ltd (ATCo) to develop a proposal for a theatre in education programme to fit inside its *Everyday Communities* programme. Child, Youth and Family manage a wide range of services to carry out statutory and preventative social work practice. ATCo is a private company with a history of using applied theatre in public education programmes.

Everyday Communities is a social change and community engagement programme to prevent child abuse, neglect and family violence. . . . The primary message of *Everyday Communities* is that communities have a part to play in preventing abuse and in caring for all children within that community. [...]

Negotiating the outcomes and their limits

In proposal documents drawn up by ATCo, the purpose and limitations of the programme and its underlying philosophy were clearly stated[:]

> *The purpose of the theatre in education programme is not to provide or teach simple solutions to the issues but to provide safe and structured*

environments for teachers and students to discuss these issues and find the answers relevant and suitable in their own contexts. The programme will allow students to think about, reflect on and talk about their own stories by investigating the story of someone else. This distancing process provides the necessary protection for students to both think and feel deeply about the issues but to do so in a protected manner. [...]

Everyday Theatre . . . was not expected to deliver the entire outcomes of the programme, but to provide one layer of it.

Everyday Theatre's structure in 2004

Particular attention was paid to developing *Everyday Theatre's* overarching structure to provide safety for all participants. This involved a four-stage engagement with each school. First, schools had to sign a contract to join the programme and agree to a range of preconditions. These included all parents being informed of the visit, and the principal and teachers signalling their commitment to the programme by agreeing to attend a meeting prior to the visit. The meeting was designed to ensure all teachers involved in the programme were aware and supportive of the work undertaken by the team . . . . As part of the safety structures, teachers at the meeting were informed they must remain with their students throughout the day. They were also encouraged to participate as fully as possible in all the process drama activities.

Dramatic structures for safety

On each day of *Everyday Theatre's* visit to a school, four classes, totalling on average 120 students, gather in the school hall to view a 25-minute performance. The performance tells a fictional story of a family in the local area. It is a complex family and the students meet its various members through the eyes of teenager Ramesh Patel, a video gamesmaster who sees life as a video game. He enrol[l]s the students as trainee gamesmasters, whose first job is to help fix the broken family game. At different times, the game requires the students to consider the perspectives of witnesses to abuse or confidantes, the victims of abuse and the perpetrators of abuse.

The teacher/actor focuses on helping the trainee gamesmasters through each level so they can gain the password to gain entry to the next level. Students work with the teacher/actors through four levels of the game, each level lasting an hour and with a different teacher/actor from the performance. Each workshop uses different dramatic conventions to explore the story and to work out answers to what might help the family. Conventions are presented as part of a video game structure. For example, at level one, students explore the narratives of the video game through two different game devices: circle story retelling and by hotseating different characters. In the circle story retelling, presented as the story wheel game, the trainee gamesmasters retell the story from a range of perspectives including family members, gossiping neighbours and visiting Martians.

Hotseated characters (played by the teacher/actor initially and then by the students) are presented within the game with on-screen buttons that can be activated by the trainee gamesmasters. Button choices include a truth button, which requires the questioned character to tell the truth. The truth button can only be played once per character and all trainee gamesmasters must agree on when they want to play it. This encourages deeper questioning and careful reframing of questions – and usually results in the truth button not being used. Another button provides pieces of writing in role from each character that had previously been prepared about life in the family. This ensures significant "facts" about each character remain consistent throughout the workshops. A third button freezes the character on screen so questions can be asked, out of role, of the teacher. This allows the teacher/actor to slip in and out of role easily.

At level two, students create still images from the family's life to explore various issues which may sit underneath the violence. Students are asked to create frozen images to entice people further into the game by selecting dramatic moments from the family's life. Thought bubble buttons on the screen allow game players to hear the family's thoughts and feelings. Other buttons allow the frozen image to be "zoomed up" so detail can be questioned more intensively.

In level three, students play a decision game in small groups, where they decide what will happen to the children in the family. The video game allows only a limited number of decisions and a very short time press. The decisions are fed back into the video game and given to separate characters. The students determine which character is selected, that character being the one who will most dislike the decision. This difficulty recognises that trainee gamesmasters are working at a high level within the game. Having given the decision, the trainee gamesmasters are asked to create ten seconds of video showing the different family members waiting for the decision to be given, under the pretext that the video is to be uploaded as part of the game about the family. Gamesmasters often work for irony, providing dialogue and action for the waiting family.

In the final and most difficult level, students recreate what they have learnt in the previous levels and present it back in video game format. Finally, each student creates the game's opening screen by choosing the line from a character they think was the most important or interesting line of the day.

At the end of the day they have the full password: "Every child has hopes and dreams" which entitles them to become gamesmasters themselves.

At the conclusion of the day participating classroom teachers and the *Everyday Theatre* teacher/actors meet and reflect on the day. A list of suggested follow[-]up activities closely related to curriculum outcomes is left with the school. A written evaluation form is completed at this point. A follow[-]up cluster meeting six weeks later allows teachers to reflect and discuss issues that have arisen in their schools as a result of the work.

Double framing for safety

[…]

The double frame used in *Everyday Theatre* sees students engrossed in completing the tasks of assisting the family but as part of a tightly run video game. The fun and excitement of playing a "live" video game provides the distancing and protection for the students to engage with the serious and difficult issues that sit underneath the game structure. Students become so engrossed in making it to the end of the level to get the next words of the password, they actively engage in challenging and difficult work inside the game structure to help the family.

The double framing allows, as Gavin Bolton (1979) suggests, for students to be protected into emotion, not from it. It provides a double protection but, paradoxically, a double opening for young people to feel the issues of the video game family. Students are motivated to engage with the drama by their desire to join Ramesh in fixing the game, and/or by wanting to help the video family. […]

Students as active theatre makers were active makers, if only for a moment, in their own lives too. In *Everyday Theatre* we were intent on making theatre part of everyday life, of democratising theatre, where everyone is entitled to be theatre makers. Via *Everyday Theatre* we consciously made the everyday extraordinary, and the extraordinary power of drama was revealed as something that can be used as part of everyday life.

Further Reading

Bowles, N. (2005). Why devise? Why now? "Houston, we have a problem". *Theatre Topics, 15*(1), 15–21. Addresses issues of discrimination and diversity in a devised TIE piece with and about lesbian, gay, bisexual, transgendered and queer young people (LGBTQ).

Carklin, M. (1997). Rainbows and spider webs: New challenges for theatre in a transformed system of education in South Africa. *RIDE: Research in Drama Education, 2*(2), 203–213. This South African work shows the transition from a school-based to a community-based TIE project that draws on traditional African performance forms.

Cassidy, H. & Watts, V. (2002). "Burn an image in their head": Evaluating the effectiveness of a play on bullying. *NJ: Drama Australia Journal, 26*(2), 5–19. Anti-bullying is a "hot topic" for TIE work (see also O'Toole, 1976). This article describes the development and assessment of an Australian TIE project in useful ways.

Haddon, A. (2013). Trust the process: Insights from making *Raft of the Medusa* with teachers. *Drama: One Forum Many Voices, 19*(1), 17–24. Haddon led a project with teachers using a painting as the catalyst that took the group through a theatrical examination of political issues.

Jackson, A. (2005). The dialogic and the aesthetic: Some reflections on theatre as a learning medium. *Journal of Aesthetic Education, 39*(4), 104–118. While largely theoretical, this essay contains a description of a TIE project on immigration and refugees in England (pp. 114–116).

Jackson, A. & Vine, C. (Eds.) (2013). *Learning through theatre: The changing face of theatre in education* (3rd ed.). Abingdon, OX: Routledge. A key anthology on theatre in education with international contributions that also looks at the historic development of TIE, ways of working, case studies and discussions.

O'Toole, J. (1976). *Theatre in education: New objectives for theatre – new techniques in education.* London, UK: Hodder and Stoughton. This seminal text on TIE is widely available in libraries and is a must-read for anyone interested in this area of applied theatre. Also very valuable for facilitators in all genres.

O'Toole, J., Burton, B. & Plunkett, A. (2005). *Cooling conflict: A new approach to managing bullying and conflict in schools.* Frenchs Forest, NSW: Pearson/Longman. These authors present a long-term anti-bullying TIE project in Australia that was delivered in a pyramid model where senior students devised and performed a play to younger students.

Schweitzer, P. (1980). *Theatre-in-education: Five infant programmes.* London, UK: Methuen.

Schweitzer, P. (1980). *Theatre-in-education: Four junior programmes.* London, UK: Methuen.

Schweitzer, P. (1980). *Theatre-in-education: Four secondary programmes.* London, UK: Methuen. The three collections of British TIE companies' scripts above are an invaluable resource. Difficult to find but well worth the effort.

Tan, J. (2005). "One island": A theatre-in-education approach in Singapore. *NJ: Drama Australia Journal, 29*(1), 45–50. This TIE project deals with citizenship and cultural identity in a South Asian context.

Winston, J. (2001). Drug education through creating theatre in education. *RIDE: Research in Drama Education, 6*(1), 39–54. Winston's case study on drug education allows us to hear the voices of teachers and students assessing the value of the theatre experience.

Wooster, R. (2010). Theatre in education: More than just a health message. *Journal of Applied Arts and Health, 1*(3), 281–294. Written by an experienced TIE practitioner, this article identifies the nature of TIE and how its approaches may be used in theatre in health education.

Questions for Reflection and Discussion

1. What strategies can you find in the four case studies presented in this chapter that address ways of creating, performing, reflecting upon and assessing a TIE project?

2. What do you perceive to be the skills required by an effective actor-teacher? What are the most important acting skills needed (see Cooper, 2013, pp. 131–141)? Teaching skills?

3. What different kinds of participation are involved in each of these case studies? Why might you use any or all of these participatory strategies in your own TIE projects?

4. Some suggest that "good theatre" is antithetical to educational needs. What is your opinion about the possibilities of creating engaging theatre while conforming to curricular contexts?

5. How do you feel about tackling difficult topics such as those seen in this chapter (anti-fascism, disability awareness, religious extremism, domestic abuse) within an educational setting?

Two excellent resources for curriculum-based drama are Larry Swartz' *The New Dramathemes* (2014), and Swartz & Nyman's *Drama Schemes, Themes and Dreams* (2010).

Suggested Activities

1. With a small group, select a grade range and take a look at the government-mandated curriculum guides in various subject areas. Find a curriculum area that you and your group agree opens itself up for dramatic exploration. Write three or four drama-based activities that promote a learning outcome and share these with other groups in a practical workshop.

2. Choose a real person who is involved in environmental issues. Research this person and create a monologue either as that person or as another character talking about that person. With a partner, take turns introducing each other in-role to the larger group. After the monologue, your partner facilitates an in-role conversation between you as the character and the audience.

3. With a partner or small group, create a professional development workshop for teachers that introduce the concepts and practices of TIE and includes a number of drama-based activities.

4. Select a fairy or folk tale and adapt it as a piece of *story theatre* that includes integral participation and also has a clear and well-defined learning outcome. If possible, perform this adaptation in a local elementary school.

Story theatre involves narration and characterization, direct address and simple theatrical devices. See Paul Sills' (1971, 2000) books on story theatre.

Web Resources

Big Brum Theatre in Education, Birmingham, UK http://www.bigbrum.org.uk/index.html

Everyday Theatre, Auckland, New Zealand http://www.appliedtheatre.co.nz/

Theatre in Education Online Links, University of Exeter, UK http://humanities.exeter.ac.uk/drama/links/theatreineducation/

TIE Company, National School of Drama, New Delhi, India http://nsd.gov.in/delhi/index.php/tie-company/

Introduction

Theatre of the Oppressed (TO) is a genre of applied theatre developed by Brazilian director Augusto Boal and codified in his text of the same name (1979), partly in response to the groundbreaking work of educator Paolo Freire and his book *Pedagogy of the Oppressed* (1970/2000) and also in response to the social and political turmoil present in Brazil at that time. Boal's theatre practice underwent a revolutionary shift during a performance when a spectator spontaneously stepped onto the stage and intervened in the action of the play. Boal realized that it was this breaking down of the fourth wall between actor and audience that is demanded in politically conscious theatre. He and his theatre company began to train themselves to work more directly with disenfranchised communities and developed an "arsenal" of games and activities that allowed unskilled participants to explore their own lives and sociopolitical oppressions (see *Games for Actors and Non-Actors*, 1992). His plans were to transform the spectator into an actor – called the "spect-actor" – through games that allowed for more self-expression before moving into theatre as process and language. Theatre became a method for communities to generate discussion and rehearse action towards real social change. Boal's TO involves a number of important strategies, the foremost known as Forum Theatre:

> [The spectator] assumes the protagonic role, changes the dramatic action, tries out solutions, discusses plans for change – in short, trains himself for real action.
>
> Augusto Boal, 1979, p. 122

> Forum Theatre consists, in essence, of proposing to a group of spectators, after a first improvisation of a scene, that they replace the protagonist [the Oppressed] and try to improvise variation on his actions. The real

protagonist should, ultimately, improvise the variation that has motivated him the most. (Boal, 1995, p. 184)

In Forum Theatre, the play is presented twice – the first time straight through. During the second time around, the audience of spect-actors has an opportunity to identify any scene of oppression with a negative outcome for the oppressed protagonist and have it re-played. During the re-playing, the spect-actor can stop the scene at any time he or she feels that things could be done differently, replace the protagonist and lead the scene towards a different solution. The scene can be repeated with a number of spect-actor interventions until an agreeable solution is reached or a variety of other perspectives on the action have been explored.

Key ingredients of Forum Theatre are the role of the facilitator, known as the Joker, the concept of *metaxis* and the importance of *praxis*. The Joker plays the key role of bridging the two worlds of the play (the fictional world) and the audience (the real world) by directly addressing both spectators and characters and facilitating their interactions. The Joker is a kind of trickster figure who is charged with keeping the dramatic process open, steering participants away from easy or simplistic solutions (Boal refers to the Joker as "the difficultator" rather than a "facilitator" [Jackson, in Boal, 1995, p. xix]) and, at times, educating the audience about the issues at hand. This interchange between the world of the play and the world of the audience is known as *metaxis* and the Joker is the all-important door-opener between these two worlds. The notion of *praxis* lies in the process of action that emanates from "reflection which in turn produces a new set of reflections, leading to the next action, and so on, in an ongoing dialectic" (Mutnick, 2006, p. 42). This is the intention of Forum Theatre, to provide a space not only for discussion and reflection but also as a rehearsal for real action towards change.

> *Metaxis*: The state of belonging completely and simultaneously to two different, autonomous worlds: the image of reality and the reality of the image. The participant shares and belongs to these two autonomous worlds…
>
> Augusto Boal, 1995, p. 43

Political upheavals in Brazil led to Boal and some of his followers being imprisoned and to Boal's subsequent exile in Argentina and Europe. During those years through the 1980s, Boal shifted his practice from the exploration of overt political oppressions experienced in South American settings to more internal psychological oppressions seen in the developed world. This adaptation of his work was published in a book called *The Rainbow of Desire: The Boal Method of Theatre and Therapy* (1995) and centered around physical and dramatic strategies that brought out the "cops in the head" of western participants, primarily the oppressions wrought by capitalism, materialism and individualism at the expense of community.

When Boal returned to Brazil after a decade overseas, he was elected to the city council of Rio de Janeiro in 1992. In his new role as politician, Boal became interested in using

[T]he challenges faced by Theatre of the Oppressed practitioners [are substantiated] when applying a third-world aesthetic language of resistance to first-world individualistic self-righteousness premised on meritocracy. The latter tends to frame the very idea of oppression as a personal problem stemming from ill-suited individual choices.

Sonia Hamel, 2013, p. 414

his theatre methods to provide a way for citizens to engage in a democratic and dramatic process focused on the creation of new laws, published in a book called *Legislative Theatre: Using Performance to Make Politics* (1998). Some issues, including anti-racism, child prostitution, geriatric care and mental health, tackled through Boal's theatre strategies by Boal and his actors led directly to the implementation of new city statutes.

It is clear in looking at the history of Boal's practices that he continuously adapted his work for different settings and communities. Today, we find variations and modifications of TO and Forum Theatre being used in many parts of the world by theatre workers assisting communities that want to take action around an agreed issue (Diamond, 2007; Hartley, 2012).

> *Our first reading is a description by Boal of a Legislative Theatre workshop he conducted in Germany. Although this is a very condensed version of the full process, we can see how effective theatre can be as a way to envision new laws. The second case study describes the work of Vancouver's Headlines Theatre in a college setting that involved students in a Safer Campuses program addressing problems of sexual harassment of female students. The author raises interesting issues around the training of the Joker as a process that should resist standardization. The third example is from a Canadian high school project giving voice to immigrant and refugee students. Finally, we hear about the use of Boal's work within a medical humanities programme in India.*

7.1 A letter from Augusto Boal
from *INTERVIEW: Augusto Boal, City Councillor: Legislative Theatre and the Chamber in the Streets*
Richard Schechner, Sudipto Chatterjee & Augusto Boal. (1998). *TDR: The Drama Review, 42*(4), 75–90.

Symbolism in Munich (letter from Augusto Boal, pp. 86–87)
    The Paulo Freire Society, so named in honor of the great Brazilian educator, invited me to show some examples of Legislative Theatre in the city of Munich [in 1997]. I explained that our experience in Rio had taken us four whole years to approve 13 new laws, and that the most we could do in only four days would be a pale and symbolic event, a hint of what might be that theatre form in the future, in the city of Munich or elsewhere.

We started our work and, over four days, prepared five small scenes about situations of oppression revealed by the 35 participants of the workshop. One of the scenes prepared by the group dealt with a very common problem in Germany – and, as far as I know, in many other European countries: [s]ome men choose a wife in matrimonial agencies, looking at their photos, CVs, and other information. Those women are recruited from countries like Romania, Thailand, and even in my own country, Brazil. Once the bridegroom has chosen his wife, she is imported by the agency with promises of marriage and a wonderful European-style princess life. Of course, those young women are very poor and full of hope – also very naive. Once the women arrive in the country, part of the agency's promise is fulfilled: they marry. Once married, the husbands – in most cases, not always – behave as though they bought a slave, and treat their wives as such, in the kitchen and in the bed. More often than not, those women don't speak a word of German and have difficulties learning the language. They don't have friends and sometimes are forbidden to go out without their men. The husbands keep strict control over them. If the wife decides to leave her husband – it is not easy but it is possible – she automatically loses her German citizenship and is sent back to her country by the police. She is punished, not him!

During the Forum that we did inside the group, the participants revealed their opinion: [i]f a crime was committed – namely, a marriage of convenience for the purpose of getting German nationality for the woman and a slave for the man – both persons are responsible for that crime, and not only the woman.

The proposition of a Project of Law became clear: the woman should be punished with the loss of citizenship, yes, but not with deportation from Germany[.] [M]ost of those women had not only economic problems back home, but political ones; in some cases, their lives would be endangered should they be deported. And the husband, considering that he was also responsible for faking a marriage, should be punished with a short term in prison, to discourage this practice. Other short scenes were made about social security, marriage of gay partners, use of public space for private activities, etc.

On the fifth day, Fritz Letsch (from the Paulo Freire Society) obtained permission to do the Forum Theatre inside the city hall (the Rathaus), and invited many politicians, including the mayor of Munich, who did not come because it was his birthday but sent his vice-mayor. The vice-mayor attended the session at the side of the secretary of the Green Party for Bavaria: those two persons were the only authorities present. Of course, we had invited everybody else but, understandably, they had more urgent things to do. The information released about the starting time for the session was wrong and some people came to the Rathaus at 11 in the morning when we were rehearsing for the presentation at 1:30 P.M. Among those persons came an old lady with totally white hair, using a cane to move around. She had been at the public lecture that I delivered on the first day of the workshop, during which I explained the functioning of the Legislative Theatre.

I remember that, during the dialogue after my lecture, another woman said that this process could have worked well in Brazil, because in Brazil we are Brazilians (meaning that we dance and sing, which is not necessarily true for some of us. . .) and that we are extroverted people. But – according to her – this could not work at all in a country like Germany, where people are more introverted, less expansive. She totally ignored the Oktoberfest! I replied that when I introduced the Theatre of the Oppressed (TO) in Europe, I frequently heard the same opinion. And yet today, the TO is practiced very intensely in almost all European countries. Of course, in each country, people have to adapt the method to their own culture, their own language, their own desires and needs. TO is not a Bible, not a recipe book: it is a method to be used by people, and people are more important than the method.

The same can happen with the Legislative Theatre: in each country, it has to find its own form for application to real situations in that country. But the woman that night held to her opinion. And the old lady with white hair and a beautiful cane at her side did not say anything. When we started the show at the Rathaus, I explained that what we were going to do had only a symbolic value: we had not done the whole procedure of the Legislative Theatre; we had not done many shows for many different kinds of audiences; we had not done the Chamber in the Street about the problems presented in the scenes; we had not done the Interactive Mailing List to consult people whose opinions might be useful in preparing a law, and whose knowledge could enlighten us. On the contrary, we wrote the Projects of Law ourselves, which positively is not the right thing to do. So, if any, the presentation at the Rathaus would have only a symbolic value.

After my introduction, we did the scenes. The audience chose three of them, including the slave-wife scene, and we did a Forum Theatre session on those three. Many people intervened, even the secretary of the vice-mayor! On the slave scene, most of the interventions were similar to ours. To close the event, we delivered our Projects of Law – someone had painted beautiful letters on a beautiful paper – to make a good impression to the Secretary of the Bavarian Greens. She was very nice to us, and said that she understood the symbolic nature of the event but, even so, she would really take those Projects of Law to the Green Legislators for consideration.

We were very happy. On her way out, the old lady with the cane and white hair approached me – she was one of the first to come in, and one of the last to leave. She called me and said:

> It is very entertaining what you have done. I agree with you and I know that this is just a symbolic action. But it was very important for me: you have shown that this is possible. And it had never crossed my mind to imagine that people, common people, people like us, could get together, make theatre about our own problems, discuss them on the stage, and then sit down and propose a new law. […] I agree with you: we have to make our desire become law!

I must say: I was happy.

7.2 Forum theatre on sexual harassment
from *Making bodies talk in Forum Theatre*
Paul Dwyer. (2004). *RIDE: Research in Drama Education, 9*(2), 199–210.

Observing Forum Theatre

In 1995, I observed a two-week workshop/rehearsal process and four preview performances of "Boundaries," a Forum Theatre project presented on the campus of Langara College in Vancouver, Canada. The project was directed by two facilitators from *Headlines Theatre Company* (one of the major disseminators of TO methods in North America) and developed with students from the actor-training programme at Studio 58, a part of Langara College and one of Canada's leading theatre schools. The development of "Boundaries" was funded under a provincial government campaign which aimed to "reduce the incidence of [physical and psychological] violence against women" at colleges and universities throughout British Columbia (Ministry of Skills, Training and Labour, 1994). In line with this campaign objective, the *Headlines* facilitators worked with the *Studio 58* actors to devise two Forum Theatre scenarios on the theme of sexual harassment which could later be performed in lecture halls and classrooms. Of particular interest for my purposes here is the opportunity which this project afforded of seeing four young performers being trained to take over the role of joker for the rest of the "Boundaries" season. [...]

Forum Theatre dramaturgy (or "boys will be girls")

Forum Theatre is based on a deceptively simple dramaturgical formula. The audience is invited to watch "with a critical eye" (as the *Headlines* facilitators would say) the struggle between an oppressed protagonist and his or her antagonist. The scenario is played through once, uninterrupted, until it reaches some kind of catastrophe. The actors then begin to play the scenario a second time, stopping whenever an audience member wishes to improvise some alternative tactic that he or she feels may help the cause of the oppressed protagonist.

For a Forum Theatre piece on the theme of sexual harassment, there is no great difficulty in guessing the likely gender of the oppressed and oppressor characters. Thus, on the first morning of "Boundaries" workshop/rehearsal process, some of the male actors involved confessed to feeling somewhat defensive: "I don't want to be typecast as an oppressor"; "I don't think all men are ogres"; "I feel like the issues are quite sticky." In response, the *Headlines* facilitators explained that since funding for the project had been obtained from the "Safer Campuses for Women" programme, the forum scenarios would focus on the oppression of women by men (in fact, the programme was simply called "Safer Campuses" but the intent – as noted above – was to support women's participation in post-secondary study). The facilitators also flagged, however, the role of what they called the "powerless observer" as an important part of the dramaturgical model: where the issues are "sticky," there can be characters (male and female) who are momentarily unaligned, capable of supporting either the oppressed or the oppressor depending on the particular tactics which intervening audience members choose to pursue.

The two forum scenarios which the group devised covered a broad range of oppressive behaviours – from the mundane (but by no means insignificant) experience of a female student struggling to get a word in edgeways as her male colleagues bulldoze their way through a group assignment, through to the more extreme (but by no means uncommon) experience of a young woman who is raped by a male acquaintance at an off-campus party. With both scenarios, the various catastrophes facing the protagonists clearly had the desired effect of stimulating a large number of audience members to intervene on stage. These interventions ranged from relatively playful attempts to deflect the unwanted attentions of a male harasser to strong confrontation and (mimed) physical violence. Situations which, in the model forum scenario, seemed quite black and white quickly turned to some much more interesting shades of grey as soon as spectators intervened.

Perhaps surprisingly, given that the focus of the scenarios was on female protagonists, a very large proportion of these interventions were made by male audience members – 48 out of a total of 92 (or 52%) over the course of the four preview performances. A much more striking statistic, however, is the difference between the interventions of male and female spectators regarding the gender of the characters they played: when women intervened, they nearly always took the part of the oppressed female characters (that is, women played women); yet when the men intervened, it was also nearly always to play a female character (men played women on 41 out of 48 occasions). Boal would generally advise against the joker allowing such a high number of cross-gender interventions on the basis that only the women in the audience could truly identify with the oppressed female protagonists (Boal, 1992, pp. 240–242). In this instance, neither the trainee *Studio 58* jokers nor the *Headlines* facilitators ever invited the audience to question the relevance of the spect-actors' gender to the interventions proposed (to be fair, neither was the issue raised by any member of the audience). […]

Boal, A. (1992). *Games for actors and non-actors* (A. Jackson, Trans.). London, UK: Routledge.

The substantial amount of debriefing within the overall performance structure of "Boundaries" (together with the fact that the trainee jokers and *Headlines* facilitators seemed unaware of this fact) is certainly one reason why Forum Theatre may be thought of as enacting an "invisible pedagogy." However, when one looks more closely at the pattern which the *Studio 58* trainee jokers were taught to follow during debriefing talk, there is no mistaking the joker's role as teacher. In rehearsals, the trainee jokers were encouraged to work from the following basic structure:

- interview the spect-actor (e.g.[,] "Did you get what you wanted?");
- interview the actors (e.g.[,] "What changed for your character? Could your

character take that kind of action?"); and
- make a brief summary for the audience (e.g.[,] "So what we learn from this intervention seems to be . . .").

Taken together, these summary evaluations amount to a compendium of recommendations for the audience to consider and thus point to the broader discourses which are being reproduced and/or challenged in this Forum Theatre event. With this in mind, here is a selection of some typical comments which cropped up during the "Boundaries" performances:

- So we can learn that by expressing your opinions right from the start then you can sort of maybe get a better perspective on what's really going on.
- I think we're seeing a lot of people stand up for themselves[.]
- So I guess what we learn from your intervention is that we can't – we shouldn't always follow our friends or give in to peer pressure. We sometimes have to go with how we feel.
- So in effect by being very conscious and open about your consciousness you can . . . educate people around you and . . . get out of situations that you don't want to be in.
- By hitting things at a very human level instead of a "man versus woman" nonsense level . . . just cutting right under it, caring . . . you managed to open things up and stop the nonsense[.]
- By insisting on your space and ... really being honest about what it is that you're comfortable with, you can avoid conflict and that's something that everybody needs to do in their life.

I should stress that my point here is not to damn the "Boundaries" jokers for lacking a more sophisticated analytical language. . . . Like anyone else, these students are prone to fall back on the clichés and common sense understandings of the dominant discourses into which they have been apprenticed. . . . At best, out of this mix comes a discourse in which the oppressors are never named as such and their actions rarely scrutinized; at worst, comes a discourse in which those who are oppressed, if only they could get in touch with their true feelings, would learn to stand up for their rights. . . . Given the generic features of the debriefing routine adopted here, it takes a linguistically dextrous and committed spect-actor to make this challenge public.

Forum Theatre may or may not be a "safe space" in which to investigate "alternative scenarios" and social interventions. It is certainly not a value-neutral space, despite the way Boal at times portrays it as a theatre of free expression, automatically empowering by virtue of the fact that spectators can transgress the "sacred" space of the stage. Against such rhetorical claims, the "Boundaries" project offers instead a salutary reminder that Forum theatre always occurs in a precise context, wherein the participants – including individuals and organizations participating as sponsors/supporters – are engaged in multiple (sometimes contradictory) forms of ideological struggles.

7.3 Igniting the social imagination

from *Theatre of the Commons: A theatrical inquiry into the democratic engagement of former refugee families in Canadian public high school communities*
J. Alysha Sloane & Dawn Wallin. (2013). *Educational Research, 55*(4), 454–472.

Currently, there is not enough action research available to identify examples of innovative practices that aim to reduce educational barriers impacting former refugee youth and their families ... Our contention is that students must develop the agency and have the freedom to ask the question, 'What kind of future do we want'? They must see themselves as capable and hopeful actors who have the courage to make a difference in a world of political apathy. ... [David] Diamond's theatre work, which coined Theatre for Living is rooted in The Theatre of the Oppressed but is more inclusive because of his refusal to adopt the binary oppositions of oppressor/oppressed. His conscious movement away from the oppressed/oppressor binaries still resonates with the emancipatory goals of Boal's work but it honours the array of complex actors who live in a given ecosystem. In a Forum Theatre event, Boal would not accept interventions from any 'oppressors', whereas Diamond sees no choice but to dissolve all boundaries between the constructs of the powerful and powerless if social change is to occur in a community. [...]

The study was located in one public high school community in Manitoba. The research process was divided into three phases: identification of the community issue and participant recruitment (Phase One), a workshop series (Phase Two), and the Forum Theatre event (Phase Three) .... All of the participants in all three phases of the study identified themselves as former refugees who had been living in Canada for at least two years. ... In Phase One of the study, 26 participants were involved in a meeting that determined the community issue for the workshops and the play. Out of the 26 participants, six were adults (four women, two men) and 20 of the participants were youths between the ages of 12 and 19 (11 girls, 9 boys). ... Participants moved into small groups to identify an issue facing the school community that was shared with the large group. After public dialogue, each member of the entire group voted to determine which issue would inform Phase Two of the study. The community issue selected was, 'Communication Barriers: What Happens When You Have No Voice', which became the content of the Theatre of the Commons workshops and the Forum Theatre Play. [...]

[A]n additional seven participants who approached the researcher upon hearing of the invitation to participate, were involved in the theatre workshops. Of the 33 participants, 26 were youth (10 boys and 16 girls) and seven were adults (four men, three women). The adults and youth came to Canada from the following countries: Afghanistan, Bhutan, Burma, Democratic Republic of the Congo, Iraq, Kenya, Nepal, Somalia and South Sudan.

Participants engaged in a five-day Image and Forum Theatre workshop to explore, in depth, the roots and impact of the community problem as well as possible solutions. Each workshop started with trust building games drawn heavily from Boal's (2002) *Games for actors and non-actors*. Muscular, sensory, memory, imagination and emotional exercises were employed to prepare the participants to work together to utilise Image and Forum Theatre to rigorously explore [the topic].

The workshop participants were then asked to create a Forum Theatre play using the content of the workshops. ... The 27-minute play entitled, 'Silos of Silence', honoured and extended the images, ideas and mini Forum plays generated in the workshops. Scenes were created based on their potential to ignite dialogue within the community and how well the scenes reflected the tensions inherent in the problem. Scene decisions were made through open dialogue and when needed, a majority vote. Seventy-seven audience members attended the Forum Theatre play, with representation by community members, parents, educators, administrators, government officials and community agencies. Audience members made a total of seven interventions in the Forum Theatre Play. After each intervention, [Alysha Sloane] engaged the audience members and the actors in critically reflecting on the interventions in her role as the 'Joker', in order to facilitate movement from micro to macro reflections on the nature of the issues at play.

There were three main strategies that were used to trouble the role of the Joker. The first strategy was to not offer praise or criticism of the participants' efforts during the workshop or the play rehearsals so that participants could offer multiple interpretations of the same image or scene without pursuing 'the right answer'. It also created an environment where it was difficult for the facilitator to be an 'all knowing authority'. Another strategy was to conduct an analysis of how many times the participants challenged the reframing of their ideas. Interpretations were repeatedly verified with the participants and corrections made. A third strategy was to demonstrate confidence in the participants' ability to work through disagreements with one another. There was no demand made that participants reach consensus or agreement, nor was there any micromanagement of how messages were delivered or received between participants. [...]

The script of the play was generated from the lived experiences of the actors who decided to create and perform in the Forum play. Interestingly, in the first rehearsal the actors situated all of their scenes inside a school, even though they had received no direction on where the scenes could occur. When asked why all of the struggles in their scenes took place in schools, seven participants responded: 'Most people have trouble at school'; 'All troubles happen at school'; 'Everything starts from school'; 'It's realistic because most of us are in school'; 'Adults can relate to all of this. They do not understand the rules that govern them in school and in Canada'; 'At school when you are the new girl it is hard'; and, 'Everyday my child comes home crying from the school'.

Therefore, it was almost inevitable that our play, *Silos of Silence*, would be situated in a school. The *Silos of Silence* script generated a Forum Theatre performance but it was also a statement about the actors' personal struggles with language barriers/no voice in the school community. Issues such as racism, addiction, disrespect for cultures and place, and the desire to appease the more established members of a community are woven throughout the play. The play was based upon six scenes. Scene one involved the introduction of six former refugee students to a classroom whose public introductions by a school principal are met with racist comments by the other students in the room. Scene two involved a young woman who finds out her best friend was spreading rumours about her, and the confrontation that ensues between the two. Scene three illustrates a confrontation that develops between the captain of a competitive soccer team and the coach regarding a former refugee's new involvement on the team during play-off season. Scene four demonstrates the clash between family and peer expectations articulated through dance. Scene five occurs in a school cafeteria in which a former refugee student is ostracised by her new classmates. During the last scene, a former refugee youth is confronted by another youth who is attempting to recruit him into drug activity. [...]

The lived experiences of the participants became the 'curriculum' of the workshops and the play challenged the participants to go into a public domain with what they learned in the hope that the audience would engage with them intellectually, ethically and emotionally. Forum and Image Theatre work perpetuated a cycle of questioning, deconstruction, analysis, debate, action and doubt that are all tenets of critical theory. This method or cycle is a provocative way to consider how children might be engaged to learn in classrooms. [...]

The study's findings indicate that spaces for diverse voices were created because the participants: had the opportunity to name community struggles; trouble the oppressiveness of the English language in the Image Theatre exercises; offer multiple interpretations of the same Images or scenes; script and share their struggles; and incite audience interventions in the second performance of the play. By extension, we believe that Forum Theatre has the potential to inform policy decisions by providing the means for multiple and diverse voices at the individual and community levels to be expressed. ... [T]he play created a reciprocal knowledge exchange between the actors and the Spect-actors. Both the actors and the audience members offered and then debated the interventions offered during the second performance of the play. The microcosm of the Forum Theatre play demonstrated how a collective consciousness about social injustice could be developed between diverse community actors to inspire social change.

7.4 Life skills in medical education
from *Theatre of the Oppressed in medical humanities education: The road less travelled*
Setu Gupta, Abhinav Agrawal, Satendra Singh & Navjeevan Singh. (2013). *Indian Journal of Medical Ethics, 10*(3), 200–203.

At the University College of Medical Sciences, Delhi, we have attempted to introduce our students to the humanities. To achieve this, the Medical Humanities Group of the Medical Education Unit has organised a series of events over the past few years relating to literature, philosophy, ethics, the visual and performing arts, street theatre, and the social sciences. The personal characteristics and attitudes required for professional life specifically identified by the MCI [Medical Council of India] for MBBS [Bachelors of Medicine and Surgery] students are "personal integrity, sense of responsibility and dependability and ability to relate to or show concern for other individuals.". Considering that these lie squarely in the domain of philosophy and ethics, it is interesting to speculate on how these ends can be achieved. [...]

The 2-day workshop in Theatre of the Oppressed that we organised was an attempt to achieve some of these goals. The 26 participants in the workshop included students from the University College of Medical Sciences (UCMS), the Army College of Medical Sciences and Amar Jyoti Institute of Physiotherapy, Delhi, and two members of the faculty from the UCMS. The sessions were conducted by the facilitator, or in TO parlance, the "Joker" – one who guides the group.

The workshop included: (i) Introduction to Theatre of the Oppressed, and rules and responsibilities of the group; (ii) warm up games/community building exercises; (iii) image theatre and other structured exercises; and (iv) Forum Theatre.

The introduction to Theatre of the Oppressed was followed by an important process – setting the container for the workshop with some "agreements" such as "listen for understanding", "agree to disagree", "step up/step back", "right to pass", etc. Of the many exercises and games described by Boal, the following were used in the workshop: Warm up/community building: Name playback, Cover the space, Fainting by numbers, 1-2-3, Zip-zap-zop, Sound and movement transformation.

Structured games and exercises: Columbian hypnosis, blind games including Glass cobra Image theatre: an introspective exercise for breaking the mind-body dichotomy, and discovering "secret thoughts".

Participants explored themes such as selection into MBBS, your first encounter with a cadaver, classroom, religion, lack of passion, and good medical practice. Forum theatre: a problem-solving technique to demonstrate the power of a community and its collective wisdom, democratic processes, and critical thinking. The group created five short plays, after identifying recent, real and unresolved moments of conflict in their own lives. Two of these scenes (Relationship and Abandoned) were selected by the audience and these were then forumed – that is, replayed to elicit their intervention and solutions.

At the end, the participants submitted written feedback of their impressions of the workshop. [...]

Community-building exercises, played in the beginning, as well as in between the sessions, had a tremendous role in eliminating the apprehension of being a group of diverse participants from different colleges, branches and semesters.

It introduced the feeling that interacting with strangers should never be difficult – an important life skill for people in the medical profession, helped in building instant rapport, a sense of togetherness and trust. [...]

Participants were able to connect the games to their lives, both personal as well as professional. Sometimes these insights went quite deep. For example, as one participant put it, "There are things that we know, emotions that we fail to acknowledge, realise ... like when we played 'fainting by numbers'. We all want someone to be always there; to catch us when we fall."

Columbian hypnosis, a game that uses the metaphor of power, provoked this response from a participant: "...in an abstract way, how a patient gives all control over himself to a doctor and how a doctor should channelize it so as not to oppress the patient." [...]

At the end of the workshop we organised a public forum theatre performance for the college faculty and students. Here, participants not only learned from their own experience as actors but were also forced to adapt quickly to the changes incorporated by the spect-actors, inculcating the skills of quick judgment and decision-making required of medical professionals when they may be in difficulty.

Our forum theatre on "Abandonment" challenged the spectators with a problem, shown in an unsolved form. The protagonist with debilitating Parkinson's disease was shown abandoned by family, doctor, and faith. The forum theatre methodology also provides a dialogic structure for deconstructing deep-seated, bitterly divisive issues with sensitivity and respect. [...]

Participating in TO is not without challenges. The literature reports potential for misperceptions, manipulation and other negative process outcomes. Challenges of the implementation phase include some changes in the script dialogue, inconsistent icebreaker activities and lack of consistency from performance to performance. We were fortunate in having an exquisitely trained facilitator with remarkable commitment to her cause. Such people cannot be mass-produced. Introduction of TO into the medical curriculum on a large scale may be problematic as it requires skilled facilitators. Mandates, forcing MH [Mental Health] onto reluctant medical educators and restrictive policies are likely to be counter-productive. Eventually, organisers at each institution should be granted the freedom to adopt what works best for them, and be encouraged to explore their own avenues.

For the participants, without exception, the overall experience was positive. The authors, all of whom participated, agree that the workshop promoted a new bonding, trust and kinship among the group. This being a mixed group of students from different institutions and semesters and two members of the faculty, it was remarkable how quickly the facilitator could inculcate a feeling of camaraderie and provide a non-threatening atmosphere.

In the Indian context, with its rigid hierarchies and social constructs, this breaking of barriers was an important lesson to learn. Teachers and students are increasingly expected to cope with diversity in the classroom ranging from class distinctions to social, caste, and linguistic disparities. In our experience, even a single exposure to the workings of TO goes a long way towards the better understanding and resolution of these issues.

Further Reading

In addition to his own texts, there is a great deal of writing about Boal's work in many settings, across many cultures and a variety of applied theatre genres. You will have already met some of this material in this text. In addition, we suggest:

Bala, S. & Albacan, A. (2013). Workshopping the revolution? On the phenomenon of Joker training in Theatre of the Oppressed. *RIDE: The Journal of Applied Theatre and Performance, 18*(4), 388–402. The authors discuss the tensions that accompany working as a facilitator/Joker in TO.

Burton, B. & O'Toole, J. (2005). Enhanced Forum Theatre: Where Boal's Theatre of the Oppressed meets process drama in the classroom. *NJ: Drama Australia Journal, 29*(2), 49–57. Presents the anti-bullying project "Cooling Conflict" that used an enhanced form of Forum Theatre; the authors analyze the four "enhancements" (three scenes, not one; multiple interventions; the fourth scene; and process drama additions) and the reasons for their use.

Cohen-Cruz, J. & Schutzman, M. (Eds.). (2006). *A Boal companion: Dialogues on theatre and cultural politics.* London, UK: Routledge. A wide-ranging collection of essays, case studies and critical discussions on the work of Boal that address the impact and implications of Boal's work by American practitioners and theoreticians with rich experience using his strategies and techniques.

Duffy, P. & Vettraino, E. (Eds.). (2010). *Youth and Theatre of the Oppressed.* New York, NY: Palgrave Macmillan. This collection features chapters by leading practitioners and scholars such as Johnny Saldaña, Christina Marin and Diane Conrad.

Woodson, E. (2012). Theatre of the Oppressed: Empowering homeless women. *Music in Arts and Action, 4*(1), 38–55. Retrieved from http://www.musicandartsinaction. net/index.php/maia/issue/view/9. This Stanford University undergraduate student conducted over 100 sessions with homeless women in a shelter. Her dedicated long-term commitment is a model for exemplary practice.

Questions for Reflection and Discussion

1. Consider the implications of cross-gender role-taking in Forum Theatre. In replacing the protagonist, how important do you consider it to be that the spect-actor identifies as the same gender as the protagonist and for what reasons?

2. Boal talks about adapting his work for various cultures and communities. Based on your reading and understanding of TO, what elements of Boal's practice need to remain consistent wherever it is done? What elements do you see as having opportunities for change?

3. In a group, discuss the implications of Boal's desire to transform theatre into a democratic arena that gives equal space to all opinions, voices and political perspectives. How possible would this be? Consider how open each member of the group would be to hearing ideas expressed by spect-actors that are contrary to their own beliefs and ethical/moral standards (see Hamel, 2013, for more on this topic).

Suggested Activities

1. In groups of four, discuss a political oppression that you see in your community (racism, sexism, power imbalance, etc.). Create a scene that illustrates this oppression at work on the protagonist and also reveals the wider social implications of that oppression.

2. Share these scenes with the class and look at each to see how successfully it holds the personal story within the broader social implications.

3. Conduct research in your local newspapers to discover the issues that are relevant to your community (e.g., sewage treatment, private use of public space, homelessness). Choose an issue. What law does your group envision that could improve the problem at hand? Create a scene that presents the problem and supports the need for the new law. Present it in a community setting to an invited audience interested in the issue, including local activists and politicians. What written documentation of this performance could be passed on to lawmakers to take to the next level of implementation?

4. In small groups, decide upon a shared internal psychological oppression that you all face, such as procrastination, ambition, pressure. Using Image Theatre, create a tableau of that oppression. Figures in the image may be oppressors or allies. Share

these images with the rest of the class, and discuss responses. You may, on a slow count of five, re-shape the images into more positive versions. Discussion is then around what actions were suggested in the re-shaping that could be taken into the real world.

5. Photographs can be a very useful tool for both reflection and reporting. For either of the presentation options above (#3 or #4), have one or more group members take a series of photographs of the work as it is happening. Select those photographs that frame moments in the process you consider evocative. After a period of time (perhaps two weeks to a month) gather together a small group of observers and use the photographs with an accompanying set of questions to elicit their memories of and opinions on what they witnessed.

Web Resources

Cardboard Citizens, London, UK http://cardboardcitizens.org.uk/

Centre for Community Dialogue and Change, Bengaluru, IN http://www.ccdc.in/

Forum Project, The, New York, NY http://theforumproject.org/

International Theatre of the Oppressed, Rotterdam, NL www.theatreoftheoppressed.org

Pedagogy and Theatre of the Oppressed, Omaha, NE http://ptoweb.org/

Theatre for Living, Vancouver, BC http://headlinestheatre.com

PART THREE

The Locations of Applied Theatre

CHAPTER EIGHT
THEATRE IN HEALTH EDUCATION (THE)

Introduction

Theatre in health education (THE) is an initiative that combines the principles and practices of theatre in education and health education to address issues of health, safety and well-being (Bury et al., 1998, p. 13). THE emerged

Australian aboriginal people generally define health thus:
"...Health does not just mean the physical well-being of the individual but refers to the social, emotional, spiritual and cultural well-being of the whole community. This is a whole of life view and includes the cyclical concept of life-death-life."

National Health and Medical Research Council (Australia), 1996, Section 2, p. 4

as a form of educational theatre largely in response to the HIV/AIDS crisis in the late 1980s and early 1990s. Traditional ways of informing people of the dangers of unsafe sex were not working (often because they were counter-cultural), and the enactive and entertaining possibilities of THE were seen to be a more engaging way of educating audiences in safe sex practices. Consider, too, the Aboriginal view of what is health; effective theatre always addresses the whole being.

Since the past two decades of the twentieth century, due in part to the growing focus on prevention and personal responsibility for health,

THE is now practiced internationally as a means of education on a variety of health issues. Some of these issues include: disability awareness (visible and invisible), drug abuse, child abuse, effective parenting, mental health, elder abuse, safe driving, sex education, safe/clean water, head injuries awareness, workplace safety and organ donation. At the same time, THE offers a new means of presenting research and models of best practice to health care workers and medical workers in the field and in training. There are also instances of mainstream theatre addressing health issues that have been performed for medical personnel as stimuli for discussion. *The Doctor's Dilemma* (1906/2004) by Shaw addresses the challenge of how to determine which patients will receive experimental treatment, in this case for tuberulosis. *Wit* by Margaret Edson (1999) follows an ovarian cancer patient's journey from diagnosis to death (*Times Colonist*, 2000, D2). These are two examples that have been used extensively in medical education. The work of oncologist and THE practitioner Ross Gray (2003) has led to remarkable shifts in health care providers' understanding of the power of artistic and narrative forms to communicate vital information: "They are the way of the future for educational and dissemination practices" (Gray et al., 2003, p. 223).

Doctors need emotional "muscle" in some ways, like an actor. They need to be open, to be sensitive, but not in a way that will incapacitate them.

Max Hafler, 2012, p. 310

THE practitioner Steve Ball (1994) sees a united philosophical basis between THE and theatre in education, consisting of seven characteristics or threads held in common:

1. Both demand affective as well as cognitive involvement.
2. Both utilize active learning.
3. Both are concerned with an exploration of attitudes and values.
4. Both involve role-taking.
5. Both emphasize self-empowerment.
6. Both are concerned with what it is to be human.
7. Both involve a community dimension (pp. 222–224).

THE's community-based process reminds us that health is not limited to individual choices and behaviors, but is a larger social responsibility. Health is contextualized by the culture, values and social, political and economic conditions of a community. As you read through the following examples of THE projects, watch how these threads are woven into the fabric of each applied theatre performance.

When I interviewed health professionals about their responses…many noted that seeing situations unfold on stage gave them the possibility of distance that they were denied in their everyday working lives… They were far from passive, engaging actively with the drama through reflection and meaning making… [I]t is important to consider the vulnerabilities and qualities of each audience before deciding how far to go in seeking participation.

Ross Gray, 2004, p. 247

THE often addresses difficult topics – "We don't talk about those things in public" – therefore, the element of ethics and safety become of paramount importance in theatre in health education projects. Note, too, how these applied theatre projects involve a freeing of suppressed voices, as in cultural taboos in various African cultures around public discussion of sexuality or, in almost all cultures, around child abuse. The careful aesthetic use of symbol and metaphor through a range of theatrical devices (puppetry, mask, or other traditional cultural entertainment forms) offer audiences a greater protection and at the same time a heightened accessibility to challenging material. THE is about raising awareness and changing behavior, and this is enormously difficult to assess. Consider carefully and log the techniques used by the researchers/practitioners in these excerpts.

> As HIV/AIDS is seen to be the progenitor of Theatre in Health Education, we begin with an example of a THE project that shows how traditional African dramatic and storytelling forms can be adapted effectively to both educate and entertain. The second case study excerpt, "Inside View" was developed for midwives, healthcare providers and pregnant women to present the different perspectives and complex questions that can arise from the choices and consequences of prenatal screening. Our final case study deals with the balance between facilitating and directing in a project with fourth year medical students designed to explore team work, emotional honesty and reconnection to the commitment to heal.

8.1 HIV/AIDS
from *Icons and metaphors in African theatre against HIV/AIDS*
Victor S. Dugga. (2002). *NJ: Drama Australia Journal*, 26(2), 63–72.

The task for the theatre is first of all to remove the issue from the private premises of human life to a public platform. In many societies in Africa, the topic of sex is not publicly discussed and, where it is, certain spectrums of the society – like children and women – may not be expected by social convention to participate in the discussion. [...]

[T]heatre creators like C. J. Odhiambo [use] narratives of old and familiar forms . . . to re-construct pressing and immediate health concerns. Usually, one or more storytellers tell the story and a somewhat "harmless" story gets encoded with issues of the HIV-AIDS scourge in ways that are identifiable to the listening public. Sometimes, the audiences of these narrative performances are incorporated into the performance as direct participants in the story or merely as chorus singers. Within this structure, certain stock qualities have been emerging including the lead character, Bodi (euphemism for "body"), who personifies the typical victim of AIDS. [...]

The use of the narrative techniques [are] re-captured in the following example:

> Bodi was born as a prince in a little town where everyone was given books at birth. At the time of his birth, the village diviner had prophesied that in all Prince Bodi's lifetime, he would require a book of only two hundred pages. Bodi was quite happy with his allotted pages until one day, he overused his pages and began to desire more pages. Finding none in his village, the prince abandons his right to the throne and travels to the city where he stumbles

123

into books in a public library. He was so excited seeing so many volumes of books under the same roof and began to read ferociously. One day, Prince Bodi walked into a bookshop and found that, instead of borrowing the books as he did in the library, he could actually buy as many books as he wanted without restrictions. He bought as many books as he wanted and kept reading until one day a strange [thing] happened to him. He could neither read nor write with the same zeal and pace that he was used to.

At this point, the story-telling facilitators interrupt the story. The audience is divided into groups and designated as village people awaiting the news of the arrival of Bodi, the library staff, the bookshop owners, etc. and asked to play-act their groups to Bodi's predicament. All the while, a pre-arranged song is sung at intervals to whet people's appetite or foreclose the immediate past or coming action in the story.

In this example, Bodi's character is used as a poetic license that frees the creative spirit of the artist. While he is an identifiable stock character in true universal concept of folk theatres, Bodi is additionally an interactive proposition that engenders dialogue and challenges the audience to expose their knowledge of HIV/AIDS. That way, wrong mindsets can be addressed, new techniques revealed and new information passed on in post-performance discussion. The story utilizes many symbols in the process of communication. The most evident is the symbol of absence – nothing about HIV/AIDS is mentioned. Instead, there are repeated references to [an] insatiable quest and hunger for books. When one follows the logic of a number of pages being allotted to the prince, one discovers that it is not a book of printed pages but a representation of life that is regulated by forces outside one's self. As the story follows Bodi's insatiable search to the point of his physical incapacitation to read, demand is placed on the audience to apply the story to the issue of HIV. It is arguable that the audience would already be aware of the theme of the story even before it starts and would therefore instantly know that the story is metaphoric. Whatever imagery is created is juxtaposed with the known facts about HIV/AIDS. Books then translate to one's partners from whom the virus could be contracted and this story can be well-received when taken to youths of school age, for whom books are daily stuff.

Like all good theatre that re-enacts and calls for the willing suspension of disbelief, no one looks at the illogicality of being given a limited number of pages at birth. Indeed, the illogic makes the story more forceful as one is ushered into the realm of the abnormal where actions contrary to one's current lifestyle are introduced. Where this technique hits the mark is its ballooning into seeking the views of the audience. The story is no longer about Bodi, but about what audiences think should or ought to happen to that character. Suggestions then end up with him being taken to the village and used as an example of how not to indiscriminately "read books." [...]

Among the Tiv of Central Nigeria, ... is a rich tradition of performances called Kwagh-Hir theatre. These performances are made up of animation of carved images manipulated by puppeteers through rhythmic movement of songs and instrumentation. Kwagh-Hir has since developed to a state festival [on the] last week of the year . . . prizes are awarded to the most outstanding groups. Participation is usually very high.

Themes of the performances are enlarged to cover every issue that draws the practitioners' attention. At [a] different point in the history of the Tivs, Kwagh-Hir was used for anti-colonial protests, for inter-ethnic or political squabbles and for social criticism. . . . A larger-than-life wooden carving of a human figure was brought onto the performance arena. It was a skinny body, smoothly carved and polished in glossy brown paint. The ribs were exposed to amplify the fact that it was the body of an emaciated AIDS patient probably at full-blown level. Three animators held the body using long wooden poles that suspended it a few feet from the ground. While music was played, they walked this body around the theatre as if to get it to speak to the audience. First it seemed lifeless but soon became intimidating as the animators simulated movements into the crowds. Then the body began to falter, displaying frailty and inability to walk properly. Soon, it was stumbling and threatening to collapse on the audience, causing them to raise alarm and shout helpful advice to the "body."

Without a word being said, the wooden carving animated the truth of devastation of HIV/AIDS. It began by projecting a super-human figure, only to bring it to a fragile less[-]than[-]human strength. It did not convey the message all by itself but built on the previous knowledge of the subject by the audience. Hence, they were able to identify the stages of deterioration that the emaciated body presented. The latent messages received about the devastation of the virus suddenly came alive in the inanimate figure as it tries to interact with the audience. Much of the credit however lay in the artistic quality of the wooden carving, its manipulators and the atmosphere generated by the music. However, the imagination and the skill of the creators and the players elicit the involvement of the audience to fully realize the communication intended. As the wooden figure was raised as an icon of AIDS, individual understanding and experience of the AIDS scourge generated other personal interpretations. [...]

Why circumvent the "real" issues with symbols? One instance of the covert presentation of facts in family reproductive [issues] . . . where a female nurse used a bottle of Coca[-]Cola to demonstrate how a condom is used. . . . Months later a man showed up with a complaint – he used the condom on a bottle as demonstrated and his wife still took in.

8.2 Prenatal screening as multimedia performance

from *Inside 'Inside View': Reflections on stimulating debate and engagement through a multimedia live theatre production on the dilemmas and issues of pre-natal screening policy and practice*
Gillian L. Hundt, Claudette Bryanston, Pam Lowe, Saul Cross, Jane Sandall & Kevin Spencer. (2010). *Health Expectations, 14*(1), 1–9.

'Inside View' was an applied theatre performance; however, it was not conceived within the generally accepted genre of theatre in health education or promotion. There were no health promotion messages concerning the use of antenatal screening. It was aimed to enable the exploration of different perspectives and raise questions for debate in this complex area both cognitively and affectively.

Prenatal screening in pregnancy for anomalies such as Down's syndrome, is an emotive and contested area. It is national policy in the UK to offer screening for Down's syndrome for all pregnant women. ... Prenatal screening is offered to all women in pregnancy and they have to give their informed consent. The information is given by midwives and other health care providers and the need for clear information and communication to underpin these decisions is paramount and well recognized. [...]

This multidisciplinary team had some shared expectations – namely to deliver a piece of theatre that was derivative from and faithful to the research project findings but that would engage and involve the public in debate on the topic of prenatal genetic screening. The data-set included a survey of pregnant women's views on prenatal screening, interviews with health providers in prenatal clinics and women and partners attending them, and ethnographic observation of clinic sessions. Three members of the research project team were members of the performance project, representing medical anthropology (GH), women's health and midwifery (JS) and biochemistry (KS). They were joined by a theatre director (CB), media technologist (SC), a sociologist (PL), a script writer (TM) and actor (KJ).

The research team members recognized the need for dramatic interpretation as well as the time and space for the creative process. The artistic team were presented with the challenge of developing a very short engaging performance (40 min) with artistic integrity that was a composite representation of the themes derived from the research data, which would present complex issues for diverse audiences. [...]

'Inside View' was written with a protagonist as a generic character of 'everywoman' representing different women with diverse narratives. The actor explored through internal dialogues with herself and the foetus, possible scenarios of different outcomes to the pregnancy relating to disability, medical technology and exploring a range of aspirations for the unborn child. Dramatic tension was not character driven but driven by the choices inherent in prenatal screening. The representation of 'everywoman' was aimed to enable the audience to identify with her dilemmas positioning her within their own context. Diversity was also represented through a number of dramatic strategies that included a voice from the past (grandmother), a radio discussion on disability rights, and the representations of three health professionals – the phlebotomist, sonographer and midwife counsellor.

The debate about pre-natal screening is one of complex cultural, moral and ethical dilemmas. The challenge for the director was to ensure that the passion for the debate remained vigorous and engaging throughout the performance without presenting a particular position. [...]

There were some hard decisions to take concerning how much information could be included, particularly scientific information within a short piece for such a wide audience.

The storyline involved a pregnant woman attending a prenatal screening clinic, and followed her physical and emotional journey through the clinic. A decision was taken to leave both the woman and the audience with unresolved possibilities and outcomes as a way of focusing on everywoman's dilemma and choices.

A mini lecture on the biochemical processes of maternal serum screening was inserted to convey not only the information, but also to parallel the didactic nature of much of the information giving to women and was congruent with a performance that took place often in classrooms or lecture theatres.

Artistically, the theatre director had to broker these different perspectives on stage and this necessarily involved adapting and modifying the script with discussion between primarily the actor and writer with the media technologist. An artistic device of a favourite but flawed coffee mug was used to convey the possibility of valuing imperfection.

> Like this mug – here's a print of the potter's thumb. And here's a bit of clay peeping through where the glaze didn't stick – that's why I brought it. It's individual. Even the potter didn't know for certain how the pot would come out. All the time it's in the kiln, it changes, becomes more itself… (Excerpt from script).

Visual technology was important throughout. At some point the audience would see a scanned foetus at 12 weeks, just as a pregnant woman on her first visit to the clinic would. An opening sequence accompanied by music with a foetal heartbeat, showed a waterfall that then transformed into the double helix of DNA. The use and reference to time both in the script but also in the visuals and [soundtrack] enhanced this theme. Set into the digitally created backdrop of the waiting room there was an interactive clock that synchronized to the duration of the time spent by a pregnant woman in a one stop first trimester screening clinic. This was accompanied by the sound of time ticking on in the sound track, and within the theatre piece were moments when time was suspended to allow the audience to have insight into the internal dialogue of the pregnant woman.

Owing to performing this piece in non-theatre spaces[,] mainly in lecture theatres without a stage to support a physically created space, the media technologist developed film of the home and clinic that was projected onto a large purpose built screen to enable the back projection that was required. Images included a domestic kitchen, driving to the clinic, footage from the prenatal clinic to frame the scenes, visualization of the maternal serum analysis using a desk top Kryptor analyser and clips of foetal ultrasound scans as well as a number of ironic still images melding the faces of two well known celebrities to illustrate the media term 'designer babies'. The visualization of the foetus using an ultrasound scan was one the main motifs and informed the title. […]

Post performance discussions

The performances elicited personal reflections that were sometimes shared spontaneously:

> It reminded me just how much I hated being pregnant on three occasions, the reason being that each time you were set up as having a test that you cannot really pass, you go there with all this joy because you are pregnant, and you are being put through a process, where people look worried and concerned and put all sorts of doubts into your head. I thought that was one of the wonderful things that emerged from this piece (Audience participant – Warwick Art Centre).

There was some understanding that the research study and the performance were different and one member of the audience commented:

> It works on a lot of different levels because it is a piece of theatre, not a piece of propaganda. It has come out of research but it is a piece of theatre and therefore it has a life of its own which may be something quite separate from the research or the things which you hoped and intended would come out of it (Audience participant – Warwick Art Centre). [...]

Health professionals in the audience also reflected on their own practice openly:

> I automatically refer women for screening, just ticking a box. From now on, I will make sure that I will discuss it with them (GP - Kings College).

Some felt that the panel discussion was an essential part of the performance:

> I think to do the play without the discussion would be wrong. But to have the discussion so that we can add things in [from] the audience is really important (Academic - London Church House).

In all the performances, the facilitated post show discussion was lively and varied and in some cases, as long as the play itself. Excerpts from 'Inside View' have been made available with facilitator briefing notes and the main research findings on the web for use [at] http://www2.warwick.ac.uk.ezproxy.library.uvic.ca/fac/cross_fac/healthatwarwick/research/pastresearch/inside_view.

8.3 Approaching a doctor's life

from *Operating theatre: A theatre devising project with fourth-year medical students*
Max Hafler. (2012). *Journal of Applied Arts & Health*, 3(3), 309–319.

Introduction

As an experienced theatre director and facilitator, when I was first approached to work dramatically with fourth year medical students at the National University of Ireland, Galway, my instincts were not to work primarily on theatre skills, but to involve the students creatively and to devise a piece of theatre based around the concept of healing. This piece was to be presented to the rest of their year, approximately seventy students, at the end of the final session…. Doctors need emotional 'muscle' in some ways, like an actor. They need to be open, to be sensitive, but not in a way that will incapacitate them. […]

Due to curricula and practical constraints, the module had to fit into the three-week window with a set number of hours. This divided into ten three-hour sessions. Nonetheless I broke an important rubric for devising, that everyone must be present, to have an earlier introductory session with only half the group available.

The Introductory Session

A whole month before the project was due to start we had our introductory session, before their end of year exams. I was not happy about a meeting which had to take place so long before the project began but we had to work within the schedule. It is also important to know that throughout this module I had a faculty member who assisted me. This doctor had considerable acting experience, provided invaluable support and was often a useful bridge between myself and the students.

The aim was to set ground rules, relax the students, give them a feel of what they might be capable of and where we might be going. I likened creating a piece of theatre to team sport to which, since it was quite a sports-orientated group, some of them related. The rules for devising and the ones I presented to the students in the introductory session were:

- That all material was confidential and stayed within the group.
- That all ideas were tried (as much as was possible).
- That no mocking or denigrating of people's ideas was permitted.
- That no one dominated. [Although the director/facilitator might have to limit the material or be trusted with taste, this prerogative was not to be used indiscriminately].
- That there was an understanding that some pieces might not be used but that each student would have opportunities to perform, and no one would be sidelined.

We began, as we were to do throughout the module with body and voice exercises, relaxation work, and group coordination and sensitivity; exercises which develop qualities which are important not only for acting, but for being. […]

There were to be two important pieces of written work; first they were to produce a poem or other piece of writing about an experience they or someone close to them had had, as a patient . They would need to write something they would be comfortable reading out. These poems, stories or songs would be the starting point for our piece. As Dymphna Callery says in her book, *Through the Body* (2007), 'Devising is really collaborative writing in the broadest sense of the word, "write"'. The second piece would be an ongoing learning journal, about the journey they travelled in creating this work.

Sessions 1 and 2: The Starting Point

All devising requires a starting point. Sometimes it begins with a concept, with movement, scenes or a song. I had chosen to ask participants to take a more literary route to begin with, to make the process less threatening…. I told the students we would not necessarily use the pieces of writing as they appeared but perhaps develop some of them into scenes, or songs…. One story became a powerful scene about a medical student meeting an old school friend who was a patient in a psychiatric facility whilst he was on placement in the same hospital. Another became a piece of choral speaking; another, which began as a poem, became a piece of revealing narrative on childhood trauma in hospital. […]

As they listened to each other's work, they started to get a sense of what they wanted to say, and several of them developed their work, often unprompted. […]

We discussed the architecture of the hospital; squares, sharp angles and corridors, and someone remarked how their experience of the hospital environment is everyday, and totally unlike the experience of the patient. It is as if they are operating in two parallel worlds.

Session 3: The creative frame, making material and an injection of humour

When the students arrived, I had marked out a rectangular space surrounded by corridors with white tape and chairs. It immediately had the feeling of a waiting room. I wanted to place the poems in the 'waiting room' environment. The deviser needs to create some kind of frame in which the students can create. The frame needs to be flexible, but it needs to be there. With limited time, this is to me, crucial. This creative frame involves both the actual space within which the performers work, and the shaping of the material they create.

A number of the poems were about waiting in the Accident and Emergency department, and one particularly struck the group as powerful. I split the text of the poem between different students and we made a piece of choral speaking as desperate people waited to be seen. I remember remarking about how much waiting there is when one is ill.

We began to develop a strong sequence where a confused and disturbed patient was admitted to hospital. The movement precision required to perform this sequence was something we returned to again and again with exercises and group awareness work.

However, neither they nor I wanted the whole piece to be grim and serious…. They created two scenes which ended up in the final piece; medical students on the rounds with an authoritarian consultant and the other, a student against the clock at an Objective

Structured Clinical Examination. They created these scenes in a basic way, but with enough skill for us to see how the scenes might work. As with the written pieces, I did not focus over-much on developing their skills at this point; that came later.

Session 4: Getting into shape and an angry moment

In this session I tried to put our current material into some kind of shape and pushed them quite hard. [...]

We started very constructively. We created the 'overture' to our piece, with the whole cast playing anxious, despairing patients, crying out for attention, looking for doctors, which rose to a crescendo. It was raw and powerful. Then when the panic rose to a crescendo, we changed the scene to a lecture about The Role of the Doctor, in which they demonstrated to their audience the various roles the doctor might inhabit. They came up with a variety of possibilities, such as the detective, the businessman, the scientist, the carer, the wise one, and most amusingly, the emotional sponge. This part of the presentation was light and amusing, but emerged from a serious exercise and discussion. [...]

In working on new material that day, there was a desire to focus on the good things about being a doctor and the students offered saving lives and curing people. I asked them to make a realistic scene around their ideas, and got some stereotypical insincere pieces I would liken to a bad episode of a television hospital drama. I feared that this might happen, but the students wanted to try it. They were rather surprised both scenes reduced them to giggles. For inexperienced actors, I have found it is often incredibly challenging to address serious issues in a naturalistic way, though the participants' instincts tell them they could do it easily, because they feel familiar with it. Sometimes a more stylized poetic approach can be deeper. We worked with a freeze-frame scenario, slowly moving from one tableau to another, and this was far more successful.

By this time, participants were really starting to relax and take risks. However, when a student whilst trying his best to do something intense and serious, was undermined and ridiculed by another, I got angry. The disruptive participant was the one who had missed a number of sessions, so quoting the ground rules was of limited use, and he found it very hard indeed to change this behaviour in a group. When you open up a person to dramatic involvement, the level of challenge this can present can be extreme. It's an illogical and emotional response, whatever their educational background, and playground behaviour took over occasionally with a few of the others, when the work got intense. I realised I had to rethink my strategy. One of this project's crucial goals was to help develop teamwork and emotional maturity, both of which they would need in abundance in their future profession. I resolved to give more breaks, and try and stop people getting too hyperactive.

Session 5: Honesty and listening

After the previous session, I decided not to start with the warm up, but to work more slowly, beginning with a conversation about how they were coping with this revealing and challenging process of making a piece of theatre. I remembered my intentions for the project. I felt I needed to slow down and be calm. I considered again the time constraints, and the emerging anxiety for them of their 'performance'.

I brought a sheet in of the running order of poems and scenes thus far. I had separated the proposed final presentation into movements, like a piece of music. Written down, it all seemed to have a reality for the students and a feeling we were making something together. I started to get a sense that they were all seeing the value of the work, and we strongly reconnected. [...]

One student wrote a poem about an early hospital experience. I encouraged him to just tell us the story using his own words, and he did so very beautifully, with an incredible intensity. The whole room went silent. I asked if he would mind very much telling us the story like that in the piece, and setting aside his poem; he agreed.

For me this was a very successful session, and as important as the performance itself. There was a realization in this session that everyone might be able to go deeper than they thought and it was as if a breath of fresh air found its way into the theatre.

Sessions 6–10: Short scenes and the ending

These sessions, running up to the performance, involved warm-ups, consolidation and some skills teaching, both in staging and writing. There were run-throughs, and working carefully through the transition or sequence from one scene to the next. In addition, I was able to see individuals and smaller groups about specific pieces of the work that I felt would benefit. [...]

When they came into the theatre after a break on the day of the performance, and the stage lights were on, they became very excited.

The performance

The performance lasted 25 minutes, and was attended as promised by about 65 students and staff members. The participants had written or devised nearly all the material. I as director had contributed my own ideas and shaped it, but most of it belonged wholly to them. We had prepared it in 32 hours of contact time.

What I had not bargained for was the generosity, and genuine wonder of the audience, as they watched their classmates reveal sides of themselves they perhaps did not know existed....The performing students achieved an intense team spirit and had explored, emotionally and intellectually, aspects of themselves that had direct relation to their chosen vocation.

Further Reading

D'Alessandro, P. & Frager, G. (2014). Theatre: An innovative teaching tool integrated into core undergraduate medical curriculum. *Arts & Health: An International Journal for Research, Policy and Practice, 6*(3), 191–204. A verbatim play was created from the diary of a 16-year-old cancer patient and interviews with his family, friends and health care team. The article surveys responses to the play by varied audiences that show its effects on both health professionals and the general public.

Gray, R. (2003). *Prostate tales: Men's experiences with prostate cancer.* Harriman, TN: Men's Studies Press.

Gray, R. & Sinding, C. (2002). *Standing ovation: Performing social science research about cancer.* (With accompanying video). Walnut Creek, CA: AltaMira. Gray is an oncology researcher who uses applied theatre in his work and documents its effect on performers and audiences.

Noble, S. (2007). Meeting myself for the first time while on stage: Learning that emerged from a community popular theatre project. *Applied Theatre Researcher, 7,* article 6. Retrieved from http://www.griffith.edu.au/education/griffith-institute-educational-research/resources/applied-theatre-researcheridea-journal/issues. Although the title suggests popular theatre, this description of a project designed to give voice to a group of psychiatric patients in Duncan, British Columbia, fits more appropriately under THE. Issues of power and identity as they affect all the participants emerge as they construct and perform *Shaken: Not Disturbed…with a Twist.*

Saxton, J. & Miller, C. (2006). The relationship of context to content in the medical model: Exploring possible paradigms. In M. Balfour & J. Somers (Eds.), *Drama as Social Intervention* (pp. 129–141). Concord, ON: Captus Press. An overview of the continuum of THE practices from the private work to the public performance.

Strickling, C.A. (2002). Actual lives: Cripples in the house. *Theatre Topics, 12*(20), 143–162. A description of a project that critiques cultural and medical attitudes towards disability and engages the audience in re-envisioning what it means to live with disability.

Walsh, A. (2012). Breaking frames: Mark Storer's *For the Best* – A case study about an artist in residence. *Journal of Applied Arts and Health, 3*(2), 217–228. A remarkable site-specific production based on interviews and artworks by children undergoing dialysis and their classmates performed by London's Unicorn Theatre, a professional children's theatre company.

Questions for Reflection and Discussion

1. From each (or some) of the case studies in this chapter, based on your understanding of good theatre, identify what you would consider to be effective as theatrical moments.

2. How do the THE case studies reflect the definition of health given in the text box (from the World Health Organization) in the introduction to this chapter?

3. In the introduction to this chapter, Steve Ball writes about the shared philosophy of theatre and health education. What other common threads can you identify that connect theatre processes with healthy living?

4. Within your group there will be a number of ethnicities and cultural backgrounds. Drawing on a cultural practice other than your own, what possibilities can you explore to represent some aspect of health or illness in a metaphoric theatrical way?

Suggested Activities

1. How might you frame a response to an imagined (or role-played) encounter with a government official who is responsible for funding your THE project? What could you say in response to his or her questions about the value of applied theatre as a way to address issues in health education?

2. Look at some current local newspapers with a view to identifying a pressing health-related issue. Write a one-page applied theatre project proposal that outlines the topic you have chosen, the possibilities for education/change, the community group(s) that could be involved as participants and the potential audiences for the performance phase. Also consider what possibilities there are for follow-up work with both participants and audiences.

3. Visual artists through the ages have recorded experiences of illness (such as plagues, famines and so on). Create a small portfolio of those artworks that engage you and describe how these could be used as potential pre-texts for dramatic exploration in the context of a THE project?

Web Resources

Are we there yet? Edmonton, Alberta, Canada www.ualberta.ca/AWTY/index.html

Caught in the Act: Theatre in Health Education Company, Kingham, UK http://www.caughtintheact.co.uk/CITA/Home.html

Corner Health Center Theatre Troupe, Ypsilinati, MI http://www.cornerhealth.org/?module=Page&sID=theatre-troupe

Theatre in Health Education Trust, Dunedin, New Zealand http://www.theta.org.nz/home/

Introduction

Theatre for Development (TfD) involves the making and performing of plays in developing communities worldwide, although the bulk of research on this topic is predominantly focused in various African and Asian countries where topical issues of relevance to communities are tackled through theatre. TfD is a potent educational tool for audiences struggling with illiteracy, as the method of delivery is both verbal and interactive and draws on popular indigenous cultural forms such as storytelling, music and dance.

Theatre for development aims to interrogate the structures of fixed reality in order to "un-fix" them. It attempts to subvert the dominant ideology, to re-order the received unities of time, space and character through fictional reconstruction of those unities.

Kennedy Chinyowa, 2007, p. 37

The TfD movement has gone through dramatic changes. Over its history, it has moved away from a somewhat colonizing process of First World theatre artists/educators, university students and/ or development agencies imposing their messages of "good" health and "good" democracy using western theatrical forms in Third World settings. In a post-colonial world, this process has been inverted so that today TfD is, ideally, locally driven with training and support offered by outside specialists and agencies, but with control of the process held by the community involved. Odhiambo (2001) says that the agenda for TfD is, "to alter and transform attitudes, habits and behaviours that are oppressive in nature and that come between a community and its imaginations towards development" (p. 86). Within this general definition we can begin to see the ties between TfD and other more politically oriented applied theatre genres, such as Popular Theatre and Theatre of the Oppressed (see Chapters 4 and 7 of this book). Also, in the wake of the HIV/AIDS crises in many developing nations, TfD has served as a form of THE in presenting plays that educate audiences about the prevention, contracting and treatment of the virus.

Odhiambo (2001) highlights the theatrical elements particular to TfD:

- *Subverting and democratizing the theatre space*; that is to say "both audience and actors have equal access to the space during and after the performance."
- *Privileging performance over the written script (text)*; the audience is offered "ample opportunities to intervene and interrogate the performance at the most critical moments."
- *Participation as a conscious act*; as well as the negotiation of the meaning in creating the performance, participation within a performance is regarded as another part of the process and not an interruption of a "final product."
- *Activating the audience: from spectator to spect-actor*; here "members of the audience, by interrupting the drama and becoming actors themselves, are made aware that they can change the direction of the drama . . ."
- *Choosing a viewpoint: the power of transformation*; "the transforming power" of TfD lies in its "ability to provide society with a lens through which it [can come to realize] . . . that reality and conditions can be changed" (pp. 89–92).

From these elements, we can see that the importance of community involvement is as central to effective TfD practice as it is in all applied theatre.

Plastow (2014) suggests that many TfD projects have goals to domesticate rather than transform participants: to change their behaviours as opposed to supporting them in finding ways to change their own lives. Plastow, an experienced western-based TfD facilitator, expresses her concerns about the lack of time spent on training that leads to TfD trainers/facilitators who simply regurgitate what they have been taught rather than work with communities in more critical ways focused on social justice and change. "No one would let a dentist loose on their molars after a two-week course, so why would the sensitive and complex business of engaging in community conscientization and dialogue be adequately passed on in such a time period?" (p. 113).

> To pretend that political contexts are not important in socially committed theatre is surely to play into the neo-liberal hands of those who wish community-based theatre to remain inward-looking, focused on individual behaviour change and divorced from an understanding of the national and geopolitical reasons for the perpetuation of social inequalities.
>
> Jane Plastow, 2014, p. 108

TfD practitioners must also consider the thorny problems of exit strategies and follow-up, recognizing not only their importance but also their difficulties in practice. Munier and Etherton (2006) returned to the site of a Bangladeshi TfD project on children's rights (sponsored by Save the Children) to find that the promised follow-up had never happened because the children with whom they had worked no longer fit the age criteria. While they felt anger and guilt about this lack, at the same time they heard from the former child participants about how much they remembered of their drama/theatre work and how much it meant to them. These "stories and discussions illustrate that it is extremely important for the initiators of the TfD process in a community to be aware and committed to long-term engagement, to see where it leads, and record what changes or impact it eventually brings" (p. 182).

Funding for exit strategies, follow-up and assessment is often ignored, under-funded or cut because the money has run out. In addition, these areas present challenges to project facilitators: planning an exit strategy often requires a project being well underway before that planning can occur; following-up can also be tricky as it may not be directly time-tied to a project. Yet if it is the will of a community to keep going, how can this happen? Assessment of TfD projects is another area that presents challenges to facilitators. The context of any TfD project is unique; therefore, how assessments are made around the perceived successes or failures of a theatrical intervention into a community must also be unique. While there are no easy answers to this challenge, close and careful attention must be paid to assessing the impact of a project on participants and audiences in a transparent and non-predetermined fashion. The concepts of open dialogue and democratic forums around community needs are key, while, at the same time, facilitators cannot afford to ignore the power relationships within a community as well as the broader economic and political pressures on that community.

> TfD is all about awareness raising, learning, communication and action. As such it occupies a specific niche in broader communication and educational strategies.
>
> Kees Epskamp, 2006, p. 6

We all would hope to change the world, but the difficulties faced by TfD facilitators in many international communities remind us that change can and does happen in small and subtle ways (Balfour, 2009). Sometimes the simple experience of theatre-making and theatre-viewing is pleasure enough to have a positive impact on the lives of those who struggle daily with poverty, illiteracy and disease.

The first case study looks at how an indigenous theatre form in Bangladesh is applied to a production that explores the issue of human trafficking. Of interest is the use of a bibek (akin to the Joker in Theatre of the Oppressed) who narrates and comments on the action of the play, and engages the audience in dialogue. Second, we see a Ugandan TfD project intended to educate citizens about their voting rights in the development of a new constitution. Note how the government oversees the project and its eventual translation into a nationally broadcast television production. Thirdly, a Pakistani TfD theatre company addresses the difficult topic of honor killings in a culture where these practices are often kept hidden. Finally, a Nigerian project involving university students living for a week in a small rural community addresses topics of environmental health and sanitation.

9.1 A Bangladesh TfD project
from *Social theatre in Bangladesh*
Nazmul Ahsan. (2004). *TDR: The Drama Review, 48*(3), 50–58.

LOSAUK (*Loke Nattya O Sanskritik Unnayan Kendro*) bases its performances on the Bengali popular theatre forms *jatra* and *khaner gan*. Traditionally, *jatra* often told mythological stories that reflect the aspirations of the people. It relies on the audience's emotional identification with the mythological hero. *Jatra* is a living form, still very popular and always changing. For many, *jatra* goes beyond theatre. It is a concept of life, a way of life. Because *jatra* is so popular, it is an excellent tool for LOSAUK. [...]

Jatra, in the hands of LOSAUK, becomes an instrument for creating awareness, social change, and transformation in Bangladesh. The extreme poverty of so many and the greed of others are the common causes of the trafficking in human lives that takes place over Bangladesh's unpatrolled border with India. Women are sold to brothels and children are taken to the Middle East to become camel jockeys. Sometimes people are murdered and their blood, kidneys, and limbs are sold. Combating these kinds of trafficking is a main goal of LOSAUK. The group begins by raising consciousness about trafficking. LOSAUK uses their short "sample" *jatras* to make people aware of the magnitude of the trafficking in Bangladesh. To develop sample *jatras*, LOSAUK conducts training workshops. [...]

A sample *jatra* developed during the five-day workshop is shown in a courtyard for a limited audience. Later, the *jatra* is brought into various communities. People assemble at first to worship, then to listen to music. Finally, the actors appear in the acting area. There is little in the way of costumes or makeup, and any minimal props that are absolutely necessary, such as chairs or tables, are procured locally. They enact a *jatra* about the trafficking of women and children. This is a real story, a true story, not something mythological.

Sometimes at the beginning of the show, photographs of trafficking victims are shown to the audience – with no explanation given. The *jatra* performers display the photographs and start a discussion with the spectators. "Do you know what these pictures are about?" "Can you guess?" After a short discussion with the spectators, the main performance begins. As the *jatra* is performed, the *bibek* – an actor-teacher – sings a song about trafficking. The bibek is both an actor and a spectator to what is being performed. The word *bibek* means "conscience" and the *bibek* is the conscience of the performance. His songs express the ethical values of the performance. . . . He rouses the conscience of both the characters and the spectators. But the *bibek* is not like Boal's Joker. The *bibek* does not solve the problem as Boal's Joker does but rather gives characters and spectators the chance to choose right or wrong. The *bibek* describes the situation but does not offer a solution. The Joker stands apart from other characters but the *bibek* is very close to the characters. He sings directly to the spectators, explaining the various possibilities and dilemmas of the good and bad characters.

Because of the combination of wit and commentary, the *bibek* is similar to the fools of Shakespeare. The *bibek* also functions in somewhat the same way as the Greek tragic chorus. In Greek tragedy, the chorus often acts as a moderator and analyzes the behavior of the protagonists. The *bibek* similarly acts as a moderator and analyst – but always without solving the characters' problems. The *bibek* opens the eyes of the spectators to what is going on.

The *bibek* is a facilitator. He introduces the themes of the performance, interacts with the audience, and converses with them throughout the performance. At the end, the *bibek* draws the attention of the audience to what the play means. The protagonist conveys the key message of combating child trafficking. He puts the message before the audience in plain language. He says that everyone should carry a passport when they immigrate, that legal immigration with a valid passport can reduce trafficking.

Rural people are fond of *jatra* because it is a very emotional form. LOSAUK chose *jatra* because it is a perfect tool with which to raise consciousness. It is also fairly easy to perform. The actors do not have to memorize dialogue; a prompter coaches them as they improvise the main story line. Musicians sitting on both sides of the performing area create an atmosphere that carries the story along smoothly. The characters enter the stage one by one, and leave the stage accompanied by specific music that signals the coming of the next action.

On 28 December 2002[,] a sample *jatra* dealing with child trafficking was performed in an open-air courtyard of Sachibunia school, a place under the jurisdiction of the Batiaghata police station of Khulna district. There were 200 men, 150 women, and 50 children present at the performance of *Haraye Khuji* (Search for the Missing) by Probir Biswas. The dialogue that created a strong emotional response in the spectators [relates the story] about a mother lost to trafficking:

- I don't know where your mother is now, Lipi!
- Your mother went to Dhaka for the job with that trafficker Ramjan.
- Perhaps we have lost your mother!

Another strong section of dialogue that shocked spectators was when Ramjan thunders:

- Ha ha ha – job!
- I shall give you such a job that you won't be able to return from there. Your job will be either at the brothel or I shall sell you to a rich man from an Arab country and I will get a very good price for you.
- Ha ha ha (*laughter*).

When the performance was over, a few spectators came to the microphone and spoke before the audience: "Everybody has to be united to combat against child trafficking, otherwise no good will prevail." [...]

The impact of the sample *jatras* on the community is strong and positive. Spectators respond spontaneously. Sometimes audiences mingle with the performers and when they see a trafficker capturing children they take action to stop him. Once someone threw a brick at an actor-trafficker as he was luring three children. The acting was so natural that the spectator just had to intervene.

Generally LOSAUK plays in communities inhabited by farmers, grocers, and illiterate and under-educated men and women of the villages and slums. These people are not only the spectators of a *jatra* but also the victims of the very abuses the *jatra* enacts.

In such places the plays are very popular. Anywhere from 500 to 2,000 individuals gather without any prior publicity. If there is some publicity, another thousand can be expected. Sometimes there are microphones to aid the actors, sometimes they have to shout. Once people in a village or neighborhood hear the music associated with *jatra*, a crowd spontaneously materializes. The very high rate of unemployment guarantees that a sympathetic audience is always ready to attend. [...]

In the film *The Constant Gardener* (Meirelles, 2005), you can see an applied theatre piece being performed. Note that each character is represented by three people, all dressed identically, as a means of projecting to a large crowd in the open air.

If the idea of the performance is properly communicated, ordinary people are moved. It is important to follow up every performance with a discussion between the actors and the spectators. The immediate response and suggestions of the spectators increases the chance that the message of the performance will get through and lead to positive action. Nothing can happen unless there is active participation. And for there to be participation, the quality of the performance must be high, its message clear and transparent.

In the sample *jatras*, opinions are invited from the spectators on how to go forward in the next scene; spectators should not feel that the performance has been imposed. Participation becomes intense and everybody shares in developing the performance. The language of the performance is colloquial.

It is a general practice of LOSAUK that different themes are communicated in different styles. Discussions and idea[-]sharing procedures are not the same at all performances. It depends on the theme and presentation. The common feature is that there is an essential issue that is put forward and performed. In some cases, audience intervention happens at the beginning, in other cases in the middle, and in still others after the show is over. Everything is adjusted to the needs of specific circumstances.

Social theatre should be judged from a social point of view. Its aim is to enable the people of the community to establish their rights in society. Indigenous forms speak to the people who have for generations made and used these forms. Adapting indigenous forms to contemporary issues is an effective way of raising consciousness and advancing particular social programs.

9.2 Education for political process in Uganda
from *A theatrical approach to the making of a national constitution: The case of Uganda*
Patrick Mangeni wa'Ndeda. (2000). *NJ:Drama Australia Journal, 24*(1), 77–92.

The performances
PUBLICITY AND THE FINAL PUSH

Prior to the performances, we had to adopt publicity strategies that targeted populated areas. Local Council and District and church leaders were approached to mobilise the people. The Commission prepared press releases for radio, television and newspapers inviting the audience. In the morning of the day of performance, the final publicity drive was done using a public address system mounted on a city council van. The publicity signature tune was the song ["]It Is Your Responsibility To Vote,["] then a "popular hit" on airwaves. Two hours to the production, the performers drove around playing drums announcing that the final hour had come.

THE VENUE, THE AUDIENCE

A big audience was a factor in meeting nearly all considerations regarding our pre-performance strategies. The consideration for venues was their centrality; being public places and meeting points of all types and classes of people....

Except for University Hall (Makerere University), where the preview performance was staged, and the National Theatre, the open air venues were ideal for the construction of a temporary stage around which an unlimited audience would sit, allowing for a theatre in the round arrangement. This was viewed as a more democratic setting, enhancing audience-actor interaction.

THE STAGE

The stage was an extended rostrum elevated to facilitate visibility. Papyrus mats marked the backstage. A second row of mats created a corridor which also doubled as dressing and back-room. The basement stored costumes, props, instruments, refreshments and personal effects of the performers.

There was no attempt to limit the audience from these areas of the stage except to leave a path for performers entering or going off stage. Seats were not provided for the audience[,] not even for the Commissioners. Everybody was "equal and level on the ground." To cater for acoustic limitations of the open air stage and the big audience, the CCA (Commission for the Constituent Assembly) provided a public address system.

THE COMMISSIONER INTERVENES

The Commissioners always kept in touch with the production and made it known to us that the showing of a scene detailing the nomination process was essential. Although we had promised to consider this, we, as directors/writers, didn't find it worthy of a separate scene. We therefore simply mentioned it in the dialogue. But during the inaugural show, the Consultant noticed this and told the actors not to proceed.

We were still considering how to handle the situation with the audience waiting when we noticed the Consultant talking to one of the actors. Other auxiliary characters had been mobilised "in a second" and, next, the Consultant was on stage "understudying" the Presiding Officer in a "make-it-up-as-you-go-along" improvisation, directly lecturing to the audience on the nomination procedure. Both the actors and directors were seeing this scene for the first time. And so, another character, another actor had been introduced and, although this scene had never been part of the original script, in this way it became an integral part of *The Shield*.

Audience on actors

During the inaugural performance, and for reasons the actor playing ECOK explained as "a spur of excitement" in the scene of vote counting, ECOK began tearing spoilt ballot papers. The audience chorused in protest. Rule 35 of the CA (Constituent Assembly) Statute classified such action as offence. "Arrest him," some demanded. The Presiding Officer chose to warn instead of arresting him because the play still needed the character.

Coming to register and vote

While playing to a capacity audience at Bugolobi with many watching from balconies, rooftops and tree tops, the actors moved to demonstrate the process of voting. Two men from the audience joined them. One explained that he had come to act while the other said he had realised that he had a civic responsibility. So he had come to register.

Yet in Rukungiri, while acting a translation of *The Shield*, members of the audience participated in the voting. It was not SUUBI (as per the script) but HOPE KISAKYE who won. The audience had exercised their "civic right and responsibility." There were hardly any spoilt ballot papers except those of the actors who spoilt them for aesthetic and didactic purposes. The audience changed the ending of this particular production and the directors had to accept the "results of their civic education."

Learning from the audience

Varying the Language Strategy

After the inaugural performance at the constitutional square, we learned from audience members that some [had] difficulty following the play. We had to mix English, Luganda and Kiswahili in the subsequent performances. While in Mityana, a predominantly Luganda speaking area, much of the play was done in Luganda, courtesy of the linguistic proficiency of the predominately Bantu cast.

The Mityana experience

Playing to an audience of about 1,000 people, this production provided the most in-depth audience/actor interaction. During question time, ECOK stimulated participation by picking on actors deliberately "scattered" among the audience. Before three of the five actors had asked the designated questions, countless hands shot up. To respond, he had to rely on his knowledge of the CA Statute, as a character and performer. He also encouraged members of the audience to participate in answering some of the questions as need arose. When he [had] difficulty, he would call on the directors. For instance, people saw no sense in the use of *either* the tick or the cross to indicate preference. The lady who raised the complaint maintained that a tick was appropriate and enough. A cross was traditionally known to signify cancellation or a fail. This was a complaint we had received everywhere the play was performed. We, as writers, had expressed reservation about juxtaposing these two symbols as alternative indicators of choice. Even the actors had resisted it in rehearsal. ECOK's explanation of these symbols as a matter of the statute met with open disapproval. Finding himself in a fix, ECOK signalled the directors to come to his rescue. We in turn pointed to the Commissioners. ECOK then said: "Let me invite someone who knows more about the CA than myself. Those good people you see over there", he pointed to the right, "those are the Commissioners responsible for elections. I call upon one of them to come and explain that matter to us." The Consultant for Civic Education promised that the Commission would look into the people's view. And, by election time, that part of the statute had been corrected, with the cross being dropped.

This was a phase when the audience, the Commission and the actors put the play "behind" and dealt with issues that impacted on the electoral process. The production had to rely on the ingenuity of the actors to bring this session to a close without curtailing discussion. This session, normally lasting about ten minutes, ran close to an hour in Mityana. Darkness was descending and the last scene yet to be performed. ECOK exploited the flexibility of the scene and put the question to the audience.

By consensus, the audience agreed to only three more questions. [...]

[These were] the last question[s] and the last of the production of *The Shield* in English. And as to whether [the] returns of this educational drive were positively reflected through high voter turnout, low ballot spoilage and voting for the right candidate, is as difficult to clinically quantify as to say they were not affected by the civic education through drama.

But, in view of the rationale behind the theatre strategy, there are certain things that stood out as conspicuously as an only tooth in an old gum. These were the mammoth audiences which kept growing in subsequent performances; the changes in voting rules that arose as a result of the alternative views of the audience; the play stimulating dialogue; the significant level of attentiveness and participation; the audience and performers identifying with the characters; its diversity in class, sex and age. These were shouting indicators on the ground.

Yet another indication of its effectiveness was that the audience never made remarks against the play but sought corrections and clarifications without accusing the production or the Commission of being manipulative.

And, finally, the Commission saw fit to adapt *The Shield* for television and translate it for performance into the major languages of the country.

It may not be too much to say that *The Shield*, as a theatrical approach to the making of a national constitution[,] was a worthwhile case for Uganda.

9.3 Women's rights in Pakistan

from *Fitting the bill: Commissioned theatre projects on human rights in Pakistan: The work of Karachi-based theatre group Tehrik e Niswan*
Asma Mundrawala. (2007). *RIDE: Research in Drama Education, 12*(2), 149–161.

Honour killings
… On behalf of the British Foreign and Commonwealth Office, the British Council Pakistan initiated in 2004 a multi-pronged project on honour killing to raise awareness. A number of initiatives were taken in the form of sensitization (workshops for the police and press), dissemination through electronic media (television plays and music video) and performance arts (mobile theatre) to diversify the outreach. *Akhir Kyun?* was therefore the theatre performance component of this multi-layered programme.

Honour killing is a term used to signify the murder of women (and men) under the pretext of restoring or reviving the "lost honour" of the family. Mostly victims of honour killings are accused of inappropriate sexual behaviour that, as claimed by the perpetrators of the murders, led to the loss of "family honour." This "inappropriate behaviour" for which hundreds of women have lost their lives can include exercising the right to marry or divorce or challenging oppressive traditions such as supporting the right of a daughter to marry through her own choice. In Pakistan[,] 1194 women and men were reported to have been victims of honour killing in 2004 alone, a figure that does not necessarily present the full picture as hundreds of cases go unreported. Honour killing is also signified by the term *Karo Kari* in Pakistan's southern province Sindh. *Karo* translated from Sindhi means "black," and in this context is used as a term of abuse for men. The term *Kari* signifies the same for women. Each province has a term for it in its own regional language, and essentially each one means the same: men and women condemned by their family and community for acts of misconduct.

Tehrik's [the theatre company] resource material for *Akhir Kyun?* was derived from manuscripts and real-life case studies collected from reports by various women's organisations and from consultations with women lawyers, activists and actors from rural Sindh. All contributors shared cases known to them or their own personal experiences. These actors had been part of *Tehrik's* theatre training workshops … and had maintained links with the group since. Their induction into the play not only enriched the performance but also added authenticity and cultural specificity in terms of local songs, language and dialect. The play is constructed around four stories and apart from the first, which is derived from one of the tales of *A Thousand and One Nights*, all of them are dramatised interpretations of case studies. In putting the stories together, *Tehrik* drew attention to the fact that men, women and children were all victims of this heinous crime, at the hands of individuals as well as various institutions such as the police, or the local village judiciary, known as the *Jirga*.... *Akhir Kyun?* is constructed around the stories of a girl, Marium... and Zainab, a 40-year-old mother who is killed by her husband because she supports her daughter to marry through choice. Zainab's case . . . reveals she was shot by her husband after a 22-year marriage for supporting her daughter's marriage. . . . She received a *Kari's* burial, which meant there was no ritual bathing or funeral prayer and her grave remained unmarked. The heinous nature of the crime is most evident in the Story of Marium, who was killed by her brothers. Her murder led to Marium being declared a *Kari*, together with the son of a poor farmer. Consequently the farmer had to pay blood money to save his son from being killed by either the brothers or through a decision of the *Jirga* [the local village judiciary]. The money extorted was just enough for the brothers to purchase a new tractor, the main motivation behind the crime.

The 60 performances, spread over a period of one year, provoked a mixed reaction amongst the audiences, ranging from vociferous approval to dismissal and verbal exchanges amongst the audience in the postproduction discussions. . . . Given the diversity of the responses, it also allowed the project initiators to identify sections of the society where support of honour killings was most prevalent. For example, the audience in Jamshoro Sindh consisted largely of intellectuals and educated people who agreed with the message behind the play. In this context, it was suggested that postproduction discussions were detrimental to the effectiveness of the play as it was probably more meaningful to allow the audience to go away with the dramatic impact of the play. On the other hand, other performances received silent responses, possibly reflecting the inhibition of people to speak up in front of their village elders or their inability to articulate their own opinions. One extreme response apparently denied the seriousness of the crime, when an audience member accused the sponsors of deliberately maligning the regions of rural Sindh and Southern Punjab and giving them a bad name internationally, in order to distract the world from more pending issues of the region.

9.4 University-community environmental education
from *TFD, Environmental degradation and health issues*
Emem Obonguko. (2010). *Creative Artist: A Journal of Theatre and Media Studies,* 4(1), 53–68. Retrieved from http://www.ajol.info/index.php/cajtms.

The University of Abuja TFD Project
TFD began in the course curriculum of the Theatre Arts Department as community theatre. For the past decade it has been practiced as such till recently it has gradually evolved into TFD.

Issues of development [and] social change in rural disadvantaged communities have always been the focus of our workshops. ... As part of the course content the students are

expected to go and stay in any rural community chosen for the workshop for that year … .
The duration of the workshop was one week.

Aims and Objectives
The project set out to achieve the following:

1.   Encourage the people to mobilize themselves and provide what the Government has not provided for them in order to make their lives more meaningful.

2.   Educate the people on their rights to demand for basic infrastructures which were basically non-existent.

3.   Raise the consciousness of the people and task them to wake up to their responsibilities.

4.   Explore the potentials of TFD as [a] vehicle for identifying and analyzing the problems of the community and to suggest through the play making process, ways and means the community may adopt to solve their problems. […]

The Gwagwalada TFD Project 2006
This study is a report of the project in Anagada community, one of [four] communities chosen. The project adopted the homestead approach that involves the practitioners living in the community. For six days the animateurs lived among the Anagada people, eating with them, sleeping in their homes, sharing views with them and so on. […]

Arrival at Anagada
The team arrived at Anagada at about 6:00 pm in the evening and headed straight to the chief's palace …. We were welcomed by the Council of Chiefs on arrival and their native dialect 'Koro' was translated for us by the council secretary. He informed us that the community as a whole was glad to have us and wished us God's guidance and success in what we came for. We were given food items, cooking utensils and shown the respective places we would be sleeping and bathing [in] a semi-rural community of less than 500 people. […]

Community Research
We woke up in the morning and began to clean the surroundings. We did this exercise throughout the duration of our stay. We discovered that the environment was so dirty and unkempt, refuse were indiscriminately dumped as well as human waste.
The youths and the children came to join us as we worked. … At the end of the day, we returned to the square outside the chief's palace which was our central meeting

point to compare notes and submit our reports. Each group was asked to use the conversational approach which allows the animateurs to converse therby sharing information and experiences. ... Problems and issues identified were:

1.   Poor electricity supply.

2.   Lack of infrastructures: housing, road, water, health facilities, schools.

3.   Lack of sanitary facilities. It was really devastating to see that even the houses were built without toilets and bathrooms which are features of a functional accommodation.

Our observations included:

1.   Lack of consideration for environmental sanitation or cleanliness. ...

2.   The women just sit in the houses doing nothing except giving birth to so many children. This we realized was because they were not educated and lacked skills and information on family planning.

3.   High rate of teenage pregnancy.

Scenario Building and Improvisation
This stage of the workshop began on the 3rd day of our stay. At this stage we found it necessary to meet with the members of the community in a central place so that we can possibily put the pieces of information gathered during the community research together.... Members of the community and the theatre/dance troupe were among the people who participated in this session.

The afore listed problems and observations constituted the major issues discussed. This process continued the next day. At 12 noon in our venue with the people assembled the rehearsal began. People were given different roles, including the children. We analyzed the story with them. Blockings were also given and they were told to say the line in the dialect. The people tried their best even with their lack of experience and skills in the theatre; even the children participants all enjoyed the process. At first most of them were shy since it was their first time, and it made the process a long and difficult one for the animateurs. [...]

The Performance
The 'play' was titled 'Environment Palaver'. This issue was more pronounced and we also felt that the dirty and unkempt environment also gave birth to other problems.. This could be linked to problems of health, lack of access road, so many cases of sick people, rise in teenage pregnancy and moral laxity. [...]

In playing out the community's story, the play was divided into stages. The performance took place in the open square in front of the Chief's house in the daytime. The community musicians brought out their drums and started playing and singing. In no time, women, youths and children had gathered and it turned into a dance and music session. When the chief stepped out and took his seat, the musicians were told to hold on for a moment because we had some things to say.

The scenario focused on the effects of lack of sanitary facilities in the community – toilets and bathrooms and people defecating on every available open space and the bushes. Children are seen openly defecating and walking off. Some by the stream and people are seen going to fetch the water. Another woman sits, eating near her child's faeces. She rises up, packs it with a paper, throws it outside and comes to resume her eating without even washing her hands. Other children are seen playing in that same spot.

The chief is seen in council with his elders. They are discussing how to get the area council chairman to donate modern farming implements to the community to improve their farming and harvest.

A group of women are wailing, some carrying sick babies and crying to the chief about the ill-equipped health centre in the community with no drugs and no doctors and some crying about their children sick with strange diseases. The council stops deliberating as they realize that they had a more pressing problem at hand. As this exchange is going on members of the audience are seen intervening and making suggestions. This stage led to the post-performance discussion without the play ending formally.

Workshop Evaluation

The 'play' sparks off a lot of questions which the people also answered for themselves. At the end of the day they agreed that a simple thing like keeping the environment clean, keeping human waste in its proper place can save the children from being sick, save money and that through community efforts the roads can be expanded to make them motorable and easier to transport their farm produce to neighbouring towns and markets for sale. 'Poohs' [diapers] were donated to the community. [...]

The chief and his council thanked us for coming to awaken and create such awareness in them and asked us to come from time to time. This brings to the fore also that programmes of this nature should not just end in one week. The workshop was over in less than a week and the question on everyone's lips was: did we achieve our goal and did we make any impact at all in the lives of the people that they will remember in a long time to come besides our presence as university people in the community? ... We left believing that a seed has been dropped in their lives that will bring about change.

Further Reading

Abah, S., Okwori, J., & Alubo, O. (2009). Participatory theatre and video: Acting against violence in northern Nigeria. *IDS [Institute of Development Studies] Bulletin, 40*(3), 19–26. A project covering many communities that looked at the relationship between religion and ethnicity and violence. The use of video to broaden the impact of the project is worth consideration as a strategy.

Afzal-Khan, F. (2005). *A critical stage: The role of secular alternative theatre in Pakistan.* Calcutta: Seagull Books.

Betiang, L. (2010). Theatre of rural empowerment: The example of Living Earth Foundations Community Theatre Initiative in Cross River State, Nigeria. *RIDE: The Journal of Applied Theatre and Performance, 15*(1), 59–78. An example of an NGO-funded programme in six rural communities addressing issues of environmental concern.

Epskamp, K. (2006). *Theatre for development: An introduction to context, application and training.* London, UK: Zed Books.

Gaskell, I. & Taylor, R. (2002). Getting the message: Measuring audience response to theatre for development. *Applied Theatre Researcher, 3*, unpaginated. Retrieved from www.griffith.edu.au/centre/cpci/atr/journal/volume5_article2.htm.   Addresses assessment of the effects of TfD with awareness of the traditions and cultures of the local community and is focused on the theatre piece itself as a communicative art.

Kumar, S. (2004). ACTing: The Pandies' Theatre of Delhi. *TDR: The Drama Review, 48*(3), 79–95. Study of a Delhi theatre company with a 20-year history that has moved from more traditional proscenium-style (often western) productions to community-based projects addressing issues such as gender, children's rights and communal violence.

Munier, A. & Etherton, M. (2006). Child rights Theatre for Development in rural Bangladesh: A case study. *RIDE: Research in Drama Education, 11*(2), 175–183. A return by facilitators to assess the impact of a project that took place several years before.

Sloman, A. (2011). Using participatory theatre in international community development. *Community Development Journal, 47*(1), 42–57. Analysis and critique of participatory theatre as a tool for TfD, arguing that community participation lies at the heart of successful practice.

Questions for Reflection and Discussion

1. Re-read Odhiambo's theatrical elements of TfD (in chapter introduction). How do the case studies in this chapter follow these elements? Where do you see divergences from his model, and to what effect?

2. Many countries, often with long records of dictatorship, depend on western governments' funding. The conditions set for this funding demand observable processes of democratization. Given this context, what tensions can you identify in case study 9.2 around presenting government-funded theatre that teaches citizens about voting?

3. TfD has historically been created in developing nations. Where do you see the potential for applying TfD models in a First World context, as, for example, with immigrant groups?

4. Based on your reading of these TfD case studies, what can you identify as the key aesthetic qualities of a successful production? When performing to largely under-educated populations, what (beyond words) helps theatre artists to communicate their stories and messages?

5. Insider versus outsider perspectives are always important, particularly in the context of TfD practice. In the report we excerpt in Section 9.4, the criticisms of the rural community that are voiced in the article might not be considered by some to be 'politically correct'. Insiders may have more license to voice their concerns overtly to fellow citizens, but how might outsider practitioners voice their identification of negative aspects of participants' lives?

Suggested Activities

1. Choose a developing nation and, in a small group, determine what novels, stories, films, plays, music and visual art (both traditional and contemporary) you can gather together that might create a cultural "toolbox" in preparation for entering into an imagined TfD project in that location. To whom might you go to advise you on your choices?

2. If you have access to computers and the Internet, go to YouTube (or another video site) and search the term "theatre for development." Select two or three examples of TfD projects. Develop viewing guides for each video and present these videos to other interested participants in your class or community.

3. Design and present a short theatre piece with the aim of educating your local audience about an issue or program created to support developing nations (for example, HIV/AIDS prevention, malaria prevention, safe/clean water, safe agricultural methods, or conflict resolution). Consider the sociopolitical and/or cultural concerns arising from these issues. How are you going to deal with these sensitive areas in your process and presentation?

4. The Abah et al. article listed under Further Reading above addresses similar issues to the Winston & Strand case study excerpt in Section 4.3 in Chapter 4. Yet the first project takes place in rural communities Northern Nigeria and the second one in British secondary schools. Compare and contrast how these two projects use both similar and different approaches to tackling the issues of ethnic and religious violence.

Web Resources

Participate: Knowledge from the margins for post-2015, UK http://www.participate2015. org/

Theatre for Development Center, Zaria, Nigeria http://www.tfdc-ng.org/

Theatre is Sunlight, Professor Jenkeri Okwori http://vimeo.com/86857551 *Note*: We learned with sadness of the death of Professor Okwori and three colleagues in a car accident in Nigeria in 2014. A pioneer in Nigerian TfD, "Sunlight," he says in this video talking about his work, "is the best disinfectant" – not simply as lighting for his plays but as a means of seeing into the dark corners of our lives.

CHAPTER TEN
PRISON THEATRE

Introduction

Theatre and drama work in prison-related contexts offers a rich diversity of forms. There are role-plays with street gangs in the United States, comedic cabarets with drug users in Manchester, human rights performances staged in Brazilian penitentiaries, and psychodramas with violent and sexually abusive offenders in therapeutic communities (Balfour, 2004; Hartley, 2012; Saldaña, 2005). From *Shakespeare Comes to Broadmoor* (Cox, 1992) to performances of *Don Quixote* in Mexican prisons (Morell, 2006), to the Medea Project with incarcerated women (Fraden, 2001; Billone, 2009), we can learn about the work that is being done in prisons through theatre and drama. Yet other examples reflect the healing power of theatre in the most despairing of circumstances: the productions staged in the prison of war camps and concentration camps of World Wars I and II. Here, through theatre, "individual identity could be reclaimed and fear transformed into freedom...the act of making art suspended the collective nightmare...helping to sustain hope, a sense of self, and the will to live" (Dutlinger, 2001, p. 5).

Prisoner: When you picked up the skull [in *Hamlet*] it really got to me; hit me right in the stomach. I've killed a person and I've done a lot of work on how the relatives must feel. I've played the role of the relatives; but it never crossed my mind until now that there is a corpse somewhere of the person I've killed. I have never thought about the corpse before.

Murray Cox, 1992, p. 149

In order to understand the context of prison life, Balfour (2004) offers a number of institutional viewpoints that have developed historically:

- The prisoner is a rational person who offends of his/her own free will, choosing to commit a crime.

- The prisoner is at the whim of internal or external factors (as in "criminal types") or social problems of poverty, lack of education, family breakdown and so on.
- The prisoner is an individual with an opportunity for rehabilitation who recognizes and can change certain self-images, attitudes, beliefs and behaviors. (pp. 4–9)

With those suggestions in mind, consider Thompson's (2003) framework for understanding how applied theatre is viewed in prisons:

- Some prison administrators consider rehabilitation as *futuritive*, in that the work is not valued in the present but for the promise of what it can achieve on the prisoner's release. However, while repeated activity can leave deep imprints, there is no simple extension to say that it can form the script for new actions.

- Other prison officials feel work done by inmates is *constative*, done to fill time or as busy work. Theatre activities may not be taken seriously or with any commitment when framed in this way.

- Ideally, theatre work done in prisons should be *performative*; that is, it should be done to have an immediate effect at the time it is being done (on self-identity, self-respect, self-efficacy) and focus on the inherent worth of participation, fun, debate, physical action and creativity. (pp. 79–101)

Paul Heritage (2004) warns about placing too much emphasis on results-based work and instrumental benefits to the detriment of what the art itself can do for the people who engage with it. We should understand that while such promotion may be a way into the institution, it may also become something that can and perhaps will constrain the potential of theatre and performance work. Prisons are set up for retributive reasons and those reasons may limit the naturally transgressive nature of theatre. For example, overt criticisms of prison life may lead to problems for all concerned. However, a fictional tale cloaked with metaphor may effectively transmit what participants want to share and tell.

Prisoner: I have just taken part in a workshop where I have cried, hugged, laughed, played in ways that I have never done in the past. I have changed totally. Perhaps next week I will have unsafe sex. I don't know why you are so obsessed with the future? What has happened now is most important.

Michael Balfour, 2004, p. 16

Augusto Boal (2006), from his experiences working in prisons, makes a very clear distinction between working in communities and working in prisons:

When we work with social groups whose ethical values we share… we do not question their values because they are our own. In the adult

156

prisons, or the reformatories for young people, the contrary is the case – we have partners who have committed acts we do not approve of. With these partners, we cannot identify, though we may be able to understand them…. (p. 114)

Boal puts his finger on probably one of the greatest challenges of working in prisons. We may wish to assist others in this environment, but the human quality of empathy and identification with others must be held with care. Janet Wilson (2013) reminds us of her pedagogical principles; to establish a safe place, refrain from judgment, maintain the freedom to disagree, and to facilitate "a shared vision that captures our collective imagination and unites the ensemble" (p. 11). To this we would add that applied theatre actors and facilitators need to prepare themselves to work in these types of settings, replacing any rose-colored glasses with a more clear-eyed acknowledgment of the complexities of prison life.

> Certain kinds of criminal activity involve skills and experiences which parallel those of artists. In a way, criminals live in a kind of parallel universe, a fictional world of their own making. To live outside the law means you're engaged in a very questioning relationship with conventional morality. To invent your own codes you need imagination, wit, bravado and courage.
>
> John Somers, in Thompson, 1998, p. 132

The prison theatre case studies presented in this chapter take us from Israel to America to Brazil. The first study examines a long-term process and public performance on questions of justice as a social concern. The second project uses Theatre of the Oppressed strategies to work with inmates on issues around fatherhood and family violence. The third excerpt describes a project in a women's prison performed for inmates using ritual as a key part of the play creation process. Finally, we read about a hugely ambitious project in Brazil that brought prison guards and prisoners together, through theatre, to present an original Declaration of Human Rights for everyone who lives and works in prisons.

10.1 Critical citizenship in prison
from *Prose and cons: Theatrical encounters with students and prisoners in Ma'asiyahu, Israel*
Sonja Kuftinec & Chen Alon. (2007). *RIDE: Research in Drama Education, 12*(3), 275–291.

A unique educational project conducted through Tel Aviv University's Community Theater program over a nine-month academic year in 2005–2006 (co-facilitated by one of this article's authors, Chen Alon) tackled the complex dynamics of the prison political system. The program focused on theatrical facilitations between mainly female students and male prisoners – two more or less homogenous groups that represent polarized social sub-cultures . . . . [T]he Tel Aviv program initiated by the head of the Community Theater Program . . . focuses on both long-term process and public performance. [...]

Meeting once a week as an integrated group, and once separately with the theater facilitators (students' group) or a social worker and education officer (prisoners), the group engaged in theatrical activities designed to produce and transform conflict and sharing sessions that reflected on these activities. Theater workshops with prison staff ensure a context of support and a space for staff to reflect on their own attitudes towards prisoners. The final performance provided a reflective site for audiences of prisoners, prison staff, family members, university students and faculty, and those who might provide future jobs for prisoners. [...]

Who is a hero?
SHAPING THE PLAY

Following seven months of group work that included the development of theatrical scenarios, the prisoners and students met together for a day-long workshop. The facilitators summed up the various conflicts they had explored so that the group could decide together upon their central premise. Exercises exposing what individuals most wanted to express to themselves, to their group, and to their society helped to formulate this premise. Several members of the group then volunteered to shape the scenarios within this structure. As the group decided that their central concerns were ethical – focused on individual choice and responsibility for one's actions in relation to their impact on others – they elected to work with the structure of a "morality play." They agreed that the journey of the piece needed to begin with an anonymous human being unrecognizable as either a prisoner or a "normative" individual. Dramaturgically, the play would commence with a peak moment in the individual's life, a celebration or emancipation from unknown constraints. The play's opening as well as its scenarios thus reflected the group's experience.

> It strikes me that theatre in prisons can perform an essential purpose. Its role isn't necessarily to educate. Neither is it to preach or pass on ideas about drug use or unprotected sex. It is to celebrate humanity for a time ... to move people to share an experience of self-recognition.
>
> Simon Stephens, 2010, n.p.

In the play, the Hero arrives at a party from an encounter with his mistress, immediately establishing the presence of an ethical crime while animating for the group the character of the mistress as figurative of the theater. The speech that the Hero makes at his party also maintained a triple meaning for the prisoners and students, as well as for the audience members who came to witness their work reflecting the thoughts of the character, the experience of the group developing the performance, and of the prisoners and students in their journey towards more ethical relationships.

> Hero: First of all I would like to thank each and every one of you who came to celebrate this important day with me . . . . Who knows better than you that it wasn't a simple path . . . but eventually, I made it, and a lot of it, if not most of it, is because of you.

The play unfolds its scenarios by adopting elements of the medieval play *Everyman* to the prisoners' experience and the group's work. In a scene reflecting a typical criminal arrest as well as the archetypal journey of Everyman, a winged Messenger takes the Hero away. Not knowing what crime he has been accused of committing, the Hero receives a 24-hour reprieve to try to find someone to take his place on the journey with the Messenger. Like Everyman, the Hero makes the request of significant individuals in his life, including his mistress, wife and daughters, the friend with whom he stole a bicycle at age seven, and his parents. Through these encounters, the group reflected on the notions of criminality and responsibility exhumed in their facilitation process.

The Messenger allows the Hero to return to the scenario in which he stole a bike at age seven, with the scenario working to illuminate the limitations of choice available in the situation. In a scene reminiscent of that explored in the significant object exercise, the Hero later encounters his daughters as young girls and as adults, one of whom accepts him while the other does not. Neither the young nor adult daughters offer to replace the Hero on his journey with the Messenger. Like Everyman's encounter with aspects of his sinful character, the Hero also encounters parts of himself that he must address in order to complete his journey, including Guilt, Memory, Education, and Self-rationalization[:] elements that the prisoners and the students had expressed they need to work through in their own transformations.

As an embodiment of their democratic process, the group also added a Chorus, designed to highlight questions emergent from their process (as well as to provide a stage opportunity for all 34 participants). Along with the Messenger, the Chorus addressed all of the crimes that were exposed within the group by both prisoners and students. "We all stole bicycles at the age of twelve, we all beat the shit out of someone until he lost consciousness, we all cheated on our girlfriends, murdered our wives, we all faked documents, sold drugs, drove without a license, hit and killed a girl on the road and ran away." The iteration of the crimes additionally signalled the act of taking responsibility for them.

In the final scene, after the Chorus sums up the ethical discussions of the group, the Messenger takes the Hero through passages of his life as possible sites of judgment for the audience as well as the prisoners.

> Hero: You want to say that no one ever stole a . . .
> Messenger: . . . a pack of gum? Downloaded a song or movie from the internet? Smoked something forbidden in India or in Israel? . . .
> Hero: So, what did I do?

Messenger: Like always you looked for someone to replace you, who will go instead of you, so now you have a choice, now you can choose again. (The Messenger hands him a knife.) So, what do you choose?

The scene foregrounds the various shades of criminality within the group (and potentially within the audience) while highlighting an ethic of individual responsibility. It leaves the audience with a question unanswered by the production about their own responsibility: "What do you choose?" Will the prisoner choose to take someone else's life or take responsibility for his own being in relation with others? [...]

ENCOUNTER WITH OTHER AUDIENCES

After relinquishing their IDs and passports at the prison checkpoint, and adjusting clothing to comply with the codes of modesty required, the audience entered the grounds of Ma'asiyahu's minimum security site. This journey upended assumptions about the prison disciplinary space. Laid out on a horizontal rather than vertical plane, the landscape featured sculptural gardens and exhibits of prisoners' photography. The gathered audience of friends and family of the prisoners and students waited by this exhibit outside the cellblock, not knowing for certain to which category each audience member belonged. [...]

The hour-long performance concluded with an equally long interactive discussion with the audience. Response to the performance by various audience members implied a grappling with their own prejudices about both groups. A prison audience found it difficult that the performance had no clear, singular message. "I didn't understand," they asked the students, "Do you forgive us or not?" Without awaiting the students' answer another prisoner spoke up, indicating that he had collapsed the choral voices into a singular truth. "Why do you ask them? You didn't see in the show? They don't forgive and they will not accept us when we'll be released." A mixed audience produced more heterogeneous discussion allowing for anger, forgiveness, and compassion. These audiences also called for more responsive action. What should be done to transform both social polarities towards a less oppressive relationship? Still betraying their prejudice towards which group is educatable, several audience members asked only the students what they had learned from the project, expressing some astonishment that the education might flow in both directions between prisoners and students.

Responses and reflections on the process continued with both groups. In meetings with their social worker following the performance, prisoners were able to better verbalize and analyze the past choices they had made while also feeling that they had accumulated practical skills to speak with rhetorical force in front of a probationary panel. The students also used the process to re-socialize themselves in surprising and subversive manners. [...]

What does it mean to become a critical citizen? It means to have the ability to recognize and transform not only individual actions, but also fields of social power. [It means to] understand society not as a given structure but as a potentially transformable site that can ultimately be re-animated within a theatrical laboratory.

10.2 Fatherhood and family
from *Notes from inside: Forum Theater in maximum security*
Tim Mitchell. (2001). *Theater, 31*(1), 55–61.

When you step into a prison you immediately notice the obvious constraints – the walls, the gates, the cells, and the regimentation of the lines and of the inmate count. There are also the less visible: the inmates' loss of privacy and control, isolation from friends and family, and the increasingly long sentences. Prisons differ from one another: high-tech centralized surveillance controls harsh new facilities while keys jangling on big rings lock up the cells of old plantation-style prisons; thick concrete and frosted windows demarcate the boundaries of a supermax while the walls of tent cities wobble in the wind. But dehumanization pervades them all. This affects the inmates the most, but it also spreads to guards and their families, administrators, and the communities that host the facilities.

For eight years I have worked in such environments through education programs in theater sponsored by two universities, Georgetown and Cornell. From 1992 to 1997 I worked in the maximum security blocks of Lorton (the Washington, D.C., prison in Virginia, now slated to close); recently, I have been working in the Louis Gossett Jr. Youth Residential Center in upstate New York. I have learned from the men I met, and I hope they have learned from me, as we have together engaged in a process of discovery that has led to some key theoretical and practical insights into theater and social change. Yet for the men inside, for me, and for the undergraduate volunteers who joined me, a tough question always looms over our endeavors: as Patricia O'Connor, the director and founder of the Friends of Lorton program at Georgetown asked the men in one of my for-credit drama courses there, "What kind of change can you know about in a place like this?"

I'd like to chronicle one change – which seems both modest and monumental – effected through Augusto Boal's Forum Theater techniques at Lorton in the summer of 1997, and through it to point to some tentative conclusions about the promise of such theater practice.

Working with community liaison Elvin Johnson, a former Lorton inmate who helped found the higher education program with Georgetown in the maximum security cellblock there, we planned to explore themes of fatherhood and family that summer by arranging to have family members bussed in from D.C. for a final interactive Forum Theater performance. Unfortunately, a change in city government and a new warden forced us to cancel these plans. Instead, each participant was allowed to bring guests from the block for the final performance, and several administrators attended as well. Here is one of the scenarios, based on actual life experiences, performed in the forum:

A man returns to his wife and his teenage son with a strong desire to reconnect with his family and to be a good husband and father. One way to get off to a good start, he thinks, would be to hold a special family dinner on his first weekend home. He imagines what it will be like – taking his long-empty place at the table and seeing his family around him again. When he returns home he tells his wife about the plan and she agrees to cook something special. But just before dinner, as he sits on the couch watching TV, his son comes into the room and announces that he is going out. "Where?" asks the man. "To be with my friends," replies the son. The father explains that he cannot go out because they have planned a special family meal. The boy begins to argue: "You've been in prison my whole life and now you want to tell me what to do? You can't tell me what to do. I'm going!" He stomps out of the house to meet his friends. The man yells after him to no avail. It is clear that no one knows who those friends are, where the boy is going, or when he will return home. As originally conceived, the father is the one with the problem here. How can he have a relationship with his son under these conditions? How could this scene end differently?

During our preparation of this forum (not the final performance), one of the men decided to replace the father right away. His intervention dismayed me but received great applause and approbation from the inmates. As soon as the son started to complain, he hit the boy hard with a slap to the face. Many of the men thought that this was a viable solution. As one of them explained, the son was making a move on the other man's power and authority. He saw the young man as the instigator, threatening his father with disrespect. Since nobody wanted to say anything against this position, we tried several other interventions, always replacing the father. One man who did so invited the son's friends in from the street and tried to include them in the family meal, but after begging off with lame excuses, the friends left with the son, laughing at the father on the way out. Another man tried to bring in the mother to contend with the boy, but after saying "I can't deal with him any more" and "This is what it's like all the time," she made only a feeble attempt to stop him, then let him go. Several others intervened, but the discussion kept returning to the first, violent solution as the best approach.

One of the criticisms commonly made about Theater of the Oppressed (T.O.) is that it often relies upon a sensitive or well-trained moderator, especially since one of the pitfalls and limitations of a forum is the danger of merely reifying the opinions held by the group. Sometimes the Joker (a moderator who can also act as a wild card) has to complicate the thinking of the group in order to touch on the soul of the matter. Perhaps this is why Boal now often refers to the Joker as the "difficultator" (Boal, 1995, p. xix). I was acting as the Joker on this occasion and finally felt that I had to "difficultate." I protested that the father's aggression immediately put the son in the position of the oppressed protagonist. I thought that his anger at his father and his reasons for wanting to go out had some basis and that it was natural for him to question his father's authority at this age. (I had the further, unstated concern that the proposed solution came close to child abuse.)

We agreed to play the scene again, this time replacing the young man. At first the interventions that followed made the son obedient and respectful. But this was "magic" –

a T.O. term that refers to the solution of a problem by unlikely or unrealistic means. For example, if the problem is poverty and the solution is finding a winning lottery ticket, that's magic. Magic is a solution that fails to engage the problem at hand, in this case, the anger and expectations of the young man. So we continued to play the scene, and some remarkable results occurred.

As the boy reacted to his father's slap, the men playing him gave real dimension to his pain and anger. The discussion took a new turn. A few in the group started to talk about their own experiences as sons and about the consequences of creating a permanent split between fathers and sons. In the end, all the men agreed that the solution and the whole situation would be entirely different if the scene were about a daughter. Though they didn't explore the sexism or other assumptions underlying this unanimous opinion, inhabiting the character of the son enabled them to investigate how someone could be both oppressed and oppressor simultaneously.

Recognizing this dual role is a serious necessity in a prison. Though a majority of prisoners are in for nonviolent crimes, almost no crimes have neither consequences nor victims. In the theater classes we generally avoid working on anything as personal as victim reconciliation or reparation because we are not in the business of therapy (and in the juvenile facility, it's flatly prohibited). However, the ability to see "the other" within any scene and to develop skills of empathy is a crucial tool for change. Echoing Malcolm X, one participant in a Gossett workshop told me, "I learned that sometimes you have to accuse yourself before you can change."

What followed from the forum scene was a lengthy discussion about how prisons can follow a person out of prison and into the family, a discussion that eventually included two other key forums from the final performance. In "The Visitation[,]" a man receives a visit from his wife, and she tells him that she has a new man and his son a new father; the two men then negotiate these roles. In "Parents' Night," a man is denied access to his son's school on the orders of his own mother; he confronts her and the school principal, seeking a new way to get back into his son's life.

Following the final performance of the Fatherhood and Family Forum, one of the participants, a leader of the Lorton fathers' support group, took me aside. He told me that he and a couple of the Lorton fathers had joined our theater class when they heard about the theme. He enjoyed the discussions about the films and texts we had looked at, but he was really moved by our use of Image and Forum Theater to show fathers facing problems reconnecting with their families before, during, and after release from prison. He told me that he was excited to return to the fathers' support group and to change what they were doing there. He explained that the men had spoken in the group about becoming anti-role models to their children. As men inside, they were examples of what could happen to their children, and they wanted to warn them not to be like them and land up in a place like Lorton. But this man had had an epiphany: [h]e now wanted his group to focus on strategies that would put the men back in touch with their children before being released, and, more important, to focus on strategies that would help inmates recognize and grapple with larger societal and structural obstacles in the way of their family relationships. He wanted this support group of fathers to reinvent themselves and to do some of the thinking we had begun in our theater class.

This was a significant moment. It is always difficult to assess the effectiveness and usefulness of these projects for men in a prison, and after a program ends I typically lose touch with the participants. Lorton is closing now, and most of the men have been scattered and shipped out. I'm not even sure who has been released. I like to think that the men take with them something of use from the theater course, and I'm heartened by studies that have shown that adults who participate in higher education programs in prisons have startlingly low recidivism rates – though these studies do not look specifically at theater programs.

Certainly, I've seen forum scenes that were unworkable – because they presented a situation in which no change was imaginable (a trial about a criminal charge with a mandatory sentence, for example) or because they couldn't generate discussion (when, for example, the presence of a prison counselor acts as a silent censor). Overall, though, I have seen theater bring humanity into a heartless atmosphere, as it enables a sense of collaboration and shared stakes among the participants. It allows individuals to stand apart from their situation and consider alternatives and, as a physical activity, allows men who are often portrayed in mainstream culture as threatening and irredeemably criminal to represent themselves in their own bodies. Through the shared experiences of people in a theatrical space, it is possible to deconstruct the self, to look at the self within a problem situation from multiple points of view, and then to put it all back together into an ability to take action.

10.3 Death and dreams
from *Agency through collective creation and performance: Empowering incarcerated women on and off stage*
Janet Wilson. (2013). *Making Connections: Interdisciplinary Approaches to Cultural Diversity,* 14(1), 1–15.

During the summer of 2009, I began a dialogue with incarcerated women who are part of an ongoing theater troupe at a medium-security prison. This dialogue culminated in the women writing and performing *A Theatrical Ritual for Incarcerated Women.* […]

Although incarceration rates overall have continued to climb over the past several decades, there has been a steady increase in stories about men in prison – but not women. […]

Collective Creation
Sherrin Fitzer has been the facilitator of a theater troupe in a medium-security prison since 2002. She welcomed me as a guest artist to work with the group and was a

collaborator and mentor throughout the entire process. When I first met the women in the troupe, I did not know how our work would evolve. Not wanting to impose additional structure on a rigidly controlled existence, I wanted them to have a choice about how we would spend our time together. I offered them a number of options including discussing plays, having an acting class, performing a play, or devising our own work. I told them I hoped we would create something together, as that was artistically exciting to me, but that it was up to them. […]

[D]uring our second meeting … the group began to explore the idea of devising a performance from personal stories. From the start, the group envisioned separate scenes or parts to the performance. The group was inspired when I expressed my belief, shared wholeheartedly by Sherrin Fitzer, that theater has the power to transform and heal and that through the act of making their private stories public, they might truly help someone in the audience. At some point in this discussion, "Diane" poignantly shared that it was "as if" the person she was before incarceration was dead and that her life had to begin anew in prison. Several other women echoed "Diane's" thoughts and the entire group seemed to identify with this experience.

I returned for our third meeting and suggested that the first part of their performance be some type of symbolic burial. The women took this idea and built upon it. Someone suggested building a coffin and assured me that they could make anything out of recycled cardboard. They started to think of props they could "bury" in the coffin to represent the death of their "old self," and they were excited to write about it in prose and poetry. […]

RUTH
(RUTH steps forward with BROKEN MIRROR)
I bury me, the old me. All that I was and all
that I hated was in my past. A broken glass of
a broken image. Yes, that was me. A girl just
existing, but never really belonging. A lonely soul
lost and wanting to be loved, but finding love
where she could and in all the wrong places. I
bury her. I bury the victim of rape, twice. I bury
the victim of an abusive stepmother, who didn't
know how to give love to another. I bury the
victim of domestic violence. I bury the drug user.
I bury all the hurt and pain. I bury all the fear
and anger deep within. Most of all, I bury the
liar that was in me, who always wanted to escape
her life and live in someone else's life.
(RUTH buries the BROKEN MIRROR) […]

While many of the women were working on their pieces for Part I, the ensemble continued to work on shaping the rest of the performance. Very moved by the image of the kitchen table from Dr. Remen's book [*Kitchen Table Wisdom*], the women wanted the second part of our performance to be set at the kitchen table. After a burial it is customary to share a meal while remembering and honoring the person who has died. Thus, Part II began with a series of toasts that were connected to what each woman had buried. For instance, "Phoebe" buried "Indecision" represented by a large question mark around her neck. In Part I, she described how her inability to make decisions had led to her crime and subsequent conviction. Her toast in Part II was "to making my own decisions." Following the toasts, the women shared meaningful memories and amusing stories, and this was the only part of the performance that was somewhat improvisational. [...]

At some point I realized that what was emerging from our process was a combination of a theatrical performance and a spiritual ritual or ceremony. [...]

Thus far our theatrical ritual included burying the past and celebrating the present. But what about the future? What hopes and dreams lived in these women's imaginations? What were the images that had the power to sustain them throughout their incarceration? To explore this, I asked the women to write a list of everything they wished for. The group then alternated reading one wish at a time until everyone's list was done. This was a unifying experience for the group when many women shared dreams for intimacy and freedom. It was clear that, with cutting and shaping, we would have the third part of our performance.

At some point I realized that since our audience would not have a program, it would be helpful to have a "narrator" to announce each part and help with the scene changes. During one session, I asked the women to think about what they would title their autobiography and each chapter of the book. I hoped this writing exercise would inspire the work on their monologues for Part I. After hearing these autobiography titles out loud, I realized that they could serve as an introduction to each character and thus a "Prologue" was born.

During the performance, the women would enter from a door on each side of the playing space with their props and stand with their backs to the audience. The first to turn and face the audience was "Diane," who said the following: "All Great Crimes Begin with A: Aggravated Ignorance." "Justine" followed with her opening line: "From the Fight through Hell, only the courageous arise!" One by one, the women turned to face the audience with a single line of introduction. Then our "narrator" entered carrying a coffin and announced, "A Theatrical Ritual for Incarcerated Women by Incarcerated Women. Part I: The Burial."

The fourth and final part of our piece was a source of significant tension. During the initial brainstorming, the group latched on to the idea of the performers changing out of their prison uniforms into street clothes for the ending. I too was inspired by this image and felt it would be extremely moving for an audience of incarcerated women to see their peers in street attire. However, I simply couldn't get past the fact that, at the end of the day, these women were still incarcerated. What were we saying to our audience by having them change? What did it mean? Was it cruel? The final part would circle back to the present, and the women would share their hard-won wisdom born out of their painful pasts. After giving this a lot of thought, I explained to the women that I couldn't justify it and had made the decision to cut it. The women were not pleased.

At our next rehearsal, "Susan" confronted me and spoke passionately about the fact that the audience will see what is on the outside and that her prison uniform did not represent who she was now on the inside. We discussed this at length, with many women agreeing with "Susan." I told "Susan" that she needed to write what she had just said in order to explain and justify this choice to our audience. Then, after further reflection, I suggested that we could form a "runway" out of the rectangular boxes that would serve as our set, and they could walk on top of the boxes, "modeling" their street clothes while sharing their wisdom with the audience. This staging would support their costume change by giving them a platform to dramatically reveal their new inner selves. The women embraced this concept and we knew how Part IV of our ritual would end. [...]

Far from a linear process, the performance was built by constructing little pieces at a time – like working on a puzzle or a patchwork quilt. My job was to listen carefully to their ideas and attempt to translate their experiences into something that might prove theatrically interesting as well as create a clear journey for our audience. And, it was essential that I respect them and trust them as much as I wanted them to trust me.

After reflecting on this process, I recognize that the role of the facilitator/director is to sustain or hold the vision. If the director is successful in inspiring a vision, then the vision belongs to everyone. It is this sense of shared purpose that keeps everyone fully engaged and participating. I became very aware that the closer we got to the performance dates in August, the more anxious the women became. Many of the women doubted what they had written. Some were resistant to finishing their parts. Some questioned the entire premise of performing their own stories and wondered if that could even be considered acting. One of the women quit. Their excitement earlier in the process about what we were creating had faded, and fear and anxiety had taken over.

I intuitively knew that they were scared to make their private stories public and that it was my job to hold the vision.

Performance

The women rallied, despite their fears, and the audience response completely surpassed all of our expectations. By the time we got through the Prologue and began Part I, the women in the audience were one with their sisters on stage. They vigorously nodded, murmured, laughed, and talked back in response. The women on stage let go and responded to the audience. It was if they discovered the power of their voices and claimed their stories for the first time. There were times when the audience applauded after every line. The woman next to me in the back had tears streaming down her face through most of the performance.

After the women told their stories in Part I, they invited the audience to participate in their ritual. Audience members had been given a piece of paper when they entered the "theater." They were invited to write down what they wanted to bury. The slips of paper were collected and ceremoniously placed in the coffin with the words, "We bury all that has broken us." A climactic moment struck a chord at the end of Part II when "Susan" said, "I wish women could support one another and celebrate one another instead of tearing each other down." Instinctively, "Susan" repeated the line for an even stronger reaction from the audience. For Part III: Wishes and Wants, the women pulled down rainbow-colored scarves that we had hung from the ceiling and, holding one in each hand, encircled their sisters in the audience, gently moving the scarves as they spoke. Then they used the scarves as a prop or costume piece as they shared their dreams. …

> SUSAN
> I want to drive up and down Lake Shore Drive
> on a summer Saturday afternoon in a fiery red
> sundress and sandals.

> TERRIE
> I want to erase my past and do it all over again.
> I want to keep the memories so I'll know which
> route to take.

> JUSTINE
> I want a comfy pair of sweats with a pint of Ben
> & Jerry's double-chocolate-brownie ice cream
> and a really good chick flick.
> […]

After Part III, transition music played while the actors went behind a curtain to change out of their prison uniforms into clothing that expressed their new selves. As each woman dramatically pushed the curtain aside and revealed her new look, there were whoops and hollers from the audience! They were imagining themselves in their sisters' shoes as the women walked the runway. The first woman to appear was "Susan" in the "fiery red sundress" that she wished for in Part III.

> SUSAN
> (Holding her prison uniform)
> […]
> This blue and white uniform says
> very little about who I was and nothing about

who I am. This uniform does not define me.
(Throwing her prison uniform over her shoulder)
This diamond in the rough has too many
differences to make to stay stuck in the wreckage
of the past. Today I am a visionary.

LATRECIA
(Meeting SUSAN on the runway and
placing a crown on her head)
Today, I crown you a Visionary.
(This pattern of crowning each other
repeats for PART IV.)

One by one, each woman modeled her new self and shared her wisdom
with the audience. These are the final words of my collaborators. [...]

LATRECIA
Today I am stretching to new heights. I have
broadened my horizons. Continually I am being
conditioned for the next level. I can feel exquisite
seeds of greatness blooming inside ready to burst
to fruition. These priceless seeds were planted
there way before I was put into my mother's
womb. I have learned to embrace and release
these seeds so they may burst forth like fireworks
on the Fourth of July – blowing upward bursting
all over the heavens in abundance. I'm soaring
like an eagle. My past is wind beneath my wings.
I'm a virtuous woman of God. I'm phenomenal,
blessed and highly favored. Today I am a queen!

JUSTINE
Today, I crown you a Queen.

(WOMEN burst into song – singing, dancing, and celebrating!)

The audience applauded and cheered all the way through a lengthy curtain call, with
the audience and performers in a state of euphoria. As an actor, director, and audience
member, I had never before experienced the oneness, the unity, the communion between
actors and audience that I experienced during this prison performance. In some
mysterious way, the performance appeared to satisfy a deep soul hunger. [...]

This collective creation … empowered the performers because of their interaction with the audience. The response of the incarcerated women to this performance affirmed the very worth of the performers. They felt seen and heard. Their stories mattered.

10.4 Human rights in a Brazilian prison
from *Taking hostages: Staging human rights*
Paul Heritage. (2004). *TDR: The Drama Review, 48*(3), 96–106.

Project Proposal Staging Human Rights

> "We committed a crime and we are paying our debt to society. But no one deserves to be treated like this – like animals" (a Brazilian prisoner cited in *No one here sleeps safely*, the report on the Brazilian prison system published by Amnesty International in 1999).

STAGING HUMAN RIGHTS is a programme being developed by People's Palace Projects with a range of partners in Brazil and the UK. It aims to work at ground level with the very people who must live and work together in prison on a daily basis. While it is acknowledged that there are very real concrete conditions that need to be improved in terms of accommodation, sanitation, and security, all reports on the prison system point to the dehumanising attitudes and environment that fosters the conditions in which abuse takes place. The discrimination against the prison population that is openly expressed in the Brazilian media ensures that public policy initiatives in prison reform are given a low priority against other pressing social needs. This in turn means that the families of those incarcerated suffer an equivalent sentence during the imprisonment of family members. By generating positive activities with the prisoners that seek to re-establish their roles as subjects and not objects within the system, the programme aims to begin a process of resocialisation within the prison that will also have an impact on their family lives. This in turn will produce different images of prisoners that can be reproduced in appropriate public media: theatrical representations, press reports on television and in newspapers.

"When prisoners forfeit their liberty[,] they do not forfeit their fundamental human rights. The Brazilian authorities have an obligation to ensure their rights are fully respected" (Brazilian prison reformer, cited in the Amnesty report). This programme aims to enable the prison population of Sao Paulo to begin to explore for themselves how these rights can be realised, so that the prison can begin to become the secure place that it is intended to be, and that ultimately society can be a safer place for all. […]

I announce that the program is also to be implemented as a pilot project for guards with the cooperation of the College of Prison Administration where they train. There is genuine disbelief. I represent for them the epitome of the sort of people that the prison directors have so often seen come from international NGOs [non-governmental organizations] to denounce abuse in their prisons. My assurances that our attention is not denunciation of abuse but declaration of rights is met with evident suspicion, but my promise that the guards will also have their space to talk about their rights has obviously had an impact. [...]

12 December 2001

In the center of the choking metropolitan mess of Sao Paulo, there is the modernist vision of order and progress that the prize-winning Brazilian architect Oscar Niemeyer designed for the Latin American Parliament. There the project *Staging Human Rights* produces its final act.

During the eight months since the beginning of the project, over 2,000 prisoners have taken part in workshops organized by the FUNAP [the State Agency for Education and Work in Prisons] education monitors. The project has been staged in 34 prisons across the state of Sao Paulo .... In 21 of these prisons the monitors successfully staged dialogues that allowed participants in different workshops to share their ideas and perform to an internal prison audience. On 10 occasions the prisons opened their gates to invited members of the public who came to debate human rights through the interactive theatre forums that were staged. More than 2,000 people saw these presentations, which included prisoners performing in the town square in Presidente Prudente and at the annual conference of prison psychiatrists in Bauru.

The final State Forum is an opportunity to bring together all of the monitors for one final act that will both demonstrate what has passed and perform what might be brought about through the urgent presence of the performers and their audience. . . . Here again was an instance when performance brought together impossible encounters: lawyers, lawmakers, guards, prisoners, their families, representatives from human rights agencies, students, and a battery of the press. And the hope behind the act lay in both its vivid present and its imagined future. [...]

The format of the project's final day of performance was simple. The 400-seat auditorium is normally home to the members of the parliament of Latin America, but for this one day its ceremonial stage has been bordered with the banners for *Staging Human Rights*. Three forum theatre plays are presented: one by the guards, one by female prisoners, and one by male prisoners. Each tells of incidences of conflict from within the prison system where the participants believe their rights have been abused. After each of the 20-minute plays has been presented, the audience is given the opportunity to enter the stage and substitute for the protagonist in an attempt to bring about change when the play is rerun. Each of the sessions is facilitated by someone from the Center of the Theatre of the Oppressed team, who had helped to prepare the casts for these presentations. [...]

The guards selected to present their play came from the prison in Sorocaba, some distance from the capital. They were not therefore the same guards [who] were escorting the two casts of prisoners. Backstage before the performance there is at first little sign of fraternization, as the prisoners arrive handcuffed and are shown to separate sides of the auditorium, away from the main body of the public. At all times they are watched over by armed guards in civilian uniform, lining the aisles. The actor-guards are to perform first and begin to take their positions onstage. Their play tells of the frustrations they experience when human rights agencies come into the prisons looking for instances of abuse. They feel invisible, both inside the prison and outside in the street. Nobody sees what they suffer and nobody listens. The play is funny and moving, and the interventions from the audience bring a blaze of anger from members of NGOs who feel that the picture presented is not an accurate portrayal of their behavior in prison. The debate is forthright, fulsome, and fierce. Quietly from the sides the prisoners are watching, fascinated to see guards dressed in prison uniforms and submitted to the humiliations of life in a make-believe prison. Horrified beside them are the real guards of the day, sensing that their own position is threatened by the subversion of order that is taking place.

Two other plays by the prisoners follow, with their desperate tales of the separation of mothers from babies and the inadequacies of the health care system in prisons. At lunch the actors all meet for the first time, sitting at tables together in the backstage area. Guards and prisoners share their fears and the pleasures of theatre, constantly monitored by the bemused guards of the day who stand dutifully at the side as the actors enjoy the familiar post-performance release in shared rites of food and drink. Perhaps in these minutes alone the promise of the project is most consummately performed. [...]

To close the event, the education monitors of FUNAP [the State Agency for Education and Work in Prisons] enter the stage to read out the 36 declarations that have been produced by the project throughout the year. At the end of each workshop and performance, the participants were asked to write a declaration of a human right that was particular and precious to them. These were edited and collated for the final State Forum and presented to the Secretaries of Justice and Prison Administration who arrived for the final ritual. The education monitors are joined at this moment by two prisoners and two guards, who read out the declarations that have been written during that day as a response to the plays presented in the parliament. [...]

The project *Staging Human Rights* set out to fight for the inalienable validity of prisoners as human beings. However, it was only through the process of the project that we realized the significance of the need to articulate that inalienability with reference to those who are perceived as the Other who denies them that right: the guards. Implicit in all declarations of rights is the relationship with another, who is recognized at that moment in which the rights are uttered. The respect for the rights of the Other, which is the basis for all such declarations, fundamentally frames the human subject in an interdependency of rights and obligations. And this is not an obligation to universal Man, but to a particular and unique other person with all her/his own demands and desires arising from the same enunciation. It is the declaration of our rights that binds us in a fight to protect the Other before we protect ourselves.

Further Reading

Davey, L., Day, A. & Balfour, M. (April 6, 2014). Performing desistance: How might theories of desistance from crime help us understand the possibilities of prison theatre? *International Journal of Offender Therapy and Comparative Criminology, 58*, 1–12. Examines the value of theatre in helping prisoners to build more positive identities and constructive life skills.

Fraden, R. (2001). *Imagining Medea: Rhodessa Jones and theater for incarcerated women.* Chapel Hill, NC: University of North Carolina. African-American theatre director Jones uses the Medea myth in working with female prisoners in San Francisco. Jones incorporates traditional myth, hip-hop, dance and autobiography that allows for connection between performers and audience.

McAvinchey, C. (2011). *Theatre & prison.* New York, NY: Palgrave Macmillan. An excellent introduction to how the prison system reflects governments' views on justice as custodial, coercive or punitive and how theatre projects happen within those contexts.

Shailor, J. (Ed.). (2011). *Performing new lives: Prison theatre.* London, UK: Jessica Kingsley. A collection of 15 case studies from American prisons.

Sutherland, A. (2013). 'Now we are real women': Playing with gender in a male prison theatre programme in South Africa. *RIDE: The Journal of Applied Theatre and Performance, 18*(2), 120–132. This article raises many thought-provoking ethical issues related to making theatre in prisons.

Taylor, P. (2012). *Theatre behind bars: Can the arts rehabilitate?* Stoke-on-Trent, UK: Trentham. This contribution to the literature on prison theatre documents the author's projects carried out in New York state prisons and looks at the issues of rehabilitation, ethics and evaluation.

Woodland, S. (2013). "Magic mothers and wicked criminals": Exploring narrative and role in a drama programme with women prisoners. *Applied Theatre Research 1*(1), 77-89. An Australian project that explores the "fluid border" between fact and fiction.

Questions for Reflection and Discussion

1. Augusto Boal says, "When we work with social groups whose ethical values we share … we do not question their values because they are our own" (2006, p. 114). James Thompson's (2001) asks: "How do we create a celebration with people who have robbed others of joy? How do we work in fantasy when some of the groups' fantasies have been performed in an abusive reality? How do we theatricalise prison's mundanity?" (p. 4). Consider these ethical questions and discuss how facilitators' relationships with participants may be challenged when working in prisons.

2. What are the necessary stages involved in gaining permission and implementing a theatre programme in a prison? What research can you do to find out how this process might be undertaken in your own community?

3. Prison theatre can include both accidental (public) and integral (imprisoned) audiences. What pre- and post-performance planning is necessary to ensure both types of audiences benefit from their experience?

4. In the Heritage case study, a prisoner is quoted: "When prisoners forfeit their liberty, they do not forfeit their fundamental human rights." In a group discussion, explore the range of opinions in response to this statement.

Suggested Activities

1. Five words or phrases are presented, each word on a large, individual piece of paper: FREEDOM; CONSTRAINTS; GUILT; REVENGE; HOPE. Each of the five small groups chooses one paper. Brainstorm images, thoughts, phrases and so on generated by the word and write your responses on the paper. After three minutes, groups rotate to the next "station," read what is written and add their own thoughts. This continues until each group has visited each paper and returned to its own station. Read what has been added to your original thinking and discuss your responses. Each group creates a found poem using the text on their paper and shares it with the rest of the class/workshop (perhaps using images and movement).

2. Paul Heritage's (2004) Staging Human Rights project has the unusual quality of including prison guards as part of the performance and dialogue. Jennifer Hartley (2012) has carried out applied theatre work in Central America with torture victims and their former torturers. What other circumstantial partnerships might

benefit from this approach (i.e., teachers/students, nurses/patients)? Generate a list of possible partnerships, select one pair and outline an applied theatre project proposal that includes both partners and present it.

3. Do an Internet search on creative writing by prisoners. Select some of this writing – fiction, non-fiction and poetry – and create a dramatic anthology based around a theme (Invisibility, Surveillance, Witness, Privacy) that has emerged in your research and rehearsal using this material. What audiences would benefit most from seeing this work?

Web Resources

Clean Break, London, UK http://www.cleanbreak.org.uk/

Geese Theatre, Birmingham, UK http://www.geese.co.uk/

The Prison Arts Coalition, USA http://theprisonartscoalition.com/category/theater-in-prison/

The Prison Performance Network, USA http://prisontheatreconsortium.blogspot.ca/

Introduction

Community-based theatre – of all the forms of applied theatre that we examine in this text – is rooted in a very particular setting within which contexts, participants and issues are all local. This form of applied theatre has a rich history and, like so much of the work, has many names: "grass-roots theatre," "local theatre," "ensemble theatre," "people's theatre." Whatever the name, the emphasis is on creating and performing the stories of communities and community members in original productions that are specifically local.

Grassroots theatre is created in direct interaction with the community for whom it is intended… The audience is not consumer of, but participant in the performance. Exemplary performance quickens the audience, the creation process challenges and vitalizes the community.

Dudley Cocke, 1993, p. 9

These stories may be celebratory or critical, or a combination of both. Community-based theatre is distinct from "community theatre" which is most often a theatre presenting previously scripted plays performed by amateurs for accidental audiences. While some applied theatre scholars/practitioners have used the term "community theatre," in a North American context, the term "community-based theatre" clarifies the distinction between this form of applied theatre form and what is generally regarded as amateur theatre.

Community-based theatre most often involves a group of community members coming together to explore and present a performance based on some shared issue or concern. However, Jonothan Neelands (1984) differentiates between *consensus* and *conspectus*; the former involves a homogeneity of perspectives, the latter a rainbow of differing opinions, all of which are to be recognized and included within a dramatic process (p. 40). In a community-based theatre project, an effective facilitator will aim for conspectus over consensus, ensuring that the voices and attitudes

[Applied theatre is] not about judging right or wrong, but rather about encouraging an understanding of ourselves and others, as well as an acknowledgment of different perceptions, if not acceptance of them.

Jennifer Hartley, 2012, p. 17

of each participant are represented in performance. These "artful collisions" (Leonard & Kilkelly, 2006, p. 31) and dissonances of identity and location allow for a theatre that challenges accepted beliefs and histories and works towards new visions of community action and social change. Within communities there are all sorts of perspectives on events that do not always agree with the public attitudes or the historic record. Theatre offers a method for presenting this broader range of "truths" that allow for open-ended reflection and dialogue with audiences.

Certainly, the challenges of listening to and working closely with a particular community demand a deep immersion, and many community-based theatre artists spend significant

[W]hen theatre is made in such intimate collaboration between artists and community, the histories, cultures, traditions, cares, concerns, questions, faiths, doubts, fears, perspectives and experiences of the community are more than present, they are essential to the plays made.

Robert Leonard & Ann Kilkelly, 2006, p. 27

amounts of time living within the communities that are sites for projects. In this way, community-based theatre work is akin to the fieldwork of anthropologists who may live for months or years with a community in order to gain access to sometimes hidden or even secret stories, rituals, traditions and other cultural practices. Members of Australia's Big hART Company, for example, commit to living with their community participants for over a year in each of their community-based art and performance projects (see Web Resources for link).

Community-based theatre projects can often be very large-scale events with dozens, if not hundreds, of participants. For playwright and facilitator Erica Nagel (2007) "an aesthetic of neighborliness meant to me that each stage would be guided by mutual mentorship, letting go of assumptions about what 'art' is and who can make it, recognition of the expertise and experience all collaborators brought to the process, generosity of time and talent, and embodied, experiential script and performance development." (p. 160).

[F]or meaningful change to occur in local communities, it cannot be triggered by ideas imported from outside by a troupe of actors, but will happen when the communities themselves are given a platform for developing ways of effecting change through critical citizenship.

Kennedy Chinyowa, 2012, p. 76

In order to manage and rehearse such projects, groups may work independently and come together only in or shortly before a performance. However, even when working with separate groupings of participants (such as school students and community members), it is important that there is some cross-collaboration so groups do not become isolated within the whole process. Various locations within a community may be used, and the audience may move from site to site alongside performers.

On performance days, community-based theatre projects may take on elements of a festival or celebration where food and drink, dances, parades and other kinds of shared activities may be incorporated into the experience.

In reviewing a number of books and case studies on community-based theatre, it became clear to us that this theatre form can fall into one of two main areas. First, it is seen as a form of activist theatre, more closely connected to Theatre in Education and Theatre of the Oppressed with an intention to intervene within a community that is facing one or more challenges (such as racism, class divisions, loss of heritage). Second, it may take on a more celebratory form, more clearly rooted in Popular Theatre, that allows for communities to come together to share and reflect upon their own histories and present circumstances. In the end, all community-based theatre should address the implicit question, "What is community?" as it seeks to understand more deeply and come to terms with this complex and contested word.

> [Community theatre] becomes true community theatre because the participants are dreaming it themselves.
>
> N'gugi wa Mirii, in Chinyowa, 2012, p. 73

The first case study is of a community-based theatre project in England involving students and community members working with a team of artists. Of interest is the focus on the experience of a group of teen participants. The second project takes us to a small Swedish community working against the loss of their culture in the face of corporate and government development. The play springs directly out of the community and is developed collectively by the participants with the aid of a local playwright and director/producer. Finally, we present a community-university theatre project that focuses on a collaboration between a student group and a war veterans' group. The innovative aspect of this project is the interweaving of the Greek play "Antigone" with spoken monologues and videotaped interviews of the veterans' experiences of war. Throughout this unique project, great care was taken to provide safety for each member of the community in the interpretation of first-person narratives.

11.1 Large-scale community play

from '*B-O-U-R-N-E-M-O-U-T-H! Our Town!' Effects on male teenagers of participation in a community play*

Tony Horitz. (2001). *RIDE: Research in Drama Education*, 6(1), 69–84.

The Bournemouth Community Play 1997

Undercliff and over Heath was situated within this community play tradition. Participants collaborated in the creation of the play "text" and included 40 15[-]year-olds from an all boys' secondary school; 35 11[-]year-olds, 30 8[-]year-olds and 40 7[-]year-olds from three separate primary schools; and a voluntary group of 20 adults and older teenagers. Each group was responsible for creating one or two scenes for the play, with the assistance of a team of facilitators, including two members of the Bournemouth Theatre in Education Team, a musician, a dancer and an artist. As well as coordinating the project, I shared the direction of the play with my colleagues in the Theatre in Education team. During the [six]-week process, I also researched each constituent group's development whilst recording my own impressions of the play's progress. Participating pupils rehearsed during the school day while the adult group rehearsed in the evenings and at weekends. Starting in the sixth week, six evening performances were given to the public.

Content

After consultation with a research group and teachers of the four schools involved, we agreed to explore various episodes in the life of the town, from pre-history to the present day. Effectively, we then decided which group should tackle which historical era, based on teachers' preferences and curricular requirements. We designed a series of inputs for each group, aimed at stimulating active responses leading to improvised dialogue and movement. Through this process, the two infants' school groups explored Bournemouth's natural environment before creating a legend about the birth of the town; the junior age group dramatized incidents from the lives of local children their age during the Second World War[;] and the General Certificate of Secondary Education Drama students devised two ensemble scenes making a statement about life in the town today, from their perspective. Finally, the community group explored the early years of Bournemouth during the Victorian era. As artistic directors, we took on the task of editing and shaping the resulting material, scripting it for later rehearsals and co-directing the end product, *Undercliff and over Heath*. By involving a wide range of young and older people in a mutual exploration of what it meant to be a member of their community, we hoped to create a strong sense of community, in which different perspectives found a voice. In terms of managing the different groups, we divided up the scenes and shared responsibility for devising and directing them amongst the three members of the Theatre in Education team, supported by a professional artist and musician. In view of my previous experience, I agreed to oversee the play as a whole and to provide a linking structure.

Form

The play was performed both inside and outside the town's principal art gallery and museum, with the audience travelling from one staged scene to another around the site, in the tradition of medieval mystery plays. There were three main reasons for this decision:

1. Our previous plays in similar open-air settings had brought positive responses from audience and casts; we now felt that this form was accessible and attractive to people unused to or deterred by the formalities of conventional theatre.
2. The local council's arts and museums officers were keen to collaborate and increase public access to the museum – which they offered us free of charge.
3. It provided a central, high profile venue that was an important historical building with a commanding view of the town centre, and the surrounding sea and landscape. [...]

Ownership of the Content

The secondary students' contribution to the play involved two scenes portraying contemporary life for the young in the town and their hopes and fears for the new millennium. This focus was predetermined by the team to give the boys a thematic framework in which they could add their own ideas and so come to share ownership of the material. We had previously agreed with the school that they would work in their usual two class groups of 20, mainly during their normal school timetable for drama, so as not to disrupt other lessons. Each group would perform on alternate nights, keeping group sizes manageable and giving everyone an opportunity to participate. No selection of participants was made on grounds of artistic ability at any stage, [a] hallmark of all our productions. [...]

The creative process began with a discussion about what the boys liked and disliked about their town. The facilitators recorded all suggestions and then led the boys through a variety of drama activities. These included: games – to encourage relaxation and concentration; exercises – to develop trust and movement and speech skills; and improvisation and role-playing – to develop theme and context. By the end of the third week, they had two scenes roughly planned; these were edited and shaped collectively over the remaining 3 weeks, the sessions including regular phases of discussion.

In terms of favoured themes, both groups wanted to celebrate the natural beauty and modern resources of the town; negatives included teenagers being unfairly stereotyped by older members of the community, who confused youthful energy and humour with anti-social behaviour. Interestingly, this gelled with what was emerging in the other scenes of the community play: from its Victorian beginnings, the town had acquired a reputation for putting on "airs and graces" and turning its back on the needs of less affluent members of the community. In the Second World War, life for children was harsh, especially for those living in a home for orphaned children. So the creative team was able to link the students' concerns with a broader theme of looking beneath the surface to search for the true spirit of the town.

The boys' first scene was staged early in the play, just after the audience had heard two elderly women (from the community group) reminiscing about Bournemouth in "the good old days." To the accompaniment of drumming, the boys entered en masse from the adjacent cliff path, pushing open a large iron gate as if "invading" the grassy acting area in front of the Victorian museum, where the audience was waiting. The two women moved quickly away, strengthening the image of the boys as rival "gangs," chanting in unison, strange staccato chants they had invented, sounding ominously warlike. But at a given moment, the impending violence was diverted into an energetic display of gymnastics and tableaux illustrating the attractions of the town, such as the beach, the amusement arcades and the pier.

During the creation of the scene, some of the boys displayed anti-social and "macho" attitudes and behaviour that appeared to confirm the original image of the scene. Sensing that this was disturbing to the majority of the group, the creative team searched for ways of countering the tendency within the scene and inserted a female character, who became another link figure for the whole community play. "Seeker" was based on our research into the lives of homeless people living in the town – a theme in which many boys had expressed interest and concerns in the brainstorming session. Initially, the facilitator role-played this character, being hot-seated by the students about her reasons for coming to Bournemouth. These were mainly positive: she wanted to start a new life and find a job and had heard that Bournemouth was a friendly place. Including this character through process drama challenged some of the negative behaviour by the students and allowed for more sensitive and thoughtful attitudes to emerge, which were then woven into the fabric of the scene by the facilitator. After the all-male group first rebuffed Seeker, as she sang a song as a busker, a few approached tentatively and entered into her inner world – mirroring her song in freeze-frame images while speaking her feelings aloud. The scene finished with their rejoining the male gang and rushing off into the museum.

Their second scene came at the end of the play and was part theatre, part ritual. The audience was led out of the Victorian section of the museum, where they had been shown vignettes of the town's history, into the modern wing. The boys met them there and performed a movement piece around an open stairwell, simulating the passage of time. After illustrating their own hopes and fears for the future of the town, they invited the audience to write their wishes for the future onto cards. These were thrown into a net, hanging from the open stairwell. Finally, the students collected all the netted wishes and took them down to the beach where they were placed in a boat and rowed out to sea. [...]

Reflecting at the end of the process, Amy, the drama facilitator, thought that she had tried her best to make the students feel *"their ideas had been listened to,"* but that it had been a hard process, at times dominated by the *"strong members of the groups."* She had found it hard to find out what the quieter members were feeling and had felt frustrated at times by some of the latter just wanting her *"to tell them what to do."*

Attending the initial brainstorming session, I had also felt unsure as to the commitment of the majority of the boys and the value they placed on their contributions. But, reflecting in their coursework essays written several weeks later, many students valued the process highly, referring to a sense of satisfaction in being listened to and having their ideas respected. Not all agreed. Rick described it as *"the toughest moment of the entire process due to the lack of confidence in the group to speak up and voice their opinions,"* though he thought things had improved when students were invited to write their ideas on paper. Most critical was Alan, who recorded that *"none of the others took the discussion very seriously as it was dominated by a few loudmouthed group members, the rest sounding rather shy."* But there was no doubting that Alan took the initial message of shared ownership very seriously. He criticized the ensuing sessions for being too controlled by the adult facilitators, even though based on the initial ideas from the brainstorming. Neil and Joe agreed, feeling that *"to start off we got told what to do"* and that this allowed some of the group to keep their distance without *"getting involved."* This suggests that they saw the consultative process as an important, practical way of sustaining group motivation, rather than merely a desirable ideological concept. [...]

As the project developed, regular "run-throughs" of the scenes brought a different learning experience. While interviewees understood and valued the need for rigorous practising, they were frustrated when poor or careless behaviour by peers made extra practice essential. Interestingly, hardly any of the other students complained of feelings of boredom with this process in their essays or questionnaires. In fact, the data reveal a fairly positive picture of rehearsals, with negative expectations confounded. The same could be said for the challenging movement skills the students were asked to master. Early in the first scene, for example, they made a human pyramid and held it steady while they called out the letters of their town – "B-o-u-r-n-e-m-o-u-t-h!" This collapsed on several occasions during rehearsals, causing much frustration and some annoyance. But both groups persevered and finally succeeded. [...]

... [T]he findings from the boy's group indicate substantial support for the claims by community practitioners. Many, though not all, boys were motivated by the prospect of a wider audience for their work; they gained valuable learning relevant to the school's curriculum objectives and in terms of their own discipline and self-confidence, and discovered a "voice" that was valued by the broader community. But in one respect in particular, the findings led me to question further our paradigm of community plays. The process revealed the weakness of the "jigsaw" approach (working with each group for several weeks and only putting them together at the dress rehearsal). The structure was practical to organise but prevented shared experience developing between the boys and other participants until the end of the process. In this case, the site did not help: there was limited space inside and outside the museum, making it impossible for all the cast to meet together in one location. As well as this, it was decided that the boys should not form part of the ensemble singing a song at the finale. They had found this extremely difficult in rehearsal and we feared they would lose concentration and distract other participants. This negative decision came from a lack of confidence in the extent to which the group was integrated within the whole cast. Though the secondary students appear to have made significant progress in bonding as a self-contained community in our production, they did not become part of the wider community of the whole cast. There was not a notable increase in "sympathy and understanding between young and old and, indeed, every section of the community"(Jellicoe, 1987, p. 5). I conclude that to develop a community play which breaks down social barriers, in the way claimed by Jellicoe and others, opportunities must be provided for all the cast to mix and feel part of a whole well in advance. The fragmented manner in which we have worked has prevented us from achieving this wider social end.

I have since modified my approach for a small-scale community play about Bournemouth with which I was very recently involved. The cast numbered 80, featuring 20 teenagers aged between 13 and 17, 50 children aged between 8 and 11, six adults with learning disabilities and three adult foreign students. Instead of devising the content and creating individual scenes in separate groups, the entire cast has worked together from the start. The play was divided into scenes[,] but constituent members of each scene ranged across ages and abilities. In this way, we hoped to break down barriers and shift stereotypical perspectives of what each age or ability group might achieve. I shall shortly be investigating participants' perceptions of this revised approach. Key questions will explore whether they have valued working together in a mixed-age, mixed-ability cast, or whether they would have preferred to have worked in separate phase groups. In this way, I hope to broaden my understanding of both the barriers and the bridges to building communities through theatre.

11.2 The 'world of systems'/the 'world of life'

from *Community theatre in a South Samic community: The challenges in working with theatre in small communities*
Tordis Landvik. (2005). *Applied Theatre Researcher*, 6, unpaginated. Retrieved from https://www.griffith.edu.au/education/griffith-institute-educational-research/research-expertise/applied-theatre-researcheridea-journal/issues.

A short description of the community of Björkevatn
Björkevatn is in a rural area. Back in 1951, it was composed of a cluster of 12 villages with a total of 174 people, which was eventually reduced to 10 villages with 39 people by 1991. Today the population of [the] Björkevatn area is about 50 people. After the Second World War, there was a strong urbanisation in Sweden. At the same time, a powerful and effective oppression of the language and culture of the Samic people occurred. Today, South Samic people don't even have a Swedish/South Samic dictionary anymore, so they have to resort to a Norwegian dictionary.

This project was born four years ago. Two women, Lena Östergren and Eva Helleberg, started the project in Björkevatnet. Lena wrote the play and was one of the actors. Eva directed, produced and performed in the show.

None of the actors in *Vattufall* spoke in South Samic; they all spoke Swedish. Many locals want to learn their old language. As a result, from 2005 all Samic theatre productions will be in South Samic. Everyone now has to begin to learn the local language if they want to perform in theatre productions organised by the Samic Theatre in Kiruna. This is a challenging goal.

The story of Vattufall/Waterfall and Björkevatn

The story of this performance is about how the world of systems penetrated the world of life during the 1950s and 1960s in Björkevatn. Locals made their living by farming, hunting and fishing. Their rights as Laps had been strengthened over generations. In this period, the Swedish government decided to develop this indigenous area for hydro-electric power production. They first sent anthropologists to document the local ways of life.

After the anthropologists had completed their research, engineers and workers were assigned to measure engineering requirements for the waterline (which is 13 metres higher than the tallest chimney). Then representatives were sent to convince the local population of the many financial benefits and improvements to their lives that they would experience from this hydro-electric project. The government's representatives visited every house, and counted every spoon, fork and knife, and every piece of furniture. Very carefully, all information was gathered and recorded.

The government invited the inhabitants to information meetings where the locals were promised a fantastic future filled with work and money and the newest modern appliances. Then the face-to-face negotiations began. The government's representatives employed money as power; for many of the inhabitants, the change from barter economy to money economy was substantial so they were only too easily persuaded. The locals used their pay-off money to buy the latest products available in both Sweden and Norway in the 1960s, including cars, typewriters and televisions – even though they had no idea of how to use many of these items. They bought television[s] without realising that there was no local electricity yet. The locals were promised free electricity for the rest of their lives – which they do now have. Unfortunately, however, the quantity of electricity they receive free is only enough to light a single lamp! Some people built new houses as close as they could to the lake, many people moved to the south of Sweden to work in factories. Others moved to the eastern coast. From the outside, it looked as if everyone was satisfied by this quick progress.

One of the consequences was fog. Another was that the local authorities appropriated local hunting and fishing rights from the South Samic people. Some even lost their status as Samic people because they farmed rather than worked with reindeer. The authorities claimed they needed to give these rights to some North Samic people who had to move their reindeer herds to the south. A barrier was placed to close the old road; it was locked and impossible to pass. At the information meetings, everyone had been promised a key to the gate, but that was only one among many promises that were broken. After about 30 years, the local people began to talk openly with each other about what they really felt about this "progress" and the negative impact it had had on their lives – particularly now that many of them have returned to the area to retire.

From a great idea to a final performance

Vattufall is an attempt to tell their story, and all scenes of the script are based on the history I have just reconstructed. The playwright, Lena Östergren, conducted detailed research. She attempted to study the official anthropological reports, but they were nowhere to be found. She read old local papers, held interviews and spoke at length with the local people. She took part in an academic course and received both response[s] and guidance from other playwrights. Then the scenes she wrote were workshopped, revised and developed in close collaboration with a local cast of 15 actors and musicians ranging in age from 12 to 72. Some of the adult and elderly participants remembered a lot of stories from the 1950s and 1960s.

The first performance was scheduled for July 2003, but during the spring one of the actors became ill and died. Two weeks after that, the playwright's father – an important contributor to the project – also died. Since this was such a small community, these events profoundly affected the group, so the production went into a temporary hiatus. It is difficult to replace personnel in a small local group like this. Eventually the grief passed, and replacements were found so that work on the production could resume. [...]

To get people involved in a project like this is easy, but to keep them involved is very challenging for a community theatre facilitator. As Eva said:

> Every time we thought we had things under control, something happened.
> We were close to giving up, but the will and desire to tell this story were
> so strong, we simply couldn't. After each crisis always something positive
> took place – as if in the fairy-tale.

When I came into the production to work alongside Eva, my task was mostly to listen to the actors' storytelling and direct them into the script and scenes. There was a double purpose to this approach. The local actors contributed to the play with their own memories (what was said by whom) while the playwright, Lena, decided what of that material would be included in the script. There were more than enough memories for several more scripts.

Storytelling was also a therapy of sorts for the local participants. Their fictionalised role in the play gave them enough protection to tell it in public. For example, "the fog comes" scene opens with an old man, Arvid, sitting in his kitchen drinking his coffee looking out over the lake where the fog drifts in. He becomes frustrated as he has been many times before and calls the Vattufall/Electricity Board. But he hears only the mechanical voice of an operator offering him several choices and asking him to confirm his choice by pressing the "star" button. He gets mad at the voice, but gets no repl[y]. He hangs up and calls again. This time he tries to listen and eventually realises his old phone does not even have a star. He takes a cell phone from his pocket and tries one more time. Of course, it's the same telephone answering voice again, so this time he decides to write a letter. He goes to his typewriter and begins to spell out: "Till Vatufall," but he types it wrong and in frustration pulls the paper out of the typewriter. This is repeated several times. [...]

In this way, during many of the rehearsals, we went deeper and deeper into what this story was really about. In many ways, it had been a taboo to confess their sense of lost identity, to confess some of the core feelings they felt about the local tradition and culture. Working in this project, the local actors began discussing these issues openly. The discussions continued during breaks. One of the greatest challenges for me was to let the actors talk – my method was to let it happen in its own time. Then I would use what was obviously important, focus and direct or lead the actors into what we were doing, and try to incorporate their perspectives into their roles or the situations.

Another challenge was dealing with the diminishing memory capacity of the old actors. I had to build their self-confidence in the scenes. There are always challenges in theatre direction which are not necessarily connected to old age, but when the actors are in the early stages of senility, things can become very difficult indeed. The more truthful an actor can be to himself in a role, the better the result will be.

The first performance

Finally the first performance came, and all went extremely well. The room where the performance took place only had seats for 40 persons, but about 55 were there from the village. Some had to sit on the stage behind the actors. During the performance, people commented out loud: "Yes, it was just like this." And they laughed. But the final scene ended with a blues that almost imperceptibly transformed into a *joik* [a Samic singing style that is deeply personal or spiritual]. It was very moving for everyone. Sitting there, my thoughts went to Augusto Boal and his experiences in the rural districts.

The audience was invited to join the cast and crew after the show, with food and drinks served. Someone from the audience thanked us because this performance had everything he could have hoped for: "Fun, serious drama, irony and sarcasm, love and poetry, power and humility. It was about life – our life and history." He was so grateful.

When all the important speeches were finished, it became dark. Believe it or not[,] we'd had a power blackout! Candles were placed on the table and now the real storytelling could begin. As mentioned earlier, storytelling is the truest form of theatre, both among Nordic people in general and Samic people in particular.

As it was told, one of the characters had his outboard boat engine sitting on the kitchen table. A lot of our scenes took place around this kitchen table while the man tried to fix the motor. This activity became the inspiration for 40 minutes of spontaneous outboard engine stories told by people in our audience. They were told in such a hilarious way that people were howling with laughter. I could not comprehend all the references, but I understood enough to follow the gist. The energy was incredible.

The power in Bjørkevatn did not return until 11.25 a.m. the next day, which was a Saturday. It was the end of April. During the night, the ground had become white with 20–25 centimetres of snow, which was unusual this late in the year, even for this part of the world. There was still no power in Mårbacka at noon, and I asked Eva if they were going to cancel the next show that was planned for that evening. "Nobody can stop us," she answered. "And least of all the Vattenfall [the Electric Power Company]! A lot of people are making coffee at home; someone else has arrived with a power generator so that we can use our theatre lights; a third person went home to get a large container holding 1000 litres of water so that we can have functioning toilets."

"See? Everything's under our control," said Eva. "They can do whatever they like to us and we don't care." They were an amazing group of people.

So this is community-based theatre the way we practise it up north. . . .

11.3 Working with war veterans
from *Devising community*
Crystal Brian. (2005). *Theatre Topics, 15*(1), 1–13.

The impetus for *The Antigone Project* was born [when a] group of theatre students... wanted to recreate, for a broader audience of students and community members as well, their experience as they listened to . . . veterans speak of the life-changing nature of combat. I suggested to this core group of five students that we devise a project which would allow them to further engage with the community of veterans in creating a work capable of communicating the thoughts and feelings stirred in them at the Veterans Day performance. The multiple goals the students wished to accomplish – forging links with veterans as well as with the campus community, deepening their own intellectual and emotional identification with the veterans' experience, and finding a theatrical structure flexible enough to allow for collaboration – could be most effectively accomplished, I felt, within the context of the applied theatre model. [...]

Three primary goals were established: 1) to intellectually and emotionally engage performers with important social issues, seeking to transform students' understandings of their roles as citizens of the world; 2) to connect student performers with communities within and outside of the university; and 3) to create a theatre piece which would attract both campus and community-based audiences. [...]

Although the students had no experience in adapting interviews into scripts, many of them were communications majors who had extensive experience with journalistic interviewing techniques. An adaptation with a documentary element offered the possibility of capitalizing on student training and expertise.

A Greek tragedy seemed the natural choice for our adaptation, since war is such a prevalent theme in so many of the plays. The students were also interested in exploring the issue of individual conscience as it comes into conflict with the dictates of the state, and they quickly settled upon *Antigone*. [...]

As a first step, potential ensemble members were invited to write an essay in which they would describe their reasons for desiring to work on the project. Those actors invited to callbacks were asked to engage in a trial act of community-building by interviewing family members and friends who were combat veterans and then [writing] monologues drawn from the interviews. The students who designed the exercise hoped it would provide the actors with the opportunity to connect emotionally and intellectually with the thoughts and experiences of fathers, mothers, uncles, grandparents, and friends who had suffered the traumas of war. Additionally, the monologues could form a pool of original material upon which to draw for the adaptation.

Although in most cases students chose to interview family members whom they knew well, many of the veterans had never spoken of their experiences in combat. Bridges were created as memories were shared – as well as varied opinions about patriotism, war, and the role the United States has played in conflicts throughout the twentieth century. In retrospect[,] it is clear that the act of dialoguing with veterans who were not strangers also provided a valuable preparation for the conversations students would conduct with the veterans of the West Haven VA [Veterans Administration] Hospital, a community with which students had had little contact. Students performed their monologues at the callback auditions and the material was collected for future use. The monologues were compelling; the core group decided that each actor who had been called back would be invited to join the company. [...]

Our next step was to set up a meeting with the veterans at which we would introduce ourselves and our project and determine which men and women wished to become collaborators. [...]

Our next step was to structure the collaborative aspect of the work. Students who had attended the presentation in the fall felt that we should invite the eight members of the Homefront Theatre group to act in our project. But after meeting with the group at the VA Hospital, the ensemble felt that our production should be informed by the feelings and experiences of a larger group of veterans. Drama therapist Mary Lou Lauricella conducted a poll of the veterans who had attended the initial meeting; approximately seventeen expressed interest in working on the project, including all of the members of the Homefront Theatre. Lauricella, however, had reservations about the idea of the theatre group members actually appearing in the production. Some of the veterans had emotional and physical challenges that ruled out long rehearsals. Additionally, the troupe worked solely in an improvisational style; she felt the stress of memorizing dialogue would not be healthy for her patients, many of whom suffered from post-traumatic stress disorder (PTSD). The ensemble vetoed my suggestion that we include the veterans' perspectives as devised text that would be acted by student actors. Struck by the veterans' characterization of their experiences in the 1970s as resembling an "ambush," students were sensitive to the dangers of co-opting powerful material generated by the vets and using it to "glorify" ensemble members' performances. The students therefore felt it vital to the project that not only the veterans' words, but also their faces and voices, be presented to audiences. After exploring various options, the media production students, ensemble members, Lauricella, and the veterans ultimately decided that the veterans could effectively communicate their message through videotaped interviews. These warnings and insights would be presented as video montages interspersed throughout the production, with the veterans thus becoming a second chorus for our version of Sophocles' tragedy. The devised monologues and video chorus segments were included with the whole-hearted approval of those veterans who had given interviews for the project.

Notes made by the students during our initial session with the veterans, as well as input from Lauricella, were used to devise the list of questions for the videotaped interviews. Each veteran was given [these] in advance of the interview . . . . [...]

Ensemble members, lacking therapeutic background, had no training in the techniques of interviewing in a clinical context, so Lauricella was present at each interview in order to create and enforce boundaries necessary to protect her clients' emotional well-being. Veterans were instructed at the beginning of the interview that they need not answer any question they chose not to address for whatever reason, and [they] could ask that the camera be turned off at any time. Each cast member conducted at least one video interview with a veteran; these conversations, conducted within the context of a two- to three-hour taping session, solidified relationships between veterans and students, enhancing the sense of community. Taping and editing the video interviews was a process that simultaneously accomplished all three of the goals we had established for the project. As students listened to the accounts of combat experience, their emotional identification with the veterans was strengthened; they found empathetic connection with the thoughts and feelings of the men and women whom they interviewed to a degree that had not occurred when researching historical accounts of war. [...]

Developing monologues from the transcripts of the video interviews would create a dramatic device for incorporating more of the veterans' experiences within the live action of the play. In both the writing and the performing of these monologues, students were moved by the experience of playing characters whose thoughts and feelings were those of the real veterans the performers had interviewed. The monologues were delivered by students who were approximately the same ages as the veterans had been when they went to war; the performers were well aware that many of the vets felt their youth had been eradicated by the combat experience. For nineteen- and twenty-year-old actors who had no first-hand experience with war, the process of identifying with "characters" who had sacrificed their youth to war was especially poignant. The abstract nature of the student performers' understanding of war was challenged by the relationships they had forged with individual veterans. By expressing their emotional and intellectual responses to these human embodiments of the impact of war, some students experienced an awakening of their own social consciousness. [...]

The monologues created from interview materials, as well as the video interviews edited by student dramaturges, provided aesthetically powerful material for the production, as our second chorus of veteran elders voiced their warnings, visions, and nightmares in ironic counterpoint to the elders of Thebes, caught up in Kreon's greed and blood lust. At talkbacks conducted after performances, audiences singled out the monologues – both those performed by actors and the video pieces – as the most powerful aspect of the production.

The visual aspects of the production were designed to emphasize the video pieces. Chorus members ringed the stage, seated on banks of risers of varying height and dressed – as were the principals – in black shirts, green camouflage pants, and army boots. White scrims, resembling Greek columns, were alternately flooded with color or used as projection screens for the speakers of the veterans['] chorus. Flute, drum, and electric guitar provided counterpoint for Brecht's choral odes. Three young women playing the messenger and handmaidens to Antigone also interspersed the action with broken fragments of war songs from the Civil War, WWI, and WWII eras. Kreon was frozen during key moments of his duplicitous oratory to the chorus by the sound of a young woman – seen in shadow through a scrim – singing fractured snatches of Bob Dylan's "Masters of War."

In addition to providing ironic counterpoint to Kreon's claims of glorious victory, the statements of the veterans' chorus were juxtaposed after certain scenes to create connections between the Greek story of ancient war and more contemporary perspectives. The scene in which Antigone describes to Ismene the burial of their dishonored brother was immediately followed by a poem written and spoken by one of the veterans who had served a year on grave registry in Vietnam:

> Chu Lai Morgue
> This building stands apart from all the others,
> A wooden leper anchored in concrete
> Poured by dead Marines
> Behind its doors ride headless horsemen,
> For death invades this place.
> It layers up in corners like old wax,
> And its drippings spot the floor in sad designs.
> In this slaughterhouse are held
> The world's most precious meats, delicacies
> To be served up to mothers' nightmares –
> The leftovers to mine.
>   – Alan Garry, Americal Division, US Army, Vietnam

Five of the monologues, delivered by actors behind scrims at the beginning of the production, provided a prologue for the Antigone story, framing it in the context of the

American war experience. Each monologue identified the speaker by name, combat division, and war; later in the production each[,] of the identified speakers addressed the audience directly via video during the chorus pieces. In this manner[,] the audience, in a visceral fashion, was confronted with the toll war and time had taken on each veteran, as the ghosts of soldiers long gone, embodied by young students, were transformed into the aged faces of suffering. […]

The talkbacks after each performance of *The Antigone Project* became another forum for community[-]building. Any veteran sitting in the audience was invited to join the acting ensemble on stage for the conversation. News of the production had spread throughout the local veterans' community, and at each performance veterans would make their way to the stage. These dialogues – emotional and sometimes confrontational – were as effective as the production itself in giving voice to the many sentiments elicited by the topic of war. Dialogue took place between Vietnam veterans and audience members (a student's parent in one case) who had protested the war. During one exchange[,] a woman in the audience apologized to a veteran who had spoken movingly in his video interview about the shame he felt when college students spat on his uniform as he walked through the airport after returning from Vietnam. She admitted that she had been one of those students thirty years before who reviled the returning soldiers, citing a specific incident in which she had told a soldier entering a diner in which she worked that he wasn't welcome. […]

Family members of the veterans accompanied them to the production and spoke in the talkback sessions, thanking a father or husband for having the courage to share long-buried trauma. The veterans spoke of feeling empowered through their collaboration on the production. *The Antigone Project* had allowed their voices to be heard as they shared the realities of war with a new generation on the brink of conflict. The sight of grown men in tears – many of them speaking publicly for the first time about their combat experience and its aftermath – further intensified the identification ensemble members felt with their "characters," an identification stronger than they had experienced in previous acting endeavors in which more traditional research was conducted.

The bridge built between two isolated communities during the devising of *The Antigone Project* provided an avenue for healing for the veterans while engaging students with a political reality which holds increasing urgency for their generation. The community built between performers and audience created a forum for campus and community-wide discussion of the challenges that confront our nation at the beginning of the twenty-first century. For the student performers, the process of empathetically identifying with another individual – one integral to any acting experience – was deepened when the work of imagination and intellect conjoined with flesh-and-blood reality. In an era in which connections are so often void of immediate human contact, the touch and sound and sight of individual suffering is potent.

11.4 Dreams over reality
from *Performing dream or reality: The dilemma of Chinese community-based theatre*
Shen Liang. (2014). *TDR: The Drama Review, 58*(1), 16–23.

Clare Dolan, the artist from the Bread & Puppet Theatre I invited to China, encountered a big problem. In the spring of 2013 she began working with migrant children and their parents in Beiyaowan, a village on the outskirts of Shanghai. These families were not migrants from a foreign country but from the Chinese countryside. Under Dolan's direction they were developing a Bread & Puppet–style parade, *Xiwang Beiyaowan* (Hope for Beiyaowan). Dolan wanted to tell a story about a residential house being torn down. The destruction of houses is a well-known public issue in China. There have been countless news reports about homeowners protesting local government officials and/or commercial developers who were demolishing their homes to implement municipal urban renewal and, of course, to make a lot of money. Some homeowners have even committed suicide in front of the public and the media to draw attention to their plight; Dolan had read about these immolations in the English media. When she arrived at the village, she saw a lot of the Chinese character *chai* (demolish) on the walls of houses and learned that the migrant families there would be forced to leave soon. She was determined to do something to help. Yet the migrant children and their parents working on the parade were not interested in the demolition story she proposed. They didn't want a big Chinese character "chai" painted on the beautiful dream house they had made for the parade, even though the house was just a large painted construction in the style of Bread & Puppet.

This disagreement puzzled not only Dolan, but also me and my colleagues and students from the Shanghai Theatre Academy (STA) who had invited Dolan to come work with the migrants on this community-based project. What was the problem? We all believe that theatre has the ability to empower people, especially those who are socio-politically in the margins – people enduring poverty, dislocation, discrimination, etc. [...]

In present day China, there is a growing gulf between the wealthy and the poor and the migrant workers and their children comprise one group impacted by this critical social issue. … Their kids do not get the same education as their peers in the city.

For the past few years, STA teachers and students have worked with migrant workers on several community-based theatre projects. *Xiwang Beiyaowan* is the most ambitious of these. It not only had the invited American artist from Bread & Puppet Theatre as project leader, it also attracted volunteers from a community center and several artists from professional theatre companies in Shanghai.

None of us realized how complex the subject of house demolition was until we ran into the problem with the parade, which revealed the feelings of the migrant children and their parents. These migrant workers have to relocate from one place to another frequently. Here's how it happens: Relatively rich local villagers rent their houses to the immigrants, turning a whole local village into an immigrant village. Then the whole village is sold to a real estate company who wants to tear it down and build new high-rises. The migrants are forced to move. Over time, the people we were working with have been driven from village to village, following the swath carved out by various urban renewal plans.

To them, it was nothing unusual, but to us, it was a story about oppression. We tried to guide the community to talk about their plight, using Augusto Boal's Theatre of the Oppressed techniques. One of the ideas was to build several puppet houses that would be torn down during the parade. When we asked the participants in the community to paint the house, they painted it with beautiful colors in a fairy-tale style, instead of making a poor looking house in a realistic style. We had to adjust the story to fit these beautiful homes. In this story, we made a big monster puppet whose name was Chai. We suggested to the villagers that they put the Chinese character "chai" in the monster's mouth. But no one would do as we suggested. This was a surprise to us because the migrants usually complied with our requests. Even the STA students agreed with the migrants. They also preferred enacting the community's dreams over criticizing the reality. They made a colorful, fantastic giant puppet and named it Xiwang (Hope). Finally, Dolan had to put the chai sign into the monster's mouth by herself.

The performance turned out to be really ironic. All the outsiders, who played the roles of supervisors, insisted on performing a conflict and were happy about Xiwang the giant defeating Chai the monster. But the community members seemed to just enjoy the pleasure of the parade itself. They liked that a lot more than the superficial story of a "successful" conflict that Dolan and the other outsiders imposed.

The whole process of the *Xiwang Beiyaowan* project was in fact based on bringing artists from outside into the community to force the community members to be aware of their oppressive situation. But the community members themselves were very happy to just have a fairy-tale dream enacted. They preferred performing their dreams to performing their reality – a preference that was shared by the migrant workers and their children who participated in two other projects organized by STA.

Around the city of Shanghai there are several migrant workers' community centers run by volunteers and supported by charity foundations. On Saturday and Sunday afternoons, the centers are open to the workers' children. In one of these centers we facilitated our *Play My Family* project with 20 kids who were all about 12 years old. In the weekend workshops we applied Boal's techniques, played drama games, organized field trips with the children and their parents, helped them tell stories about their families, and guided them to write short plays of five minutes. Finally, we devised a one-hour play based on their short plays and performed it for their parents. [...]

In another project, *The Barbers*, a documentary and environmental theatre project we did with adult migrant workers in barbershops, we found a similar preference among the participants. The majority of male barbers and female shampooers in Shanghai are from rural areas or small towns outside of Shanghai. ... [We] conduct[ed] interviews and then wrote a play based on the workers' stories. We performed this play in barbershops in front of the barbers and shampooers whom we had interviewed. Most of them came to the city with the same dream – to struggle to make money and get residence papers that would allow them to stay for good. But in fact they don't know how long they will be allowed to stay in Shanghai.

One story was about a barber who had experienced many difficulties when he came to Shanghai. But he did not want to dwell on the painful past. One night, he had a dream about visiting his hometown and giving a haircut to his mother, who had been strongly against his choice to go to the city to become a barber. We enacted that dream scene. It was beautiful and audience members were deeply moved. In the discussion afterwards, the barbers asked us to move beyond performing their dreams for the purpose of reconciling with estranged friends and family. They wanted plays not about their current lives of suffering, but about how to successfully attract more customers, to fulfill their dreams of remaining in the city. They wanted to learn more "social performance skills" in order to appeal to prospective patrons. Increasing their business would help them *fulfill* their dreams. [...]

[I]t is very difficult to evaluate how and to what degree any community-based theatre really helps people to build their community. When we go to a community to propose a project, we face a lot of choices and have to make all kinds of decisions. Essentially, we need to figure out what would be the better way to serve the particular community we are among.

One question often raised during our work is: What kind of stories about their community should we guide them to tell and enact? Stories about the history of their community, current situations in their lives, or stories about their dreams for a better future? All of the above? What would it mean to them if they enact their struggles to earn a living? What would they get if they enact their dreams for a brighter future? In what sense would the performances they do affect their future? Since most of the young migrant workers and their children would like to stay in the city instead of go back to their home villages, would it be helpful to the migrant workers' kids if they perform their dreams onstage? Even though most of their dreams may not come true, it is the dreams that keep them going in the present. We must choose the stories carefully. [...]

When we first went to the communities, we had the simple idea that helping people tell their own stories of oppression would help them gain the self-confidence needed to cope with their difficult reality. We took a certain risk to do so, because "Harmonious Society" as a political slogan is highly valued in China – and what we were doing would not promote harmony but rather the recognition of and resistance to oppression. To our surprise, so far the government – which is always alert to people's expressions on sensitive issues – has not pressed us to do anything differently. But we have faced quiet resistance from the migrant community we work with. They are habitually reluctant or even opposed to enacting their harsh reality, opting to enact their dreams for the future. I believe this is because those who come to our theatre workshops have never lost hope. [...]

The community-based theatre we have been doing can help in this respect in that we teach the participants performance skills that can be used as social communication skills.

Some of us may need to more resolutely cross the border between aesthetic performance and social performance to dedicate more time to helping community members in their social activities. Yet for those who are happy to attend the weekly theatre workshops, even learning some domestic social skills through theatre can result in better communication with family members, an invaluable improvement of quality of life. [...]

In short, we have found out from these cases that many community members prefer performing their sweet dreams to performing their unpleasant reality. Hence our reflection: Because community members are so keen to perform their dreamed future, as long as we have no real power to solve their daily problems, why don't we help nurture their imaginations so they can better look forward? The questions are still there, of course: Is it possible for people to realize their dreams without fully expressing their current suffering and oppression? Is it possible for them to achieve reconciliation with those discriminating against them without going through a struggle? The answers to these questions lie mostly in the realm of social performance studies, rather than in aesthetic performances. Maybe I should ask my students, at least some of them, to change their careers to become journalists, lawyers, or better still, government officials who might actually have the power to create change.

Further Reading

Cohen-Cruz, J. (2005). *Local acts: Community-based performance in the United States.* New Brunswick, NJ: Rutgers.

Cohen-Cruz, J. (2010). *Engaging performance: Theatre as call and response.* New York, NY: Routledge.

Haedicke, S.C. & Nellhaus, T. (Eds.) (2001). *Performing democracy: International perspectives on urban community-based performance.* Ann Arbor, MI: The University of Michigan Press.

Leonard, R.H. & Kilkelly, A. (2006). *Performing communities: Grassroots ensemble theaters deeply rooted in eight U.S. communities.* Oakland, CA: New Village Press.

Salverson, J. (Ed.). (2011). *Community engaged theatre and performance.* Toronto: Playwrights Canada Press.

Van Erven, E. (2001). *Community theatre: Global perspectives.* New York, NY: Routledge.

The six books listed above offer excellent introductions by the authors/editors and many case studies from North America and around the world.

Muriri, S. (Summer 2013). Easter rising: An article about The Poole Passion (TPP). *Drama: One Forum Many Voices, 19*(2), 24–30. Describes an annual project involving 70 community members and artists in Poole, UK.

Nagel, E. (2007). An aesthetic of neighborliness: Possibilities for integrating community-based practices into documentary theatre. *Theatre Topics, 17*(2), 153–168. A useful discussion on the lack of aesthetic in the work applied theatre does in terms of how we see both the art itself and the artists who engage with it.

Nogueira, M.P. (2006). Reflections on the impact of a long term theatre for community development project in Southern Brazil. *RIDE: Research in Drama Education, 11*(2), 219–234.

Nogueira, M.P., Goncalves, R.M. & Scheibe, C. (1996). Community theatre in Florianópolis. *RIDE: Research in Drama Education, 1*(1), 121–128. The two articles above offer reflections of a community-based project in Brazil over a ten-year period.

Walling, S. (2012). The tree of community art practice: Reflections on a resident art practice in Vancouver's Downtown Eastside. *Alt.theatre: Cultural Diversity and the Stage, 9*(4), 21–25.

Questions for Reflection and Discussion

1. How would you begin to go about researching a community in which you would like to work? What sources of information are available in print (archival and contemporary) and in personal contacts?

2. What benefits for a community do you see arising from the creation of a community-based play? As a facilitator, what strategies might you employ to highlight and promote these benefits?

3. Jan Cohen-Cruz writes that community-based theatre "is about not just the play but the play in its community context" (Leonard & Kilkelly, 2006, p. 5). How is this process different from mainstream theatre practices, and what are the implications for organization and facilitation?

Suggested Activities

1. Select a geographical area of a maximum ten-block radius with your own home location as the centre point. Determine and list how many different communities lie within this area (senior citizen's homes, schools, libraries, recreation centres and so on).

2. How might you discover what issues are central to each of these communities? Where can you see some potential performance sites in this area?

3. Identify a concern in the community-based on your research. What partners or community groups might be interested in addressing this challenge? Create a promotional kit (leaflets, advertisements, posters, media) for a community meeting designed to bring these groups together to consider a community-based theatre project.

4. To prepare for this meeting, plan at least one activity-based game or exercise that will lead participants into a shared sense of community and purpose.

Web Resources

Big hART, Australia http://bighart.org/

Claque Theatre, Tunbridge Wells, Kent, UK http://www.claquetheatre.com/

Jumblies Theatre, Toronto, ON http://www.jumbliestheatre.org/

Roadside Theater, Norton, VA http://roadside.org/

Vancouver Moving Theatre, Vancouver, BC http://vancouvermovingtheatre.com/

Introduction

A good definition for museum theatre is "the use of theatre and theatrical techniques as a means of mediating knowledge and understanding in the context of museum education" (Hughes et al., 2007, p. 680). Within that definition lie a number of performance possibilities:

- A theatre performance presented to help people understand a particular time period or issue. For example, a transportation exhibit at the Smithsonian in Washington, DC demonstrated life in the United States in the 1950s. After the performance, the actors came out of role to discuss the show and its time period with the audience.
- First-person interpretation is one form of museum theatre in which the interpreter takes on the role of a particular, usually historic, character and interacts with museum visitors in-role. These interactions may be dramatically framed or unframed. An unframed encounter is when an interpreter only functions within the historic time period and does not acknowledge the present day. At other sites, a framed encounter is when visitors are asked by an interpreter if they'd like to meet someone, in this way acknowledging that he or she will perform for them as a "witness" (Rokem, 2000) from the past.
- Historical reenactments can be theatrical recreations of historic events, often involving a large number of participants. In 2001, for example, UK artist Jeremy Deller led a large group of around 1000 people through a reenactment of a 1984 mining strike confrontation between miners and police he called *The Battle of Orgreave* (Correia, 2006).
- Collective role-playing, also known as "second-person interpretation," is when

the audience as well as the interpreters are working in-role together. The audience may put on costumes and participate in activities related to the historic site – for example, playing maids in a historic home (Rosestone, 2012), or playing fugitive slaves in a history park (Magelssen, 2006).

- Third-person interpretation is when the interpreter performs in-role but at the same time "walks alongside" the role acknowledging that he or she and the visitor are able to dialogue across two different time periods (Boucher, 2011). This process has been described as a blended sensibility "not yet present, but rather present imperfect" (Talbot & Andrews, 2011, p. 182).

Museum theatre, much like any applied theatre form, presents many challenges. One of the primary ones is that of moving a casual museum visitor into either an audience or participatory role. Museum theatre audiences may be the most accidental audiences found in all of applied theatre, as they are not usually coming to a museum for a theatre experience. However, research demonstrates that when a museum-based performance does gather the attention of an audience, it can be an effective learning tool that people tend to remember (Jackson & Rees Leahy, 2005). Another challenge lies in how much perspective or multiple points of view can inform the historical storytelling enacted by performers.

> In putting the learner[s]-the visitor[s]- at the centre of the experience of learning, rather than simply placing information in front of them, museums have been part of a larger move… to ensure that visitors are not just 'targeted' but are considered participants in the process.
>
> Anthony Jackson & Jenny Kidd, 2008, p. 3

Actors working in museum settings need to be aware that museums, which are mainstream institutions, can be very traditional; therefore, it takes a great deal of negotiation, research and tact on the part of theatre artists working in these settings to bring a more complex set of understandings to the process. It is also challenging to negotiate if and how actors may work with historic artifacts from a museum collection. A third challenge is the discipline required to repeat scenarios and monologues multiple times every day, plus the added challenge of being an effective improviser who can respond to visitor input while maintaining a role.

There are clear tensions in the heritage community that sometimes convey a suspicion of all things theatrical as "fake" and a belief that everything of heritage value must be "authentic." This brings into question how somebody enacting a historical figure, or a fictional character within a historic timeframe, is representing the "truth" while at the same time conforming to the mandate of a particular institution. Again, as in all applied theatre practices, the negotiation and preparation that happens beforehand is paramount in importance. Research has demonstrated that where a high investment is made in training, the visitor response has been extremely positive, both in appreciation of entertainment value and in perceived learning (Malcolm-Davies, 2004, p. 285).

The case studies presented in this chapter offer three very different museum theatre projects. Polly Williams looks at the challenges and rewards of the guided tour as first-person interpretation in which the power of place, in this case the National Coal Mining Museum for England, generates belief and connection for visitors. That power can be seen again in Scott Magelssen's description of a one-time only historical reenactment of a slave auction at a historic site in Virginia and makes for compelling reading that raises many useful questions. Finally, Debra McLauchlan shares a Canadian museum–university partnership from the point of view of the facilitator. She encounters and negotiates institutional and student resistance to the project.

12.1 In the present looking at the past
from *Performing interpretation*
Polly Williams. (2013). *Scandinavian Journal of Hospitality and Tourism, 13*(2), 115–126.

[A] key means of interpretation for the industrial museum or heritage site is through the production of experience – that attempts to give a sense of "being there" in the past and to understand what it was like to be a worker then. Privileging the visitor experience has important implications for the sense of authenticity which was formerly located in the "real things in real places" that museums possessed. The focus on the experiential, transforms the sense of what *is* real into what is *felt as real* by the visitor, and so authenticity is shifted from the material to the existential realm. [...]

[The research site] the NCMME [National Coal Mining Museum for England]- a former colliery site in Wakefield, West Yorkshire ... has a range of buildings and artefacts from the early nineteenth century to the late twentieth century within a 17 acre site. A combination of restored and conserved buildings and traditional museum gallery display spaces are housed in both original and rebuilt spaces, but the external appearance of the site and its buildings are designed to look as they did when the colliery closed in 1985. The NCMME has a very popular underground tour led by ex-miners that takes place 134 meters underground in a real operational mine, with all the installation still in place, and this too is designed to look "as if" it were left behind when the mine stopped producing coal. The "realness" of the mine space is very much augmented for the visitor by the sensory effects of descending underground in a cramped "cage" in the dark. The floors are uneven, the roof very low in places, the temperature drops and we have the feeling of being immersed within the mine. The

[A] distrust of theatre as misleading and insubordinate, concerns over authenticity, and a relatively narrow use of performance techniques coupled with persistent financial limitations, seem to constrain the theatricality of the practice [of museum theatre].

Jennie Sutherland Clothier, 2014, p. 223

miner-guides who lead these tours are extremely popular with visitors and are regarded as experts: "they've got all the information – and the merry quips that they put in – you know that they've been there and done that" (Visitor 18, interview, February 20, 2008). [...]

Research ... indicates that performance practices associated with the guided tour can be organized into the following broad categories:

- *Scenography*: guided tours utilize the "staged" space that is arranged to be "as it was" at some point in the past.
- *Characterization*: guides will sometimes produce fully formed and acted character roles based on people from the past – or more often than not – suggest a more shadowy "character", by simply wearing a costume.
- *Narrative*: guides use storytelling that draws on personal history, myths and legends as well as instructional narratives designed to educate the visitor.
- *Collective experience*: tours may use elements of practices associated with significant collective experience such as ritual.

Characterization

The museum guided tour is generally regarded as having performative qualities rather than as *being* a performance, mainly because the tour guide is being themselves rather than assuming a character, and because the content of the tour is generally believed to be factual information. However in the guided tours mentioned here, guides are costumed and assume a role which is in-between being themselves and being a "character" from the past. [...]

The role of the miner-guides at the NCMME is ... complex. They are themselves acting as guides but they also represent their former working role as miners as well as standing in for all the other miners in the past. Many of the miner-guides interviewed mentioned that working at the museum was "like" it was working in the pits before the strike in the 1980s and there is the sense that this is a set aside space for them where they can "be" their former selves. The question of whether this is their "real" self, or is a persona based on their idealized picture of a miner, is reflected in the complex array of roles that the men assume both in front of each other and in front of visitors.

Assumptions about the need for entertainment rather than education have led to historic sites being faced with a "double mandate": to act as both an entertaining tourist attraction and an educational resource and often end up caught between the two, satisfying neither objective.

Malcolm-Davies, 2004, p. 278

Narrative

The "banter" of the miner-guides is a characteristic form of narrative which they bring from their former working lives. This can be described as a joking or teasing way of talking to colleagues that can be a way of cutting others down to size as well as maintaining a sense of camaraderie. This banter – with each other and to a certain extent with visitors can sometimes alter the status of the "facts": "sticking to the subject matter totally, it would be very dire, very grim, so you break it up by putting some stories in that's happened to you, to just make it a bit more light-hearted" (Miner-guide 7, interview, November 27, 2008). … The attempt to "lighten" what might be unpalatable information related to death and disaster at these industrial sites produces a mixture of instruction and entertainment. It can destabilize what might be regarded as the "truth" in the guides' historical narratives, but any potential misrepresentation of the facts that might be conveyed by a particular tour delivery is balanced by an insistence by other aspects of authenticity. The miner-guides can "get away" with a fictionalized version of history, because they *are* the real thing: they talk from experience, and they know what they are talking about. As well as this, the insistent material authenticity of the … underground regions with their part real/part reconstructed artefacts along with the authority of the museum ensures that visitors do come away with the impression of having been in contact with "real" history. However it is the tour-guide's narrative that makes the history *seem* real. Both visitors and guides stress that on their own, the tour spaces and artefacts would be nothing without the narrative to bring them to life.

Collective Experience

These guided tours require their participants to be both actors as well as audience for their tour-guide's performances. Visitors actively perform the tour as they follow the suggested choreography of the guide and they enact appropriate responses to the stories they are told and scenes they witness. Tour parties are bound together in a group experience as they are prompted to feel the emotions associated with the harsh lives of miners and apprentice children. The following sections analyse the elements of liminality and ritual present in the guided tours in question that I would argue, facilitate this sense of collective experience. [...]

Being underground is literally disappearing from the world and may feel like being buried alive. It also represents the underworld of death and the afterlife. The fear of the dark, of small spaces and of being buried alive may lurk at the back of many visitors' minds, or may become overwhelming. Occasionally once underground visitors are too frightened by the space to continue on the tour and have to be brought back up again. [...]

In the case of the underground tour, the building that we enter to reach it – called the lamp room, is organized in a heavily demarcated way with barriers, signs and arrows and is clearly a threshold region as we seem to be neither any longer in the museum, nor on the tour. This is the place where the ex-miners begin the tour but it also seems like the place where they used to collect their lamps, and begin their day. The lamp room seems authentic as a workspace but actually it is not a former lamp room and has been "set-dressed" by the museum to seem like a left-behind space. [...]

At the NCMME, we are held in a waiting area and may not proceed with our tour until our guide has looked us over and explained the rules. We then have to hand over all our valuables and any items with a battery, and exchange them for a hard hat and a light and battery pack. This could be regarded as a levelling process where the signs of our pre-liminal status are destroyed and signs of our liminal non-status applied. This changes our role from museum visitor to something more along the lines of a junior employee. We lose our customary autonomy and are led in a pre-determined pattern, at a set time. The tour is a series of crossings we make: from the lamp room into the cage, from the cage to the pit bottom and from stopping point to stopping point. One of the key features of a transition ritual is an enhanced sense of *communitas*. On the tour we are bound into a temporary community which produces us as a civic body which is part of the civilizing role of the museum, but I think also to enact the working class identity that was so dependent on this sense of community. We are encouraged ... to *feel* for the original inhabitants of these places and to have a sense of empathy for their harsh working conditions. If we can do this and imagine ourselves "there", we temporarily bind ourselves into their community and our lives are joined with theirs. [...]

The value of the guided tour in the industrial museum is to produce *extra-visibility* through the limiting of access to the resource being toured, and through the medium of the guide who allows us to see these environments through their eyes, made rich with their imaginative recreations and memories. The journey as a metaphor is acted out by these tours which suggests the passage of time from the past to the present, the connections between home and work and between family and community and gives us a way of looking again at our own lives, work and families.

12.2 Re-examining history through museum theatre

from *Making history in the second person: Post-touristic considerations for living historical interpretation*
Scott Magelssen. (2006). *Theatre Journal, 58*(2), 291–312.

The 1994 Publick Times Estate Auction at Colonial Williamsburg [was] staged by what was then Williamsburg's African American Interpretations and Presentations Program (AAIP) ... The auction reenactment, which included the dramatization of the sale of four slaves, drew substantial criticism from several groups, including the Southern Christian Leadership Conference and the NAACP. Protestors occupied the stage with the characters throughout the performance, condemning the auction as a demoralization of human dignity. This controversial reenactment was a moment of living history in which several performative and historiographic issues came to a head, specifically in the collision of the remembered pasts of the institution, the interpreter, and the museum visitor. In this space, a ritualized commemoration of a past identity (a site of potential) was forced into the structures of institutional history.

The auction conveyed and condensed several stories: Lucy and Daniel, married by common law, were sold to different bidders from counties fifty miles apart, their marriage and family broken up. Sukey, a laundress, was purchased by her husband, a "free Negro," who was able to outbid a wealthy white landowner. Another slave, a carpenter, was sold to a white bidder along with his tools. The staged auction lasted about thirty minutes, but by the end, a clear set of important themes and lessons had emerged to tie the stories together: (1) Whites bought and sold blacks like livestock; (2) Sometimes freed blacks could outbid whites to purchase and free enslaved individuals; (3) Sometimes white masters' desire for profit and/or frugality overpowered the bonds between two human beings. Several other narratives were possible, but unable to be contained in a dramatic presentation that sought to convey selected historical information and ideas in the most immediate and successful way possible. These other potential stories were left out of the narrative because they would not fit easily into the dramatic structure of singular plot, conflict, rising action, and denouement.

Audience members picked up on the missed opportunities in the talkback that followed, when AAIP Chair Christy Coleman (who also played Lucy in the performance) fielded questions from the audience. "Where do you show African Americans as fighters?" shouted one voice from a contingent of protesters holding banners demanding, "Say No to Racist Shows." Coleman responded that the AAIP shows resistance in all of its programming at Colonial Williamsburg, both active and passive (deciding not to work for the master one day, saying "I'm sick," or breaking a hoe). This answer did not, apparently, appease the dissatisfied spectators. Another question was hurled from the crowd: "Where was that today?"

The auction reenactment had negative effects on the costumed reenactors as well: in a May 2000 telephone conversation, Christy Coleman Matthews, now president of Charles H. Wright Museum of African American History in Detroit, spoke to me of how extremely difficult it was for the interpreters, who normally interact with visitors in the first or third person, to shift to a more traditional theatrical approach for the 1994 estate auction. According to Matthews, the interpreters experienced extreme emotional exhaustion, much of it caused by the need to internalize the characters' emotions in the performance, since, historically, the slaves on the auction block were not allowed to speak. When living history programming employs traditional theatre practices, the interpreters find the experience of immersing themselves in characters to be psychologically and emotionally more draining than their regular job of historical interaction. "They couldn't wear their interpreter hat [during the auction]. They were used to relying on both theatrical tricks for suspension of disbelief and the story told as an interpreter. . . . They had to dig into their personal psyche. That was a new experience for these people." Matthews cited this distress as the reason why the estate auction was only performed once. "The staff didn't want to do it," she said, "because it was too emotionally draining." The participants, both black and white, were taken aback by visitors' strong emotional responses to the reenactment and by their own emotions, which they had to repress in order to stay in character.

The estate auction failed to meet either interpreter or visitor/spectator expectations, and the museum's ethical, performative, and historiographic responsibilities were poorly defined. Acts of memory that would have been more personally empowering for contemporary performers and audiences, though not found in the Virginia Gazette records upon which the auction was based, could not be incorporated. The spectators, though, rather than passively accepting this institutional history, were instead allowed to unmask and voice the limiting conditions, because the liberating environment of protest enabled them to do so.

It is vital that the largely undocumented history of black oppression and experience continue to be voiced at such an educational institution and historical tourist [destination] as Williamsburg. But is there a way to do this that would allow more discussion and exploration than that which is available in a living history sound-bite like the estate auction? [...]

"Second-person interpretation," a relatively recent term in the living history field, allows visitors to pretend to be part of the past and offers possibilities of co-creating the trajectory of the historiographic narrative with the staff, rather than merely passively consuming it. The vast bulk of this type of programming at living museums, though, does not involve any kind of impersonation or assuming of character on the part of the visitor. [...]

Second-person interpretation is becoming one of living museums' most foregrounded programs. Social history, the wave of revisionist thinking that swept through the industry in the 1970s and 1980s, has much to do with its emergence. Museums have since changed the focus from displaying the lives of the Founding Fathers and have made significant steps toward showing the rest of the story, the mostly unrecorded histories of women, children, racial and ethnic minorities, and the very poor. Hence, second-person activities are geared toward hands-on learning about the kinds of crafts and chores these individuals would have done throughout their lives. Activities almost always include basket weaving and candle dipping. Musket drilling is conducted at Colonial Williamsburg using wooden sticks as dummy rifles. Other activities might include building a stone wall, throwing a pot, making ribbon, weaving on a loom, or working a plow. In summer 2001 at Living History Farms in Iowa, my fellow visitors and I were each given a pair of work gloves, stamped with the museum logo. The gloves served as a take-home souvenir, but we were encouraged to use them throughout our visit to the museum. For example, the interpreters at the 1850 Farm were using daub to patch holes in the walls of the log cabin homestead where the weather and hearth fires had dried and crumbled the earlier layers; they encouraged us to try our (gloved) hands at it. [...]

Often, too, reenacted historical events (as opposed to the generalized common practices like ballgames and square dances) require the occasional crowd or cast of thousands in order to approximate an accurate picture of what originally transpired. Colonial Williamsburg makes heavy use of crowd participation, which often simply means that visitors chant lines on the cues given by the first-person reenactors. One June afternoon in 2000 (7 November 1769 in the Historic Area), I was one of the hundreds of visitors gathered for the "Convening of the General Assembly." After Williamsburg staff hand-picked a selection of middle-aged men from the audience to represent the burgesses marching through the gates of the Capitol building to begin that year's session, the crowd was led in a rousing chorus of "Rule Britannia!" in order to demonstrate that, at least in 1769, ties between Virginia and England were still strong. That was Sunday. By Tuesday morning of that week, we had skipped to April of 1775, and the crowd was enlisted in protesting the British Governor's middle-of-the-night removal of gunpowder from the Public Magazine; later that day, we jeered at the burning effigy of Alfred, Lord North, in protest of growing British sanctions.

With the exception of the 1994 estate auction at Colonial Williamsburg, there is no question about whether one will comply with the rules of these games, post-tourist or no. So effective is the tourist realism and family fun that to go against the grain and voice alternative histories, or to question the agenda of the institution (or to assume a character not assigned by the interpretive staff), would make one a spoilsport.

12.3 Museum–university partnership
from *Digging a ditch with undergraduates: A museum theatre experience*
Debra McLauchlan. (2008). *NJ: Drama Australia Journal, 31*(2), 83–94.

[I]n January 2003, the Museum Board of Directors formally approved my proposal to create an on-site theatre project using university drama students as playwrights and performers. The Board outlined three requirements: (1) that I would personally take charge of the project, (2) that the museum's education coordinator would select the topic of the play, and (3) that the production would increase museum publicity through media coverage and a preview performance for local politicians and museum supporters. The Board took responsibility for advertising, creating and distributing a program, financing and organizing an opening reception, and supplying a small production budget to cover extraneous costs. [...]

In March, I met the museum's education coordinator to discuss potential topics for the play. A few weeks later, on the advice of teachers who regularly visit the museum with their classes, the coordinator decided on the topic of the Welland Canal for three reasons: (1) Lock 3 of the canal sits behind the museum, and artifacts about its history are located throughout the site; (2) the topic complements Ontario Ministry of Education guidelines for both social studies and science in Grades 4 to 6; and (3) the production would coincide with the canal's 175th anniversary. The coordinator requested a one-hour performance, with pre- and post-show discussion time, for seven Friday mornings in March and April. She assumed responsibility for advertising to schools, scheduling school visits, communicating with teachers before and after the performances, collecting feedback, and creating a study guide package to accompany the production. [...]

In St. Catharines, the museum is accessed through an open foyer, overlooking the Welland Canal, with a permanent [three]-tiered riser close to the exhibit entrance. The exhibit area is a narrow, winding avenue of niches and display cases, some fixed and some moveable. Potential performance spaces included the façade of a shanty inhabited by canal workers, the helm of an old tugboat, a replica of a sea captain's office, stacks of barrels, and a large topographical model of the region. The curator took responsibility for providing costumes and print material about the Welland Canal. [...]

Ten months before the performance would be staged, preliminary arrangements with university and museum personnel were complete, and initial contact with potential audiences had been made. Groundwork of another sort now demanded attention. Meticulous planning would be necessary to enable the university students to learn about museum theatre concepts, research the Welland Canal, and devise and rehearse a one-hour performance in the short time available. Seven weeks of the 13-week course were already committed to performance, leaving six [three]-hour in-class sessions for the creation of the play! I made a few decisions to alleviate the scarcity of time issue.

First, I envisioned that the play would begin and end in modern-day scenes involving the entire class, the opening to occur on and around the foyer riser, and the closing to re-enact the annual Top Hat Ceremony that welcomes the first boat of the season through the canal each spring. The bulk of the play would be developed from topics selected by the students, working simultaneously in self-determined groups to build individual scenes of approximately seven minutes. The scenes would be linked by a narration strategy, also to be determined by the class, that would move the audience from one area of the museum to another. Next, after scripting their scenes, each group would schedule two [two]-hour rehearsals with me outside of class time. These focused sessions would provide uninterrupted opportunities to block and polish every section of the script. Finally, a local actor who frequently interprets the historical figure of William Hamilton Merritt, primary founder of the Welland Canal, agreed to visit the class, in character, during the first session. As Merritt, he would provide rich details about the canal's inception, while also modeling principles of first-person interpretation. [...]

The first class consisted of introductions and warm-ups, a course overview, the in-role visit from "William Hamilton Merritt," and a structured exploration of possibilities for the opening scene. Of 18 students enrolled in the course, 14 were present. Although some displayed a knowledgeable approach to preliminary play-building tasks, others lacked the skill level in dramatic exploration that I had expected from a third-year group. [...]

The final hour of class was devoted to the opening scene. I distributed factual information about the Welland Canal ("the ditch", as its creators labeled it) which groups translated into movement-with-narration vignettes. By fortunate coincidence, each vignette included depictions of a lock, water, and a boat. Merging the vignettes and staging them on the museum foyer riser would comprise the opening scene of the play. [...]

We returned to the opening scene. After creating precise gestures for "lock," "water," and "boat" characters, we agreed on the order and transitional movements for vignettes devised during Week One. The role of Lockmaster Winston emerged as a character who would introduce the play and help narrate scene transitions. We choreographed an opening chant – "Inch by inch, meter by meter, we'll dig a ditch and dig it deeper" – that would bring performers into the performance space. [...]

For the second half of class, we traveled to the museum and met the site's educational coordinator, curator, and board chair. After touring the facility, students were free to decide what topic interested them about the canal, what classmates would work together on developing a scene about their selected topic, and where their scenes would be performed. The curator presented copious print material as research aids... Over the next two weeks, we hammered out tentative scenes for the play. [...]

Meanwhile, as [Napp-]Schindel (2002) predicted, the museum denied access to authentic artifacts for use as theatrical props. In the end, actors performed certain actions in front of authentic objects, while either miming their use (especially in the case of shovels and other digging implements) or replacing them with replicas (especially in the case of documents). [...]

Napp-Schindel, D. (2002). Museum theatre: Telling stories through objects. *Stage of the Art*, 14(4), 10–16.

The play eventually developed into eight scenes that moved both chronologically and physically through the museum's exhibit space. Incorporating dance, song, mime, monologues, stylized movement and tableau work, it balanced episodes of despair with comic moments of light-heartedness, and included gender-blind depictions of both real and fictional characters. It ended as it began, in a full-cast scene set in present time. [...]

Aside from the initial visit, the class did not return to the museum until dress rehearsal, when we competed for space and time with both a work crew engaged in noisy repairs and a couple of bus tours. With the preview performance hours away – and an invited audience of media, city and tourism officials, university faculty, museum board members and supporters – no one had assumed responsibility for setting up seats in the foyer! Last-minute recruitment of labor went unnoticed by the audience, most of whom warmly applauded the show and praised its professionalism and entertainment value. Problems, however, demanded attention before the first performance for children. [...]

First, museum staff noted a couple of factual inaccuracies, one minor and a more significant one that prompted an additional rehearsal. Secondly, the curator wanted an actor to refrain from using a specific cart handle, requiring some restaging of a scene. Thirdly, docents worried that children's potential exuberance for the play might incite them not only to infringe on spaces, but also to touch objects restricted to the public. As a solution, the educational coordinator would make a welcoming speech before each performance, outlining rules of expected conduct in the museum. Children would also be supplied with small seating mats that would define their personal spatial boundaries.

Cast members complained that the preview had ended without a formal curtain call. A customary bow seemed inappropriate within the non-traditional setting of the final scene, which positioned the audience as crowd members in the Top Hat Ceremony. Yet, the ending of the play had seemed awkward without a mechanism to signal audience applause. We decided that I would speak a line at the end of each performance to thank everyone for attending. Afterward, the cast would bow and applaud the audience as a cue for the audience to return the applause. [...]

A potentially more serious concern emanated from a few museum supporters who complained that sections of the play were inappropriate for children. In particular, they wanted to eliminate the action of a husband slapping his wife, as well as any references to racial or religious hatred that sparked riots during the Welland Canal's construction. Although not in favor of sanitizing history, museum staff felt obliged to placate the supporters and asked my opinion about toning down these sections of the play. Fearing not only a revolt from the cast but also a severe wound to the play's integrity if I complied, I suggested a compromise that the museum supporters accepted. The script would be performed as written; however, during the post-show chat the actors would (a) demonstrate the stage slap technique and (b) denounce racial and religious intolerance in the play as unacceptable beliefs not shared by the performers in real life. [...]

Response from the seven school groups who attended the play was highly positive in terms of its entertainment value and professionalism. Obvious warmth developed between actors and audience in almost all performances. Most noticeable in post-show questioning was the children's interest in specific characters' reactions to dramatized events. The production achieved the museum's goal of increased school visits and publicity, with the result that the "Theatre for the Community" course has continued as a partnership between the museum and the university Dramatic Arts Department.

Further Reading

Bridal, T. (2004). *Exploring museum theatre*. Walnut Creek, CA: Altamira.

Clothier, J.S. (2014). Authentic pretending: How theatrical is museum theatre? *Museum Management and Curatorship, 29*(3), 211–225. An excellent survey of museum theatre practice that raises important critical issues in the field.

Hughes, C. (2014). Theatre performance in museums: Art and pedagogy. *Youth Theatre Journal, 24*(1), 34–42.

Jackson, A. & Kidd, J. (Eds.). (2011). *Performing heritage: Research practice and innovation in museum theatre and live interpretation.* Manchester, UK: Manchester University Press.

Jackson, A. & Rees Leahy, H. (2005). "Seeing it for real …?" – Authenticity, theatre and learning in museums. *RIDE: Research in Drama Education, 10*(3), 303–325. A look at the kinds of learning achieved in museum theatre education with children.

Magelssen, S. & Justice-Mallory, R. (Eds.). (2011). *Enacting history.* Tuscaloosa, AL: University of Alabama Press.

Malcolm-Davies, J. (2004). Borrowed robes: The educational value of costumed interpretation at historic sites. *International Journal of Heritage Studies, 10*(3), 277–293. This article looks at the value of costumed interpretation and the importance of sufficient training time for first-person interpreters.

McCalman, I. & Pickering, P.A. (Eds.). (2010). *Historical reenactment: From realism to the affective turn.* Basingstoke, UK: Palgrave Macmillan.

Rosestone, S. (2012). Thought-provoking experiences for secondary students. *Ethos, 20*(3), 20–22. Presents three drama and performance programs at former gold mine Sovereign Hill Museum in Ballarat, Australia.

Tzibazi, V. (2012). Primary schoolchildren's experiences of participatory theatre in a heritage site. *Education, 3*(13), 1–19.

Questions for Reflection and Discussion

1. In the three case studies you have just read, how does participation differ in each of these museum theatre activities? How do the different levels of participation potentially affect the learning intended in each project?

2. Re-read the concluding paragraph of Scott Magelssen's case study in which he describes how second-person interpretation usually offers little or no space for spectator-participants to resist the narrative they are recreating. What are some

possible strategies that might allow for more diverse opinions on historic events to be voiced in a museum setting?

3. Reflecting on one selected case study, identify what meanings could be drawn, what connections to the information could be made, what elements of surprise were evident (as in seeing something in a fresh way) and what possibilities exist for raising new questions.

Suggested Activities

1. Make a list of the museum and heritage sites in your area and find out, on the Internet or by phoning the Education Director, if any museum theatre has been or is being done. (Note that science centres and art galleries may also offer first-person interpretation and/or theatre performances.) If possible, make arrangements to attend a performance or interpretation and document it via notes and/or interviews with actors and institutional staff. Use these data as part of a post-performance analysis that examines the balance between entertainment and education.

2. Visit a local museum or heritage site with a view to determining possibilities for interpretation, presentation or interactive role-play in that setting. Write up your idea as a short proposal, keeping in mind the mandate of the institution and any potential challenges you can foresee.

3. Decide upon a museum or historic site as a setting for a first-person interpretation. Research the time period. You may want to identify a historic figure or create a composite fictional character. Write, rehearse and perform a monologue with a strong narrative that includes opportunities for audience interaction. In presenting this first-person interpretation, what educational opportunities are present for audience learning? If possible, present these monologues within your chosen museum site.

Web Resources

International Museum Theatre Alliance [IMTAL] http://imtal-europe.net/

Kentucky Museum/Western Kentucky University, USA https://www.youtube.com/watch?v=Z_jvfwmrl5Y

Performing Heritage Research Report, University of Manchester, UK http://www.plh. manchester.ac.uk/documents/Performance,%20Learning%20&%20Heritage%20 -%20Report.pdf

Timeline Theatre, Chicago, IL http://www.timelinetheatre.com

CHAPTER THIRTEEN
REMINISCENCE THEATRE

Introduction

Reminiscence theatre uses the strategies and techniques of drama education to generate the recall of memories and experiences of the elderly. Often these experiences are simply shared and enjoyed by the group. Sometimes stories and experiences, stimulated by drama activities, are developed into performances that may be played either by the elderly themselves or by professional actors. This is reminiscence theatre: "dramatizing and making theatre from memories" (Schweitzer, 2006, p. 13).

The plays that are built from those shared reminiscences are generally performed in spaces that we would not recognize as theatre spaces but are ones in which the audiences feel comfortable. These plays have a double purpose: to generate memories and to use those memories to engender further memories and story-making from their audiences. The raw materials of the scripts are the tape-recorded or written recollections of older people, gleaned from group discussions, individual interviews, improvisations or pieces of writing. These stories are reflected back to an audience made up of the very people whose stories are being performed, as well as to their families, other seniors and their guests. Audiences are most often small groups so that seeing and hearing is easier for both players and watchers. After the performance, the serving of food and drink enables conversations that reflect the memories of the audience as they interact with the stories they have heard and the performers they meet.

> [Reminiscence Theatre] passes lightly over the relentless, recurring search for funds, the prodigious workload and the versatility required to work with older and younger volunteers, professional and non-professional actors, musicians, teachers, artists and health and social care staff of varying abilities, ambitions, talents and temperaments.
>
> Faith Gibson, 2006, p. 11

Variations of this model may be intergenerational and may happen in one of three ways. First, a group of young people elicit stories about life memories from seniors, dramatize these stories and then perform them for the seniors themselves. Second, a theatre group made up of senior players may choose to perform their reminiscences for young audiences who gain a deeper understanding of their grandparents' or great grandparents' generations. Third, as seen in one of the case studies that follows (Petheridge & Kendall, 2012), young and older people come together to present stories about the history of their communities and their senior members. These mixed generational projects may be performed for varied audiences, especially the community itself.

With improved diets and good healthcare more people are living longer, yet we still struggle to make those later years productive and engaging. Today, the quality of our later years is an important area of research, and we are discovering that the needs of the elderly are the same as for humans of all ages: affirmation of their presence and value in the world.

Meaning-making rituals – what Myerhoff (1992) refers to as "definitional ceremonies" – could become "powerful tools" in the self-construction of elder identity; without them, it may be difficult to see one's later life as a fulfilling time (p. 113). Part of engendering that sense of fulfillment lies with the creation of time and space for memory prompting, storytelling and communicating. The value of reminiscence theatre is that it reframes the stories of the elderly into performances that provide meaning and confirmation, not just to those whose stories are being told but also as prompts for the stories of its senior audiences and, often, their caregivers and family members. For these latter groups, reminiscence theatre pieces can become invigorating stimuli to promote reconnection and respect for the past through the conversations that ensue after the performance.

> Revisiting aspects of their own lives in the company of others, singing and talking together, appeared to shore up people's sense of identity at a time of increased vulnerability, and enable them to engage at least for a while in pleasurable exchanges around remembered shared experience.
>
> Pam Schweitzer, 2013, p. 42

What we have described above reflects the approaches of a number of reminiscence theatre companies of which The Age Exchange in London, England has the strongest reputation. It is known for the variety of programs that it offers, the quality of the work itself by "in-house" or professional performers, and the international connections that it makes through its outreach activities, such as The Memory Box project (Schweitzer, 2006). There is, however, an equally strong body of work located in the United States and referred to as "senior theatre" (Basting, 1995). Senior theatre, not to be confused with reminiscence theatre, can be an extremely

> In writing about children's theatre, Brecht said, "It is no different with grownups. Their education never finishes. Only the dead are beyond being altered by their fellow-men (sic). Think this over and you will realize how important the theatre is for forming characters."
>
> Bertolt Brecht in Willett, 1964, p. 152

demanding vaudeville-style production that capitalizes on the talents of older adults (e.g., *The Geritol Follies* [Canada] or *The Geritol Frolics* [United States]). Senior theatre can also refer to the performances of scripted plays by senior actors. Western Gold Theatre, founded by Joy Coghill, produces "outstanding professional theatre that expands horizons and enriches the lives of mature artists and their audiences" (Western Gold Theatre, n.d.).

In Victoria, BC, Target Theatre, which has the motto "empowering seniors by overcoming age stereotypes," combines both kinds of theatre (Target Theatre, n.d.). In addition to working with scripts, the company has a repertoire of applied theatre pieces, often commissioned, addressing such issues as dementia, elder abuse, incontinence, death and dying. These plays are performed and facilitated at conferences for audiences of social workers, doctors, police and any who have a direct interest in the issues presented.

In our first example, an oral historian working with The Age Exchange examines the purposes of storytelling in terms of its truth and intentions. These are issues that any facilitator must consider when working with people's stories, whatever their age. Our second case history offers an example of work from the Uhan Shii Theatre Group, a collective of non-professional elder women under an experienced theatre director. This excerpt describes only one part of a much larger work, "Echoes of Taiwan", that focuses on cultural identity and traditions through reaffirmation and critique. The third study is an examination of an intergenerational project in London with over 200 participants of all ages. The project shows how this kind of theatre creates a place for participants to engage with their community as active citizens. Finally, an Australian research study on widowhood led to the development of a play performed extensively across the country that explored the challenges of this kind of significant transition.

13.1 Interrogating reminiscence
from *Reminiscence and oral history: Parallel universes or shared endeavour?*
Joanna Bornat. (2001). *Ageing and Society, 21*, 219–241.

The Good Companions are a London-based group of older people, nine women and one man, who devised a play *Our Century and Us* with Pam Schweitzer, a well-known producer of reminiscence projects in the theatre, community and institutional settings. The play dramatizes their memories through their words and, in so doing, presents a history of the 20th century which is both personal and public. Some memories are collective, others are quite individual. With songs and stories the play begins at the time of the performers' births in the 1920s and early 1930s, tracks through their growing-up years, their World War II experiences, their working lives and the changing pattern of family life, up to the present day. It is designed for audiences of older people, deliberately making links with audiences through shared experience and reinforcing messages with the help of contemporary songs and music. I was co-organiser of an international conference on "Biographical Methods and Professional Practice" held in London in October 2000. We invited *The Good Companions* to present this play as part of the programme.

As a member of the audience, I have a first-hand impression of the dynamics of the event. My understanding of the process has been further built up from reports and interviews with those involved. The experience was both moving and enlightening. Although we were confident about the skills of the performers and the relevance of the play to the content of our conference, we were worried that a group of amateur players, older people at that, might not be well received by the delegates. We should have addressed our own prejudices instead. The performance was wildly received by a group of academics, whose emotional responses belied the objectivity and detachment of their own highly professionalized presentations. Clearly something was at work here. The stories narrated by the performers had meanings which communicated across national and international boundaries with people whose backgrounds and ages implied quite different experiences of the 20th century. The performance ended with a standing ovation and lively discussions between the audience and the ten performers. . . .

During the play, one of the women takes the stage on her own to describe her experience of divorce in the 1950s. She describes the stigma, the exclusion and rejection which her erstwhile friends and neighbours visited on her. The other performers then joined in with brief exchanges to illustrate this cold and wounding behaviour.

The background to this scene was complex, as we discovered. In devising the play, the performers had discussed at some length how personal the play should be. In particular, in playing out her own real experience of divorce, was this actor in danger of "re-living" her humiliation and pain? In the end the scene was included and, in my view, the play was the better for it. Divorce in the middle years of the 20th century was difficult for many people, men and women. The performers recognized this and, for a while, the balance of the play shifted away from celebration and humour.

The process of arriving at this particular scene involved interrogation, on an individual and group basis. More than that, the scene inevitably interrogates audiences that include people who themselves are divorced or who have to come to terms with their own actions in relation to divorcing neighbours and relatives. The process of reminiscence is also interrogative and, while the individual account stands out as a performative act (whether in a play, a group or in a one-to-one exchange), the extent of that interrogation is set by the individuals taking part. Indeed, the background to the performance illustrates that people arrive at some kind of reconciliation with past life events by taking different paths. *The Good Companions* actor who played out her experience of divorce had not previously found a way to talk about this painful experience. The process of interrogation from her group members[,] and the shaping of the account for wider audiences, provided her with the means. Working in a reminiscence context enabled her to find a method, in this case a public performance.

In summary, this review of the methods of oral historians and reminiscence workers suggests that there are aspects which can usefully be shared. Awareness of the influence of age and life stage on how a story is narrated can help to broaden oral history, giving it relevance in policy and practice terms. Identifying the dialogic and interrogative nature of oral history helps to remind us that participation involves agency and decision-making, and that the interview is essentially an interactive process involving two parties, each with their own agendas and purposes.

13.2 Memory and transgression
from *The subversive practices of reminiscence theatre in Taiwan*
Wan-Jung Wang. (2006). *RIDE: Research in Drama Education, 11*(1), 77–87.

The background and context of the Uhan Shii Theatre Group

Taiwan has been ruled by different political regimes, undergoing colonisation by Japan and "re-colonisation" by the Kuomingtang nationalists (shortened to KMT) immediately after the Japanese occupation in the twentieth century. Culturally and historically, Taiwan has been influenced by Chinese and Japanese imperialism as well as "modernized" by Western neo-colonialism, and the hybrid culture of Taiwan indicates this post-coloniality. It was only after the lifting of Martial Law in 1987 that the Taiwanese began to reconstruct their own multiple histories and, as part of the process of decolonization[,] started to renegotiate a more secure sense of their own identities. The Uhan Shii Theatre Group was founded in this emerging movement of cultural decolonisation in the 1990s. [...]

The Uhan Shii Theatre Group is the first Taiwanese theatre company exclusively dedicated to the performance of the oral histories of community-based elders. By recovering and performing their buried memories, the company reconstructs Taiwanese historicised identity and, in the process, reaffirms it. [...]

In *Echoes of Taiwan VI – We Are Here*, [which] premiered in 2000, a migration epic story of Hakka (the second largest ethnic group in Taiwan) was delivered for the first time on the Taiwanese stage in the Hakka language. The story spans the past to the present, from the countryside to the metropolis, and the experience of Hakka women is the main focus. These women use their Hakka dialect to tell their life stories and project themselves into a public space, thereby countering their previous absence in public and creating a new spatial reproduction. They employ the Hakka language and singing to reclaim a space for Hakka women whose experiences and voices had been previously marginalised by the double oppressions of [Kuomintang]'s nationalism and patriarchy. They share their personal stories of migration, showing how they make a living in the metropolis and how they have moved from the confines of the domestic place to the public space. Furthermore, their numerous tours (the production has toured to remote Hakka villages for more than

50 performances and has travelled as far as Wupertale, Germany in 2001) has meant that their stories have been seen on various public platforms both in and out of Taiwan.

Echoes of Taiwan VI – We Are Here reveals the hidden tradition of adopted daughters in Hakka history for the first time on a Taiwanese stage. Some of the female cast are "adopted daughters" themselves, some of their mothers and sisters were "adopted daughters" who were given to another family in exchange for their labour. Sharing collective memories of this exploitative system of adoption helps them to come to terms with their suffering. In turn, the performance enables them to show the inner feelings of these exploited daughters through dramatic narratives and singing. In the scene of "Wrapping the Wound for the Little Girl," enacted by an all-female cast, they pass a long white strip of cloth towards each other slowly. It occupies and involves the whole stage and symbolises a cleansing meandering river. It represents a healing ritual to comfort their traumas. The healing space sometimes extends beyond the stage and reaches the audience who may have endured similar afflictions.

The production also portrays how Hakka women break free from their domestic constraints and economic dependency. Women start to make a living to support their families by tailoring or selling merchandise, and this is shown theatrically in Jyu-Ing's and Yu-Ching's stories, both of whom are self-reliant Hakka mothers and career women in real life. They either walk out of their domestic space and create their own career in the public domain or transform their domestic space into their workplace. In contrast with the confinement, financial worries, suppression and anger that Jyu-Ing had to put up with at home, she dances with her customers, using her tape-measure and mannequin to celebrate the economic independence she has gained by transforming her home into a tailor's studio.

In the last scene, the circling parade "Opening up the Bundle of Memory," projects the Hakka women's memories into the auditorium. Each woman opens a blue bundle, which traditional Hakka people wrap up and carry around their shoulders when they embark upon a far[-]away journey, and she shares her most treasured memory with the audience. Xiou-Ching's memory is a family photograph in which her mother holds her tight and loves her dearly; Jyu-Ing's blue bundle contains her diary which accompanies her migration journey from village to city. One after another, they circle around the auditorium and pass on the blue bundles to children as passing on their Hakka heritage. The procession encompasses the space with their memories of migration and projects them into their prospective futures. This play has toured around the metropolis and remote Hakka towns twice in the past five years with the intention of re-inscribing Taiwanese history with Hakka women's oral histories and re-affirming their identities through theatre practice.

These examples illustrate how the Uhan Shii Theatre Group not only presents the traditions of Taiwanese culture, but also subverts them by new representations of contemporary female experience.... . The presentation of the Taiwanese stories performed by the women themselves also subverts the "orientalist" imagination about Asian women and challenges passive stereotypes with which they are sometimes associated. Although the director Peng Ya-Ling never stresses their political aim as a "feminist group" (Wang, 2004), the process of women acting their own stories is part of a continual process of striving towards social justice and gender equality. Through these cultural and theatrical strategies the company intends to transcend binarism and open multiple choices and spaces for different voices in Taiwan.

13.3 Intergenerational reminiscence theatre
from *The process and impact of intergenerational theatre making*
Jonathan Petherbridge & David Kendall. (2012). *Quality in Ageing and Older Adults,*
13(4), 301–306.

Brenda sits at the back of the air raid shelter – she has a chair unlike the other younger shelterers, who are squashed down on the stone floor. Around them the air raid is at its climax and, partly in defiance and partly for something to do, the people begin to sing Underneath the Arches, which seems appropriate. A young girl with red pigtails is exhorted to get up and dance – she taps with some skill as the others watch. This is also Brenda, but as a ten year old, some 70 years ago. As the older Brenda watches her doppelganger a third manifestation is heard, the voice of Brenda recorded two months ago telling the story of how she would dance in the shelter for the entertainment of the community. And another community is watching now, an auditorium full, some are friends and family of the cast, many are from the neighbourhood and among them are people you do not often see at the theatre – older people, silver haired, singing along and commenting on the action with some authority – and why not, not only were they there, they also helped create the show.

Brenda not only contributed to the script but ended up in the cast. Oh and helped with the marketing. Provided some props … and got reviewers along and came to the House of Lords to pick up the United for All Ages plaque which the project was awarded. And Brenda is not in the prime of life, she lives alone on the top floor of a block of flats around the corner from London Bubble Theatre Company, and has tried to join various drama projects but they would not have her – "something about insurance" she tells us. But thank heavens Bubble and Brenda found each other because both parties and many other have benefitted enormously.

London Bubble creates theatre in partnership with their community. The company runs a range of groups for all ages, year round. They deliver projects in schools to children who are having communication problems and large-scale performances to audiences in public spaces. They deliver over 600 events a year. Running through the company's work is a belief that theatre is a social art that can connect people and create well being.

The air raid scene was part of *Blackbirds*, a show that emerged from an intergenerational oral history project called Grandchildren of the Blitz. The project ran over 18 months and involved over 200 people in a range of tasks from map making to cooking via storytelling and hairdressing. Funded principally by the Heritage Lottery Fund the project set out to share, and explore, some of the events that befell Bermondsey during the bombing of 1940–1941, popularly known as the Blitz. It was driven by a theatre company who have been working in the area for 26 years, London Bubble. They started by connecting children with older people who had been their age during the Blitz. The children were armed with solid state recorders, microphones and a training in oral history. In pairs the young interviewers talked to 19 older people and were shown photographs, artefacts and of course were told stories. These stories were transcribed by other volunteers and posted on a newly built web site (www.grandchildrenoftheblitz.co.uk) along with maps, articles and images. If the project had stopped at this stage some good would already have been done – new encounters, some friendships and knowledge had been shared and there was a wider awareness of what had happened to the streets we use daily and the people who had endured this trauma within living memory. But the gathering of the testimony was only the first of three stages as the intention was to develop the stories into a script and then create a full production to be shared with a local audience.

The second part of the journey saw an intergenerational group of 25 community actors drawn from the Bubble's workshop groups, collaborating with a specialist writer and director to turn the testimony into scenes. To begin with this did not work, various attempts to re-enact stories or present action that illustrated the recorded voices trivialised the material and made poor theatre. After a handful of sessions a different tack was taken and the focus fell on one street, Mayflower Street, situated behind the company's rehearsal room, leading down to the Thames and now full of small modern houses. Iris, a retired teacher and Bubble stalwart, visited the local history library and found the names of the families, a record of the bombs that had hit and an account of a parachute bomb that had caught on a Wharf side crane that stood at the end of the street, dangling there unexploded for days. The group visited the street, shared the history and divided themselves into households. Now the testimony had a context, the actors had a world to work on and the script started to take shape.

The stories that had been gathered were personal testimonies. They were more than words or photographic images, and finding an appropriate way to share them was difficult. Some were gruesome, some funny. There was the mundane, the obscure and the appalling. But they were human, flawed, wonderful, and occasionally, annoying. Working with an ever growing cohort of community actors, who were themselves flawed, wonderful and occasionally annoying, felt appropriate. And, theatre, rather than a book or exhibition, seemed the right medium. The show would gather a live audience to attend to actors sharing events that had scarred local people and the local area. Performance was big enough to contain and do justice to the stories. Rather than the stories overwhelming us we would deal with them together.

The process also addressed many of the issues that can keep generations apart. Technology, accessibility, not having a reason to talk to someone from a different age group, the assumed difference and distrust of that difference. All these melted away in the face of a shared task. To take technology for example, lapel microphones and recording devices were used in the interviews, a web site became a repository of testimony and messages, the web site became the subject of a small road show to homes and lunch clubs, showing older people how to explore the site and leave comments, and finally the production used projection and a sophisticated sound track to evoke the period and retell the stories.

The script which was now called *Blackbird ...* was being worked on by a loose collective of 40 – children as young as 8, teenagers, adults and super adults in their 80s. Bubble have created intergenerational projects before and it usually leads to a wonderful working dynamic where children take more responsibility and adults are allowed to play. But it also means that all have to look after and support each other through rehearsals, line learning, car sharing and illness. The success of the production rests partly on the togetherness of the cast. But it was also important to look beyond the rehearsal room and as the project developed it became clear that some of the original older contributors could not, or did not want to, perform. The response was a series of practical workshops, exploring wartime life skills, under the umbrella title *Make Do and Mend*. These had two valuable outcomes: firstly older people re-connected with the project, secondly young people learned about hair, make-up, dancing and cooking. All of which added authenticity and depth to the production. And it was fun – at Christmas, a party was preceded by a workshop making wartime Christmas decorations, and again, this simple shared task provided an excuse for older and younger to exchange skills and stories with a shared purpose and outcome.

Blackbirds was performed 16 times to a total audience of just under 1,600 people. The tour of local venues was originally intended to include just six performances, this was extended twice and all but a few performances sold out – this was a "hot ticket". [...]

At the curtain call at the end of *Blackbirds*, photographs of the older people who had told their stories were projected on to the back wall of the stage. Often one or more would be in the audience sometimes with friends or family, and it was a true moment of community as they were applauded for the contribution they had made not only to the project but also to the war effort in Bermondsey. [...]

The process of the extended and open conversation between generations brought benefits and well being to all. As Brenda will tell you:

> We sheltered mostly in the railway arches, which are still there, on the other side of the road. The one we used to use was the metal working factory, sheet metal, cutting metal for industry and we went there at night for company and this was heaven to me because I always wanted to entertain; singing and dancing and being on the stage was my aim in life. So I pretended that I was in the theatre. I had no costume of course but it was all in the mind. I used to go a lot behind all the machinery, pretend that I was in my dressing

room, and then I would come out and sing and dance to the people who were sheltering and it cheered them up; and it took their minds off the raid. They would join in; so you see you couldn't shut me up ....

13.4 Uncharted territory of widowhood
from *Translating research findings into community based theatre: More than a dead man's wife*
Susan Feldman, Alan Hopgood & Marissa Dickins. (2013). *Journal of Aging Studies, 27,* 476–486.

Giving a voice to older widowed women
[The researchers in this project] encouraged older women to talk about widowhood from a broader perspective than the conventional focus on loss, grief or health problems. It was considered important to describe how older women themselves make sense of the shift from being married to widowed and to link these accounts to wider social, cultural and relational contexts. [...]
A whiteboard and butcher's paper were used to record key points of discussion. Detailed field notes were kept, and every discussion was tape recorded and subsequently transcribed in full. These processes generated two main types of data. One form comprised lists of issues and themes generated in all of the group sessions, schematic diagrams of the web of inter-relating factors and issues identified by the groups themselves, and a rank ordering (by the women) of the key issues that they saw as impacting on their lives as widowed women. The second consisted of a rich dialog that had taken place between the women – it is this second level that provided the basis for the dialog within the play (Feldman, 2005). [...]

'Wicked Widows' – A play about widowhood
The theatre production 'Wicked Widows' was created from the data and findings of Susan Feldman's doctoral dissertation *More Than a Dead Man's Wife: Older Australian Women Talk About Widowhood* (Feldman, 2005) and translated into a play by a leading Australian playwright and actor Alan Hopgood. [...]
The storyline concentrates on what the women said about their shift from wife to widowhood following the death of their spouse and in particular addresses issues of identity and being a single older woman who now bears the label of "widow". The themes of the play are drawn directly from the research findings generated by the study and include the three dominant themes as already mentioned, combined with sub-themes including overall social and emotional wellbeing.
'Wicked Widows' has toured many urban and rural communities, the performances attracting approximately 6000 individuals in over 40 locations .... The play runs for 60 minutes and has been staged in a wide range of venues including small rural halls,

churches and community centers. At times the audiences ranged in size from less than 30 people to capacity crowds of over 400 in community arts centers and theatres. [...]

From research to theatre: Script development

As an integral component to the process of script development, Alan constructed the characters of three widowed women of different ages and lengths of time since the death of their husbands. He then created a series of dramatic situations into which particular narrative conversations of the 58 study participants could be compressed. [...]

The setting of the play is a restaurant and the meeting of the three women over lunch. As the story unfolds, the focus shifts to one of the woman who – as a 'widow virgin' – does not want to be there and has been tricked into coming (ostensibly for her own good). It is because of her presence that the other two characters are able to tell their own stories, slowly engaging the third character in the conversation through the use of humor and gentle persistence. Through the telling of their personal stories two of the women (constructed from the research narratives) are eventually able to reassure the third woman, settle her, and by the end of the meal she is comfortable enough to share her very recent and still raw experiences of widowhood with them. [...]

Central to the women's experience of widowhood was the concept of independence and autonomy. This was expressed through talk about their reticence to accept help from family and friends. Reliance on others was seen by some as a risk to their independence – even in the face of deteriorating health.

Issues such as needing assistance with transportation, continuing to drive despite their deteriorating health or the challenges of public transport usage were examples used by the women, who navigated the balance between protecting their independence and accepting help from those around them. This narrative and its translation into script can be seen in Table 1. [...]

Audience reception

[A]udiences described how they found the play enjoyable, true to life, useful in learning about widowhood, affirmed and acknowledged their experience and afforded them an opportunity to reflect on their circumstances and life journey. Additionally, the forums facilitated by both the playwright and the researcher, which followed each performance, more often than not generated lively and lengthy audience discussion with individuals contributing their personal experiences and observations, despite the potentially challenging and difficult topic concerning the death of a spouse.

The actors returned to the stage during these forums and participated in the discussions. On many occasions members of the audience directed questions about how they prepare for the role of older widowed women and in particular asked if any of them had in fact been widowed themselves. [...]

Table 1

Independence and autonomy (asking for help).

Research data	*Wicked Widows* script
Jenny: Well I will tell you, and that is asking for help. Asking for help.	JENNY What's become more important to you all since your husband died?
Group: ((Long laughter))	CAROL Asking for help. When you've been independent all your life that's very, very hard. If I haven't got the car, people say — "Can I give you a lift home?" And they go right out of their way and you feel you're imposing and they're doing you such a favor.
Group: ((Individual women indistinguishable)) Yes, we know how hard that is.	
Paula: When you've been independent all your life that's very hard, very hard.	MILLIE Or it didn't fit into their time table to take that extra time to get home.
Ruth: It is <u>very difficult</u> if you've been independent all your life, even though I never drove before. There's a real struggle to start saying to people 'I need help'. Because I've got diabetes, asthma,	CAROL Then they start telling you how expensive it is to run a car.
osteoporosis and <u>suddenly</u> all these things are really very up front for me now, and, yes, asking for that help, it's very difficult =	And then you say — "oh, I know."
Paula: =Yes, I know people say to me, can I give you a lift home? and they're right out of their way and you feel that you are imposing and they're doing you such a favor. And then they start telling you how expensive it is to run a car. I think you	"You know? Have you got a car?"
are better off being independent =	"Yes."
Priscilla: = Excuse me but I don't mean to go to your friends, you can go to lectures, it is about how to manage these things and other things.	"Why aren't you driving it?" – without saying – "Instead of taking us out of our way when it's so expensive to run a car!"
Q: Paula, were you talking about the same thing or something a little bit different here?	And you can't say — "Because I thought some generous person like you would be happy to give some old duck like me a lift instead of making it look like a pain in the arse."
Ellen It's difficult, but is it important?	What do they expect me to do? Ride a bike? (to MILLIE) Would you ride a bike?
Paula: Yes I feel it is. Yes I do.	
Priscilla: Excuse me, how do you mean by asking for help, be it medically or from your friends?	MILLIE If I'm in the right place, alongside the river. CAROL I think it's stupid to ride bikes. Too dangerous.
Paula: No more to do with perhaps needing to get that lift because I've driven all my life.	
Annie: Oh yes. Oh yes.	MILLIE Taxis are worse. CAROL Taxis aren't dangerous.
Paula: Some days the asthma's not really good and yet I <u>still want to maintain my contacts</u>.	
Priscilla: Have you gone to any specialists <u>or what</u>?	MILLIE No, you try to get one for a short journey. That look you get. There's danger behind that look!
Paula: Oh yes I have all of that. What I'm talking about is to go and say to a friend I'd love <u>to go to this and can you give me a lift</u>. Yes you can do it but it is relying on others.	
Group: ((Individual women indistinguishable)) Yes, yes, Not good to do that.	

[T]his project recognizes that theatre has the potential to acknowledge the universality of the human condition and in particular the aging experience by encouraging audiences – friends, family and community – to think both about their own aging and to consider what life might be like for them as individuals who have outlived a spouse.

Further Reading

Gjaerum, R. (2013). Recalling memories through reminiscence theatre. *InFormation: Nordic Journal of Art and Research, 2*(2), 214–243.

Kelin, D.A. (2005). *To feel as our ancestors did: Collecting and performing oral histories.* Portsmouth, NH: Heinemann. Useful information on the important and tactful ways of engendering memories and respecting the stories.

Mangan, M. (2013). *Staging ageing: Theatre, performance and the narrative of decline.* Bristol, UK: Intellect.

Nicholson, H. (2012). The performance of memory: Drama, reminiscence and autobiography. *NJ: Drama Australia Journal, 36*, 62–74. Retrieved from http://search.informit.com. au/documentSummary;dn=340948664097419;res=IELHSS.

Schweitzer, P. (2007). *Reminiscence theatre: Making theatre from memories.* London, UK: Jessica Kingsley. The text pretty well covers the waterfront. Pam Schweitzer, who began her career in Theatre in Education, has been working in reminiscence theatre for over 20 years, and this is a compendium of her experiences with many case studies.

Strimling, A. (2004). *Roots and branches: Creating multigenerational theatre.* Portsmouth, NH: Heinemann. A practical text that includes workshop and playbuilding activities with an appendix of monologues and scenes.

Questions for Reflection and Discussion

1. Who is the oldest person you know, what is your relationship with this person, and how much do you know about her or him?

2. When is old, "old"? What may be some of your biases and fears around aging?

3. What are some foundations for ethical practice when working with senior participants, some of whom may have impaired memory? What do we need to keep

in mind if a participant shares a painful memory that has strong dramatic potential?

4. In a culture that focuses on celebrating youth, what responsibility do reminiscence theatre workers have to counter the invisibility of the elderly? What positive examples of vital and engaged seniors can you contribute to the discussion?

Suggested Activities

1. Working collaboratively with others, identify two potential partner groups (e.g., an elementary school, high school, youth or university group and a neighborhood senior care facility) for an intergenerational reminiscence theatre project in your community. Write a letter of invitation to each, outlining the structure of the project and its benefits to those involved.

2. Working with a partner, generate a list of questions from which to conduct an interview focused on eliciting life memories. Using these, carry out an interview – ideally, with a senior member of your family. You might like to practice first with another pair.

3. Gather some examples from film, television, plays and other sources (novels, short stories, etc.) where senior characters are *central*, rather than peripheral. Present your research in a creative way – dramatically or visually (as in a poster) – in order to generate a discussion. How are these characters portrayed? What are the stereotypes and prejudices often embedded in these representations?

Web Resources

Age Exchange, The, London, UK http://www.age-exchange.org.uk/

Reminiscence Theatre Archive, UK http://vimeo.com/user14979645

Senior Theatre Resource Center, USA http://www.seniortheatre.com/

Target Theatre, Victoria, BC http://www.targettheatre.ca/

Western Gold Theatre, Vancouver, BC http://www.WesternGoldTheatre.org

PART FOUR

Challenges for Practice

CHAPTER FOURTEEN
PARTICIPATION, AESTHETICS, ETHICS AND ASSESSMENT

Introduction

You will have noticed in every case study that participation, aesthetics, ethics, and assessment are present in some form or other. These four motifs raise issues that are central to the practices of applied theatre. Much of what this chapter addresses falls with the designation of "contested" applications, in the sense that while most agree that these four areas are significant, there is often disagreement about who or what they represent in applied theatre and how to go about structuring the work in ways that address these issues. Certainly, as a first motif, **participation** throughout all stages of a performance project is an ingredient that makes applied theatre work markedly different from mainstream theatre. Big Brum Theatre reminds us of that when, in its mandate, it speaks of the fluid boundary that allows audiences to become active participants within the safety of the fictional action (Big Brum Theatre, n.d.).

> [D]rama is a politically incorrect and corrupting medium; it corrupts the certainties of received truths and identities with both dangers and possibilities... It even-handedly shows the commonalities as well as the differences: our common humanness within the very otherness. But of course, like the contents of Pandora's box, drama is powerful and it is morally neutral so we have to be careful how we use it.
>
> John O'Toole, 2004, pp. 11–12

The second motif is that of **aesthetics**. Lowell Swortzell in Jackson (1993) regretted the difficulties he had in "trying to like" Theatre in Education performances, but he found it hard to accept the poor production values and the seeming lack of aesthetic sensibility. Why should schools not expect the very best production values, he wondered? In current applied theatre performances, his objections can still hold true, but Denzin (1997) suggests that we "suspend normal aesthetic frameworks so that co-participatory performances can be produced" (p. 121). Whatever conclusions we come to, Jackson (1999), in discussing the educational experience of theatre, points out that the "aesthetic dimension must form an integral part of any serious evaluation" (p. 51). Feelings cannot be separated from thought or intellect, but are, to put it crudely, the "glue" that makes things stick in the memory and accumulated remembered experiences comprise our learning (Damasio, 1999, pp. 54–56). Aesthetic learning enables us to see not only ourselves but also to reflect on the perspectives of others, helping us to wonder and imagine things "as if they could be otherwise" (Greene, 1988, p. 3). Does that mean we have to see aesthetic appreciation differently in applied theatre?

Small miracles and changes [in applied theatre] suggest a need to check against unrealistic claims, and to ensure that the aesthetic is interdependent with the possibilities of social engagement.

Michael Balfour, 2009, p. 356

"It has been claimed that the aesthetic enables individuals to reflect on the contrast between the conditions of everyday life and human potential and, as such, it acts as a powerful means of educating the political imagination" (Nicholson, 1999, p. 83). But the imagination, as we all know from our own experiences, can generate negative as well as positive visions. Applied theatre practices tend to be seen as always beneficial, and certainly, it is unlikely that anyone would want to engage in a social practice that was not so. Yet theatre is, as O'Toole (2004) says, "morally neutral and so we have to be careful how we use it" (p. 12). And as Eagleton (2008) reminds us, a lethal weapon is the result of an act of the imagination. The implications of that recognition demand that we pay more attention to the **ethics** suffusing our work than perhaps we have heretofore. We need to be more careful, for example, in examining the way in which power is held and distributed, whose agendas are really being served by what we do, and how we leave the project sites.

Lastly, how do we value what we do? By what criteria do we judge the effectiveness of the work? What are the implications of short-term results when laid against what traces remain years later? What claims can we make for "transformation" when the money has run out, the project is over and the facilitators have moved on? What is the language we are using to describe what we do and how is it helpful? What language is demanded by those to whom we are accountable? How can the languages of others assist us to make our case and how can we negotiate these languages so that everyone is clear about the results? Such questions lie at the heart of our fourth motif: **assessment.**

Assessment is an important element in the acquisition of funds and in justifying those expenditures. More significantly, how we assess, what we assess and how we frame our assessments are central to effective research that will, in turn, promote advocacy that can stand on firm ground. At a purely personal level, we have a need to find satisfaction in what we do. With appropriate assessment, the field of applied theatre will grow and develop. Without it, the field will always remain vulnerable, subject to the economic bottom line and the whims of those who can help us to make this work happen: institutions; communities; donor organizations; and the prospective participants themselves.

Of course these four motifs are always bound together, but this chapter attempts to separate them so that we can see them more clearly. We acknowledge that, in doing so, something may be lost.

14.1 Participation

The goal of the participatory component of applied theatre practice is one in which all those engaged with the performance (community sources, players and audiences) are moved to become active and reflective through "wrestl[ing] with the consequences of their choices and actions" (Haedicke, 2003, p. 79). In the traditional mainstream theatre (especially that of the western world from the late nineteenth century on), audiences have been defined by their passivity, their submission to "theatre rules." We ask our audiences to come on time, sit still, refrain from talking (either to each other or to the actors), refrain from eating or drinking, to pay attention and to suspend their disbelief. In order to help the audience to focus and to discourage any interaction, we place them in rows facing towards the stage, an arrangement that also makes it difficult for them to move around. They sit in darkness while the stage is lit in order to command their attention to the place and action that matters. While there is an understanding that a performance needs an audience in order to complete the act, and that what is happening on stage is a reflection of the human condition of which the play and actors are representative, audiences in mainstream theatre are often viewed merely as "bums on seats" rather than as co-creators in the meaning-making (Butsch, 2000; Prendergast, 2008).

Paulus (2006) suggests that only when theatre is prepared to refocus its attention on the audience by waking them up and allowing them freedom of movement and choice; only when "the rules of audience etiquette" are rethought and the audience is regarded as co-collaborators, can the "flow of energy that can only happen live in the presence of both parties" actually occur (p. 335). When it is clear to the audience that their presence is both appreciated and necessary, effective participation practices should allow audiences to decide the level of their involvement for themselves (p. 340). For performer-participants in applied theatre, whose lives and words are the material of the performance, questions of ownership may arise. And while Jackson (2000) reminds us that this work is so localized that it does not generally "outlive its historical moment" (p. 104), ownership can be a point of ethical contention if it is reproduced as script or as material for scholars; for example, in conference presentations and/or peer-reviewed publications.

> In a productive postshow, audiences talk back, talk to each other and (with good facilitation) also listen to one another, making sense together of common experience...
>
> Janna Goodwin, 2004, p. 317

When audiences become participants, we must honour the culture, rituals and characteristics of their context in order to enhance the flow of meaning. The audience is the source and the judge of the process and the performance. Their feedback needs to be constantly encouraged and not seen as something that only happens at "appropriate" or "safe" moments. For facilitators, this level of participation can be very difficult, as it requires an open mind, ability to put aside one's own agenda(s), and the grace to see value in critical responses.

Participation in applied theatre is not just confined to audiences, however. For many applied theatre companies, their partnerships within the local community are central to their practice, especially when members of that community become resources for the information upon which the work is based and may also be performers in the project. Time must be taken to ensure that each of the parties involved are clear about "what's up" and how everyone will be included within the communication loop. Maiter et al. (2008), in their examination of the ethics of community-based participatory action research, point out the importance of this kind of contextual knowing for strengthening community partnerships that can only be productively built through taking time to build relationships and communicative networks (pp. 307–310). Central to this partnership must be the recognition that things may turn out differently from the original expectations. If people are included in the design and planning as experts in their own cultures, they will be aware of these shifts – when they occur, how the direction has changed and why. To accept engagement with a creative process means that surprises are to be expected; how the partnerships are to be kept informed must be a part of the structuring of the project. One of the most important elements of feedback is that the stories and words that are drawn from the community must be "served back" to them before public performances as a way of checking the authenticity of the work and receiving permission for use. It is here that those whose stories are involved have the opportunity to withdraw them if they are not comfortable with having them played publicly. This is one of those matters that mesh participation, aesthetics and ethics; scenes that are aesthetically "right" may have to go because, ethically, it would not be right to use them.

Often, in addition to building a relationship with the community, there will be a partnership with a funding body, donor organization or institution. Again, the agendas need to be opened up for scrutiny and a continuing means of information exchange agreed upon. This does not mean that, having proposed and been accepted, the facilitator(s) are expected to be in touch with funders constantly and, indeed, such a thing may not be possible for many reasons. But the context that surrounds an applied theatre project must be a participatory one for all involved if the work is to be effective and seen to be effective. The best working partnerships are those in which the conditions for participation are followed. Dudley Cocke (2004) writes eloquently about these issues in his discussion of how art interacts

> Whether an applied theatre practice allows for the more radical possibilities of participation within a project depends on the ideological intentions of the project (and the interests being served in it), the scope of the work and the openness of the creative strategies offered.
>
> Sheila Preston, 2009, p. 129

with democracy in applied theatre work. And recent books on ensemble theatre making also offer excellent strategies for encouraging and maintaining full participation (Britton, 2013; Bonczek & Storck, 2013; O'Connor, 2010).

By participating in building and/or performing a fictional or parallel world, audiences (and players) gain the kind of distance that sets them free from their own bodies, specific situations and lives. It is this distance that allows participants to explore areas that, in real life, may have remained hidden or unexamined, perhaps through ignorance or fear (Haedicke, 2003).

14.2 Artistry and aesthetics

In traditional theatre, the focus is on the artistic making with a trust that if done "well," those attending the performance will have an aesthetic experience. Actors and directors meet together to interpret a scene artistically but, of course, the receptive aesthetic is at work in the process of creating a piece of theatre as much as it affects an audience's response. Maxine Greene (2001) defines this experience as new connections made, new patterns formed, new vistas opened; after an aesthetic experience, "persons see differently, resonate differently" (p. 6). The idea that "aesthetics" refers to the sensory, centring on the visceral and physical (Neelands & Goode, 1995, pp. 42, 44), places the practices of applied theatre as part of what Eric Booth (1999) calls "the everyday work of art," where the aesthetic lies not necessarily in an escape from reality but often in a return to it. When we find ways to talk about our hopes and dreams, our desires and wants and to share these through theatre as process and as product, we discover that we can make a difference to other's lives. In applied theatre, this can make it extremely difficult for any viewers who do not share the context – who come to the work as "outsiders," as accidental audiences.

> We should be clear about the fact that the Aesthetic Process is not the Work of Art. Its importance and its value reside in its stimulation and development of perceptive and creative capacities which may be atrophied in the subject—in developing the capacity, however small it may be, that every subject has for metaphorising reality. We are all artists, but few of us exercise our aesthetic capacities.
>
> Augusto Boal, 2006, p. 18

In the early days of what in Canada was then called "popular theatre," a group of women created a play from their experiences of domestic violence. The work was incredibly powerful for them, their small, mainly female audiences, and for the facilitators. The women were persuaded to show their play as part of a conference of theatre scholars. But the scholarly audience had difficulty hearing the actors, the acting was unskilled and the production values completely absent. They saw the presentation as raw and unframed; they were confronted with a theatre experience they did not recognize and the subject matter was presented without the distancing devices of traditional production, leaving the audience with no idea of how to respond. For that accidental audience, there was no "aesthetic" present. And yet for the integral audiences who first saw the work, there was an immediate recognition that promoted a powerful response both at a feeling and a thinking level. What creates this apparent dichotomy?

In mainstream theatre that is required to connect with an accidental audience – whoever it is that happens by – the work of transmitting the message can be extremely difficult. You will remember, of course, being told that the first 15 minutes of any play are the hardest – hardest for audiences "getting the picture" and hardest for actors helping them to do so. A traditional performance experience follows the taxonomy of engagement (Morgan & Saxton, 1987) by first attracting your interest, then engaging you (generally through its theatricality, force of argument or subtle manipulation of the elements of tension, contrast and/or symbolization). Once engaged, you have to be held long enough in the logic of what is happening for you to commit to the "idea" or world you are seeing and hearing; only then can you begin to internalize, unconsciously laying your own experience against that of the play to discover its truth by gathering its meanings – another way to say you begin to "get the message" (pp. 21–29).

> In terms of practice, a sole concentration on social utility is in danger of abandoning the terrain of sensation: of the aesthetic concerns for beauty, joy, pleasure, awe and astonishment.
>
> James Thompson, 2009, p. 129

In applied theatre, the first three parts of the taxonomy are almost always already in place; that is to say (unlike, for example, that audience of bewildered scholars), an integral audience is already interested and engaged (we recognize this, it is about us and concerns us). For the most part, they are committed to the content (if it's about us, we should listen) whether it is a celebration or a critique, and so the messages begin to arrive almost at once.

Christine Bailey (1987), writing about what is now called reminiscence theatre, says, "Those who feel the art object ... is a self-contained entity separate from its extrinsic contexts, will have difficulty seeing [applied] theatre as an artistic medium." "The seeming banality (at times), of [applied theatre] presentations," Bailey suggests, "is minimized because the audience is sympathetic to both the presentations and their sub-texts." As a result, she goes on, "an interaction takes place between performer and spectator that is an integral part of the process ... [and] for those involved, it is an aesthetic experience. The intensity and degree of that experience varies from individual to individual and depends on the degree to which performers [and audiences] connect with the performance" (pp. 19–20). It is the full aesthetic impact of a performance that makes itself felt, as Jackson (2005) puts it, through the "'liveness' of the event, the emotional resonances it can offer, the dialogues that can be generated [either within or after the performance] and the complexity of texture that defies easy closure" (p. 117).

14.3 Ethics

"Ethics" refers to the principles or values by which a culture or group agrees to function, as in professional codes of conduct. "Ethical" refers to the ways in which someone functions in accordance with the cultural values or standards of the group. "Morals" and "morally" can be used interchangeably with ethics and ethically (see any dictionary definition), but for most people, morality suggests a set of values that has some sort of religious connotation (Hart, 2000, p. 96). We need to remember, however, that there are many people today who are extremely ethical and yet would not admit to a religious belief.

> [T]here is always the need to be vigilant about whether the practice is accepted as a generous exercise of care or whether, however well-intentioned, it is regarded as an unwelcome intrusion. It is easy for trust to become dependence, for generosity to be interpreted as patronage, for interest in others, to be experienced as the gaze of surveillance.
>
> Helen Nicholson, 2005, p. 160

All of us, whoever we are and wherever we live, conduct our lives by a set of standards. The standards under which we operate – often without even thinking about them – may be very different from those that govern the lives of the people with whom we are working. As facilitator Hartley (2012) remarks, "Learning not to judge success by my own understanding of what that is has been difficult and will probably continue to be so" (p. 143). Applied theatre practitioners work with groups in their cultural contexts all the time and that "being inside" means that the ways in which facilitators conduct themselves are open to scrutiny. Facilitators generally are invited or appointed to work with a community, usually one with which they are not familiar; for instance, in a facilitating role, you may need to work in an institution such as a prison or a museum or with a group of people in a country different from your own. Even before you begin this work, you need to be clear about your own understanding of what is important to you, what it is that you value and see as fair, what it is that you are prepared to give up. You need to create a sense of safety for yourself and others that will free you and them to work at optimum.

Equally, the group and the individuals within that group may be governed by different views from you (and from each other) of what is important and valuable. You need always to be aware not only of those standards but what the implications of living within those standards mean. No group of people is wholly homogenous and it is helpful to discover how the community defines itself as a "community" – what does that mean to them and how is it manifested? For example, you may see the independence of women in a very different way from the societal group with whom you are working.

> [The work] was not about judging right or wrong, but rather about encouraging an understanding of ourselves and others, as well as an acknowledgment of different perceptions, if not acceptance of them.
>
> Jennifer Hartley, 2012, p. 17

Always the work follows what it is that the group *together* with the facilitator develops and sometimes that work begins to move in directions that are different from what you had in mind. How prepared are you to follow the group's interest and, if it applies, to support that shift when reporting back to your funding agency? This is a particularly difficult question if the work you are doing is funded by an agency that has its own agenda, standards and educational history. In HIV/AIDS education in Africa, for example, there has been difficulty with the government funding received from the United States. This funding is generous and well-intentioned; however, when the condition of funding promotes abstinence over condom use the funding recipients may find themselves between the proverbial "rock and a hard place" (Dalrymple, 2005).

Ethical practice depends upon *reflection* as a key means of intra- and inter-personal discovery, not only for the facilitator but also for the group. But many may not find reflection very easy or desirable, in that it may pull up issues that have been deliberately hidden or cause participants to see things about themselves that they have heretofore self-censored. Safety in these instances is both imperative and an ethical requirement if insight is to be encouraged and supported. Maiter et al. (2008) suggest that reciprocity and trust are fundamental to effective ethical practice. Trust must be carefully built between facilitator and group and between the participants so that an atmosphere is built in which everyone feels comfortable in expressing their ideas, feelings and actions without censure. With trust established, the feedback loops can then become reciprocal – exchanges that are open and in which the power is equally shared. Power-sharing is possible because everyone is aware and informed about the process as it is taking place. While this is easy to describe in words, it is extremely difficult in practice (Prendergast & Saxton, 2013, Ch. 4).

Whether we are facilitators or facilitator-researchers, "the very last thing we might aim to do is 'dominate' but the ethical dilemmas we invariably face demand that we choose to acknowledge and trouble the power inherent in our ... roles," writes Gallagher (2006, p. 97), reminding us that we facilitators must ever be aware of our status positions. Awareness through continuous reflection is one way to keep our work, ourselves and our fellow-participants in ethical balance. Gallagher also reminds us of Conquergood's (1985) four "ethical pitfalls" – the Custodian's Rip-off (using texts [often sacred] without permission); the Enthusiast's Infatuation (trivializing the lives of participants by allowing our enthusiasm to prevent us from becoming deeply involved in their cultural setting); the Curator's Exhibitionism (presenting the material as a kind of curiosity for others to wonder at); and the Skeptic's Cop-out (refusing to face up to the "ethical tensions and moral ambiguities of performing culturally sensitive materials") (p. 8).

In the end, ethical practice is about being aware that "every time a text is performed, a performance ethics is enacted" (Denzin, 1997, p. 120), reminding us to ask the question, "What are we doing here in someone else's cultural context?" and to take responsibility for what is interpreted, what points of view are espoused, and who it is that makes up our audience (p. 121). Denzin concludes by writing, "empowerment begins in that ethical moment when individuals are led into the troubling spaces once occupied by others.

In the moment of co-performing, lives are joined and the struggle [begins] anew" (p. 122). How we co-perform is, Denzin suggests, a matter of seeing that what we perform is "dialogic." He means that we need to be aware at all times that we are not "speaking about," but rather, "to and with others, keeping [the work] open-ended; critiquing, interrupting and empowering" (p. 121). Through those facilitated dialogues emerge the questions that participants need to ask and the language with which to ask them. The ethical demands of applied theatre practice are energy, imagination, commitment and the ability, as Greene (1995, p. 31) puts it, to decentre ourselves in the interests of the greater good – a good that derives from the participants' communally agreed-upon agenda.

14.4 Assessment/Evaluation

How can we assess the impact of applied theatre work, not just in terms of what an applied theatre performance transmits (the learning) but also in terms of its aesthetic impact (the reception)? Elliot Eisner (2007) is perhaps the most helpful when he writes, "there is no hard and fast distinction between assessment and evaluation, but there is a tendency to think about assessment as pertaining to judgments about individuals and evaluation as pertaining to the appraisals of programs" (p. 423).

By risk I'm referring to bold choices that challenge the status quo, that subvert the expected, that attempt to reveal new layers of meaning, that provoke questions, that disorient and reorient us. They are bold choices that, given their ambition or volatility, might not pan out as expected.

Jordan Tannahill, 2015, p. 18

Whatever the kind of theatre we practice, one of the most persistent questions is, "Well, how did it work?" In applied theatre practice, there are many things that we could talk about in answer to this question and many areas of assessment and/or evaluation. Each of those areas can be fraught with difficulty because, as Nicholson (1999) points out, whatever we are assessing or evaluating is "bound" by the context, the conditions and, we would add, the capacities of the participants. Paul Newman (2008), in an interview once remarked that "in films, the definition of 'good' is always murky" – indeed an appropriate adjective when we are discussing how and what we value in the arts.

[C]reative individuals alone do not make creativity happen. They need access to the right information, and they need access to resources. If any of these three elements of the system are not functioning properly, the system… will not adapt creatively to its environment.

Mihaly Csikszentmihalyi, 2009, p. 410

In mainstream theatre, success is judged by the response of the critics (solo voices also bound by their own context, conditions and capabilities) and, contingent upon that subjective judgment, by the financial returns that must both cover the costs of production and the investments of backers. In applied theatre, judging success is very different, depending upon the type of project; it is the nature of the project that will dictate, to a greater or lesser degree, the sorts of evaluative procedures that can be undertaken. The three major project types are: those that are generated in response to a perceived need; those that are funded for a specific purpose; and those that are created for research purposes. In each case there will be an assortment of guidelines, goals, aims, objectives and purposes – some will be set out specifically and others will be more general in their descriptions. For each type, facilitators will need to address the question: How will this (goal, objective, aim, purpose or outcome) be demonstrated?

The following supplementary questions apply both to any project as a whole and to each element of a project as it emerges. Evaluation considers everything from the initial meetings and setting up, the research, development and rehearsal phases, the presentation itself and, of course, the organization and facilitation of the interactions with the audience at the presentation as well as those interactions that may take place before and/or after the presentation (see also Prendergast & Saxton, 2013, pp. 193–203).

- What will be seen?
- What skills will be required in order for that to take place?
- What will be looked at specifically in order to consider (and value) the effect?

These questions refer only to the actual elements that make up the event. Beyond that, facilitators will need to consider such things as:

- The degree and quality of participation
- The rhythm, form, pace and structuring (aesthetic)
- The risks, trust, sharing and caring of participants (ethics)

These, in turn, are balanced by:

- The conditions that surround the creation of the event (space, time, support and so on)
- The skills that are brought to the work by the facilitator(s)
- The response(s) of the audience
- The ways in which the participants and the project may be provided for after the facilitators leave (exit strategy/ies)

One of the least-addressed, but not the least important, planning points are the exit strategies; in exiting from an applied theatre process, practitioners are ethically bound to create – preferably in collaboration with participants – an action plan that aims to continue the process following their departure. A "good" project should contain "clear evidence of effective planning to sustain [the partnership] beyond the funding support" (Burnaford et al., 2001, p. 240). This is where field notes, in the form of a log and/or reflective journal, become key.

All this sounds a bit like counting the angels on the head of a pin and, for that reason, many practitioners do not pay much attention to assessment and evaluation because, in the end, they know that whatever they may value and offer in proof, they can often be wrong. For example, Ross Prior (2005) points out that one of the difficulties of group playbuilding is that shared meanings may not be shared at the deepest level; that players can "own" the work but not necessarily the content (p. 62). His experience is paralleled by final year drama student collectives who created, over a number of years as their final assignment, excellent pieces of playbuilt work about drinking and driving, supported by MADD (Mothers Against Drunk Driving) and local police organizations in Lower Vancouver Island. All those who supported it deemed the project successful: teachers, including the facilitating teacher, and outside agents, present not only at the performances but also at the talkback and workshop sessions. They all agreed that the audiences learned a great deal (demonstrated by the questions they asked), were thoughtful and concerned (as shown through their improvised scenes in follow-up workshops), and were able to generate useful suggestions for further action (writing). But despite the participants' research, their commitment to the project and the demands of touring to local schools, they themselves, it was later discovered, did not follow their own advice. Anthony Jackson (personal communication, July 2008) has noted that same disconnect and suggests that this may be because "school" and the "real world" are seen as totally separate: what participants learn in school is not seen as being connected with their lives outside. Although it met all the criteria, can the drinking and driving project be truly judged a success? This example does not, however, reduce the need and the importance of considering project evaluation as a fundamental component of effective practice and, importantly, central to advocating for the field itself.

> Even after the grant is over, and the "passion" of the funding subsides, you gave birth to a child that needs nurturing.
>
> Jorge Merced, in Sato, 2005, p. 55

> Heisenberg's theory of uncertainty... dictates that anything under observation will change its course as a direct result of being observed. If that is the case, can anything be observed with any accuracy, be it the movement of particles or the interplay of human motives?
>
> Richard Eyre & Nicholas Wright, 2001, pp. 331–332

Assessment is not something to be done only by facilitators. Participants need to be included in assessment/evaluation processes, not simply as resources for feedback but as designers of that feedback. In this way, participants feel a sense of true ownership of the project over its entire course; they are enabled to feel that they are people who are capable of doing and not simply of being done to. Journaling, interviews, focus groups, a series of follow-up sessions (see Jackson's elegant research on the effects of museum education projects, 2000, 2002, 2005; Jackson & Kidd, 2011) are all valuable means of recording, discovering and validating raised awareness, changes in behaviour and action taken or advanced. In the end, we are guided by the ethical principle that an "aesthetics of cultural democracy be considered in the light of its intentions and values and evaluated on its own terms; Rustom Bharucha's question – 'Is it right?' – is primary" (Little, 2008, p. 3).

There are many who make claims for applied theatre's transformative powers. "Transformation" is a theatre term used to signify an "apparently miraculous change in a stage set" (Stein, 1966, p. 1505) and the verb "to transform" is a synonym for "to convert." Until there is a way to assess, quantitatively and/or qualitatively, such theatrical power, we are on stronger ground when we limit our claims to what we know applied theatre can do (Balfour, 2009). It is a theatre that, in the words of Kate Donelan (2007), provides "space for social dreaming" (n.p.). It encourages participants to create dialogue through imagining and enacting possibilities. It is a theatre that does not tell what *must* be done but, rather, in offering a multiplicity of perspectives, invites questions that may, perhaps, initiate action in the search for answers (see Paterson, 2001, p. 65). As Tony Kushner (2001) reminds us, "art is not merely contemplation, it is also action and all action changes the world, at least a little" (p. 62). It is possible that, as Paul Heritage (2004) points out, too much emphasis on results and the instrumental benefits can submerge the very real power of what art itself can do for the people who engage with it. "Do no harm" applies equally to the art form itself.

> In 20 years of activist theatre I do not believe I have raised anyone's consciousness, or liberated them, or brought them new understanding. I have, however, been changed with and through others, and they I hope, with and through me... in theatre, as in life, we develop one another.
>
> Bertolt Brecht, in McDonnell, 2005, p. 73

Summary

Motifs are distinctive ideas that recur as forms or shapes in a work of art. The four motifs presented in this chapter – participation, aesthetics, ethics and assessment – are recursive constants in any applied theatre process. We acknowledge the contestation and murkiness of these areas and recognize that debate around these motifs will continue – the mark of a growing and vigorous field. These debates continue since the publication of the first edition of this text, and will do so in future as they lie at the heart of applied theatre practice. The art that lies within this practice is reflective and dynamic, giving us the social spaces in which to dream. Applied theatre presents us with a mirror of our lives and is the imaginative tutor of our future possibilities and action.

Further Reading

Participation

Haedicke, S. (2003). The challenge of participation: Audiences at Living Stage Theatre Company. In S. Kattwinkel (Ed.), *Audience participation: Essays on inclusion in performance* (pp. 71–87). Westport. CN: Praeger. This chapter uses the work of the Living Stage Theatre company that lies more firmly in the semi-private than semi-public (see King, 1981). However, their use of professionals as facilitators provides valuable insight into those processes.

Paulus, D. (2006). It's all about the audience. *Contemporary Theatre Review, 16*(3), 334–347. Paulus describes two shows that, like the reading above, blur the line, this time between semi-public and public, but what the author has to say about how audiences can be engaged through contemporary methods is very useful information.

White, G. (2013). *Audience participation in theatre: Aesthetics of the invitation.* New York, NY: Palgrave Macmillan. This recent study theorizes audience participation in both immersive theatre and applied theatre contexts.

Aesthetics

Boal, A. (2006). *The aesthetics of the oppressed* (A. Jackson, Trans.). London, UK: Routledge. This text is a whirlwind ride in Boal's inimitable style, through his years of practice. Many useful examples of his practice and the philosophy that underlies it.

Samson, F. (2005). Drama in aesthetic education: An invitation to imagine the world as if it could be otherwise. *The Journal of Aesthetic Education, 39*(4), 70–81. A thorough description of the use of Ping Chong's documentary theatre to develop an understanding of aesthetic education in pre-service teachers and teachers in the field attending a Lincoln Centre Institute course.

Winston, J. & Haseman, B. (2010). The aesthetics of applied theatre and drama education [Special issue]. *Research in Drama Education: The Journal of Applied Theatre and Performance, 15*(4). A themed edition featuring articles by many leading theorists and practitioners, including one by Nic Fryer that examines the related issue of assessing devised performance (pp. 547–562).

Ethics

Bishop, K. (2014). Six perspectives in search of an ethical solution: Utilising a moral imperative with a multiple ethics paradigm to guide research-based theatre/ applied theatre. *Research in Drama Education: The Journal of Applied Theatre and Performance, 19*(1), 64–75. Based on conversations with six leading theorists and practitioners, Bishop identifies key ethical areas for facilitators to consider: justice, critique, care and professionalism.

Maiter, S., Simich, L., Jacobson, N. & Wise, J. (2008). Reciprocity: An ethic for community-based research. *Action Research, 6*(3), 305–325. For practitioners and researchers, this is a rich discussion of procedures for setting up and maintaining a communicative network with a focus on power-sharing.

Shaunessy, N. (2005). Truth and lies: Exploring the ethics of performance applications. *RIDE: Research in Drama Education, 10*(2), 201–212. Apart from the interesting issues raised by the basics of theatre performance (it is all a "big lie"), there are two useful case studies that examine the "lies" in practice and the ethical questions that derive from them.

Assessment/Evaluation

Eisner, E. (2007). Assessment and evaluation in education and the arts. In L. Bresler (Ed.), *International Handbook of Research in Arts Education* (pp. 423–426). Dordrecht, NL: Springer. This synthesis of the problems of assessment/evaluation should be required reading for anyone involved in measuring outcomes in applied theatre.

O'Connor, P. & Anderson, M. (2015). *Applied theatre: Research: Radical departures.* London, UK: Bloomsbury. The first section of this book addresses evaluation and impact assessment in applied theatre, focusing on the value of reciprocity in and with communities.

Robinson, K. (1993). Evaluating TIE. In A. Jackson (Ed.), *Learning through theatre* (2nd ed., pp. 251–266). London, UK: Routledge. Although the date is early, this discussion and examination of the "areas of evaluative action" is really indispensable, particularly as it uses a Theatre in Education programme as its model and is therefore rooted in the realities of the practice.

Questions for Reflection and Discussion

1. As theatre audiences are challenged with higher levels of participation, what alterations to actor (or director) training might need to be made to reflect this change?

2. If audiences are to be recognized and involved, what practical implications are there in constructing a presentation and its audience intervention strategies?

3. What other kinds of theatre have encouraged audience participation and what was the quality of that participation? What can we learn from these historical antecedents?

4. Two useful questions from Shaughnessy (2005) to chew upon: (1) When is it right to make the private public? (2) The actor is a master of pretence, mimicry and artifice; what are the ethics of using these methodologies when we are working with real lives? (p. 202).

5. Some other questions worth thinking about: Who decides what stories are told? Who decides whose stories are told? When may a discussion about a presentation not be safe for the participants? What needs to be done to make it safe?

Suggested Activities

The situation: A funding agency has provided information and project guidelines for facilitators they have hired to work with homeless men in an effort to help them build job-seeking skills. The facilitators have consulted widely with social agencies and drawn up a plan that will extend over ten weeks, with a possibility of some kind of presentation – to whom and what about will be decided by the participants. As the facilitators meet with the community and get to know them, it becomes clear that the need the agency sees as being important is not what the men have identified. Libraries and other public spaces do not tolerate people who have simply come in to get out of the weather; the men are constantly being moved on. They need a place to go to be warm in the winter, dry in the rain, and out of the weather. They need somewhere that is open daily where they can remain for as long as they need until it is time to seek the night shelter. Keeping warm and having a safe place are two most basic of Maslow's (1968) hierarchy of needs. Without these assurances, finding a job is, for the men, an exercise in futility, not to mention that they have a tendency to see the whole "exercise" as an opportunity for "do-gooders" to slum a little! It is clear to the facilitators that the funding agency is not up to date with – and perhaps not sympathetic to – the needs of this constituency.

1. What research do you need to do to familiarize yourself with the issue of homelessness? What areas of importance can you identify to bring forward to your group?

2. With your group, search out an agency that works with people who are homeless or vulnerable to homelessness. What do they believe to be the needs of their

clients? What is the agency's mandate? How might an applied theatre project support or perhaps challenge this mandate and the agency's operations?

3. Search out a potential group of participants, preferably with the cooperation of the agency. What do these homeless people identify as their needs?

4. With your group, create a proposal for an applied theatre project to work with this clientele. As you do so, consider the following:

    a) What information would be helpful to you in deciding what to do? What strategies might you use? What exit strategies are available?
    b) Identify any potential ethical dilemmas that facilitators may face.
    c) Outline a procedure for addressing these possible shifts in intentions.
    d) Consider how you will go about dealing with shifting intentions with your own group members, with the funding agency, with the clients, with the community at large and with the local government.
    e) Look at the assessment instruments used by the agency and use it as a template for an assessment instrument. How will you include the participants in designing your assessment procedures?

5. Present your proposal and ask the funding agency to provide you with feedback as to how they see the project as appropriate to their mandate.

6. If the funding agency or participants suggest a shift in focus, what changes would need to be made to the proposal, keeping ethical issues in mind?

7. Continue to revise your proposal until the agency, participants and you, as facilitators, are all comfortable with the guidelines for the project.

8. If it is possible, implement your project.

The quality of reflection usually reflects the quality of the experience but, strangely enough, even a rather flat or mundane experience can often be lifted into something much greater than itself through reflection. The act of simply thinking about something with other people can enable insights into things that were not apparent while inside the experience; when reflection happens together, shared insights deepen and extend that experience. When there is no time for reflection, the opportunity is lost, and at the same time, we lose the ability to see ourselves and our actions in relation to our community and the environment. Shared reflections help to build, extend and enhance collective visions. To slight or forget reflection as an imperative element in the operation of applied theatre is to lose the opportunity to exercise what Antonio Damasio (1995) calls "our unique human properties" – the ability to anticipate what may happen, make plans, look after ourselves and other people responsibly and maintain our lives with thought and care (p. 10).

> [O]nly humans are capable of observing themselves in action. By observing myself in action, this dicho-tomization allows me to change my way. That's why culture is possible: because we humans are capable of looking at ourselves in action... We observe ourselves and say, "If I am here I can go there. If I have done like this, I can do like that."
>
> Augusto Boal, in Delgado & Heritage, 1996, p. 35

The heart of the reflective process is the space it provides to bring into existence a personal relationship with the material. Reflection allows time to consider the moral attitudes, principles and beliefs that lie beneath actions and to see these in relation to the views, actions and feelings of others. Reflection lets us see how ideas are mediated and how thought is changed when it becomes concretized through action. Eric Booth (1999) notes how hard it is for

> But if theatre is a reflection of the world we live in, it's also a reflection of the world we hope to live in. It's a space of potential and possibility.
>
> Jordan Tannahill, 2015, p. 19

people to reflect. Many have an ingrained bias against such an activity, deeming their thoughts not worth noticing. For facilitators, reflection can be one of the most difficult activities to initiate but, once begun, as Booth points out, participants "come to respect experience-awareness as a skill that directly taps into the feeling of being alive" (p. 54).

If, as Allen (2006) says, the arts enable the kind of distance and viewpoints that help participants to understand where they have positioned themselves, the potential for change will only occur through reflecting on what has happened in the safety of a metaphoric world that the theatre experience has created. When groups reflect they bring past experiences into relationship with the present and, in so doing, are better able to see where it is that they want to go. This sense of the future generates motivation and hope and is important for building a sense of identity within the group and for each member of that group. Reflection develops the skills of assessment, helping participants think about their work and to see how what they have been doing has substance and purpose; that is, their work has real value. Reflection helps participants to organize their thoughts and legitimizes the place of feelings within their own work.

> The arts allow those who practice them and those who consume them to imagine alternative states of mind and being. This is a political function of art. Imagined communities allow us to get critical distance and critical perspectives on our own political condition and potentially to transform it.
>
> Garth Allen, 2006, p. 291

Reflection:

- encourages participants to think about how and what they could have done differently;
- presses participants to consider that no action is without implications for themselves and others;
- enables them to be aware of the innovative ideas that can emerge when they work together;
- encourages participants, through a safe and trusting environment, to develop their critical and analytical skills that, in turn,
- builds participants' aesthetic and artistic standards.

Through reflection, participants have an opportunity to consider the ethical and moral implications of their work and to set those considerations within the wider contexts of their culture. It is, writes Doll (1993), the "only reliable guide to further action" (p. 141).

> There are temporary stopping places [in reflection], landings of past thought that are also stations of departure for subsequent thought.
>
> John Dewey, 1933/1971, p. 75

The best reflection is recursive, functioning in the same way that the theatrical rehearsal process works; that is to say, by going back and back again over things experienced by the group,

Jerome Bruner (1990) in *Acts of Meaning* writes about our two "dazzling" intellectual capacities: first, the ability to "turn around on the past and alter the present in its light, or to alter the past in the light of the present" and, second, the capacity "to envision alternatives, to conceive of other ways of being, of acting, of striving."

pp. 109–110

Reflective thinking engages imagery as the fluid language of the mind that disrupts the automatic ways in which as adults we tend to become limited by inflexible descriptive summaries of experience.

Daniel Siegel, 2007, p. 326

Theatre is not just a place, not simply a profession. It is a metaphor. It helps to make the process of life more clear… [W]hen the population assembles in a special place under special conditions to partake in a mystery, the scattered limbs are drawn together and a momentary healing reunites the larger body, in which each member, re-membered, finds its place.

Peter Brook, 1998, p. 196

participants are enabled to see how their ideas, thoughts and feelings work together to build the group's sense of efficacy in the world. But such reflective activity is not something that works for the participants only. Reflection is an essential strategy for facilitators: it is something that, with more and more experience, can be used in the midst of what is happening – reflection-in-action (Schön, 1984). Reflection-on-action is more easily acquired: here the reflection is on what has happened in order to know how to move the work forward; on what worked or was not effective; on one's own ideas, thoughts and feelings; on what needs to be done again, and what needs to be let go. As Freire (2000) argues, action without reflection is unproductive both for ourselves and for our participants (p. 87). And reflection is not something to be used only for closure; it must occur throughout the process, building new awareness upon which the work can capitalize.

In his discussion of genius, Malcolm Gladwell (1999) writes that the best candidates are those who have "the ability to rethink everything they have done and imagine how they might have done it differently" (p. 60). Such reflection is not limited to the genius; it also makes effective the work of applied theatre facilitators and their groups. And those groups include the audiences to which the act of theatre is applied. While it may not always be applicable or, indeed, politically safe to reflect with the audience, reflection – generally speaking – is an important extension of the performance for everyone concerned.

In reflection, the first simple thoughts, as they bounce back and forth, become more complex ideas as they mix together. Within the richness created through reflection can always be found new ways of thinking about ourselves and the world; within those thoughts lie the unlimited opportunities for healing, as the community is re-membered through the act of theatre.

Further Reading

What are the books and journals that you would like on your bookshelves to help you build your understanding and strengthen your practice?

Questions for Reflection and Discussion

What questions would you now want to pose to colleagues for discussion?

Suggested Activity

With your group, create a number of scenarios that mark your learning in applied theatre and share them with the class.

BIBLIOGRAPHY

Note: Sources quoted in the text are listed here and may also be found in Further Reading.

Afzal-Khan, F. (2001). Exposed by Pakistani street theater: The unholy alliance of postmodern capitalism, patriarchy, and fundamentalism. *Social Text*, *19*(4), 67–91.

Allen, G. (2006). The arts and the cult of performance. *Arts & Humanities in Higher Education*, *5*(3), 291–304.

Anouilh, J. (1951). *Antigone* (L. Golantiere, Trans.). London, UK: Methuen. (Original work published in 1942).

Arnold, R. (2005). *Empathic intelligence: Teaching, learning, relating*. Sydney, NSW: UNSW Press.

Arrabal, F. (1973). *Le panique*. Paris, France: Union générale d'Édition.

Bailey, C. (1987). "Soul clap its hands and sing": Living History Theatre as a process of creation. *Activities, Adaptation, Aging*, *9*(4), 1–43.

Balfour, M. (Ed.). (2004). *Theatre in prisons: Theory and practice*. Bristol, UK: Intellect Books.

Balfour, M. (2009). The politics of intention: Looking for a theatre of little changes. *Research in Drama Education: The Journal of Applied Theatre and Performance*, *14*(3), 347–359.

Balfour, M., Bundy, P., Burton, B. Dunn, J. & Woodrow, N. (2015). *Applied theatre: Resettlement: Drama, refugees and resilience*. London, UK: Bloomsbury.

Ball, S. (1994). Theatre and health education: Meeting of minds or marriage of convenience? *Health Education Journal, 53*(2), 222–225.

Barnhart, C.L. (Ed.). (1965). *Thorndike-Barnhart comprehensive desk dictionary.* New York, NY: Doubleday and Company.

Basting, A. (1995). The stages of age: The growth of senior theatre. *TDR: The Drama Review, 39*(3), 112–130.

Beckerman, B. (1990). *Theatrical presentation: Performer, audience and act.* New York, NY: Routledge.

Big Brum Theatre. (n.d.). Retrieved from http://www.bigbrum.org.uk.

Billone, N. (2009). Performing civil death: The Medea Project and theater for incarcerated women. *Text and Performance Quarterly, 29*(3), 260–275.

Blau, H. (1965). *The impossible theatre: A manifesto.* New York, NY: Collier.

Boal, A. (1979). *Theatre of the oppressed.* London, UK: Pluto Press.

Boal, A. (1992). *Games for actors and non-actors* (A. Jackson, Trans.). London, UK: Routledge.

Boal, A. (1995). *The rainbow of desire: The Boal method of theatre and therapy* (A. Jackson, Trans.). London, UK: Routledge.

Boal, A. (1998). *Legislative theatre: Using performance to make politics* (A. Jackson, Trans.). London, UK: Routledge.

Boal, A. (2006). *The aesthetics of the oppressed* (A. Jackson, Trans.). London, UK: Routledge.

Bolton, G. (1979). *Towards a theory of drama in education.* London, UK: Longman.

Bonczek, R.B. & Storck, D. (2013). *Ensemble theatre making: A practical guide.* New York, NY: Routledge.

Bond, E. (1996). Preface: Notes on imagination. In E. Bond, *Coffee* (p. xxxxiv). London, UK: Methuen Drama.

Booth, E. (1999). *The everyday work of art: Awakening the extraordinary in your daily life.* Napierville, IL: Sourcebooks.

Boucher, D. (2011). Telling ourselves to ourselves: Reinterpreting historical interpretation. Unpublished non-thesis Master's paper. University of Victoria, BC.

Bray, E. (1991). *Playbuilding: A guide for group creation of plays with young people*. Sydney, NSW: Currency Press.

Britton, J. (Ed.). (2013). *Encountering ensemble*. London, UK: Bloomsbury.

Brook, P. (1968). *The empty space*. London, UK: Penguin.

Brook, P. (1998). *Threads of time*. Washington, DC: Counterpoint.

Bruner, J. (1990). *Acts of meaning*. Cambridge, MA: Harvard University Press.

Burnaford, G., Aprill, A. & Weiss, C. (Eds.). (2001). *Renaissance in the classroom: Arts integration and meaningful learning*. Mahwah, NJ: Lawrence Erlbaum Associates Inc.

Bury, A., Popple, K. & Barker, J. (1998). "You've got to think really hard": Children making sense of the aims and content of theatre in health education. *RIDE: Research in Drama Education, 3*(1), 13–27.

Butsch, R. (2000). *The making of American audiences: From stage to television, 1750–1990*. Cambridge, UK: Cambridge University Press.

Butterwick, S. & Selman, J. (2003). Deep listening in a popular feminist theatre project: Upsetting the position of audience in participatory education. *Adult Education Quarterly, 54*(1), 7–22.

Cahill, H. (2010). Re-thinking the fiction-reality boundary: Investigating the use of drama in HIV prevention projects in Vietnam. *Research in Drama Education: The Journal of Applied Theatre and Performance, 15*(2), 155–174.

Carlson, M. (1993). *Theories of the theatre: A historical and critical survey, from the Greeks to the present* (Expanded edition). London, UK: Cornell University Press.

Cheeseman, P. (1970). Introduction: Documentary theatre at Stoke-on-Trent. In P. Cheeseman and the Victoria Theatre Company, *The knotty: A musical documentary* (pp. vi–xx). London, UK: Methuen.

Chinyowa, K.C. (2007). Frames of metacommunication: Examples from African theatre for development. *NJ: Drama Australia Journal, 31*(1), 33–43.

Chinyowa, K.C. (2012). Building critical citizenship through syncretic theatre: A Zimbabwean case study. *Journal of Peacebuilding and Development, 7*(2), 67–78.

Clothier, J.S. (2014). Authentic pretending: How theatrical is museum theatre? *Museum Management and Curatorship, 29*(3), 211–225.

Cocke, D. (1993). The aesthetics of community-based artmaking. Unpublished essay.

Cocke, D. (2004). Art in a democracy. *TDR: The Drama Review, 48*(3), 165–178.

Coleridge, S.T. (1817). *Biographia literaria.* Retrieved from www.english.upenn.edu/~mgamer/Etexts/biographia.html.

Conquergood, D. (1985). Performing as a moral act: Ethical dimensions of the ethnography of performance. *Text and Performance Quarterly, 5*(2), 1–13.

Cooper, C. (2013). The performer in TIE. In A. Jackson & C. Vine (Eds.), *Learning through theatre: The changing face of theatre in education* (pp. 131-141). Abingdon, UK: Routledge.

Copfermann, E. (1972). *La mise en crise théâtrale.* Paris, France: François Maspéro.

Corman, S. (2013, March 21). The difference beween story and narrative. Tempe, AZ: ASU Center for Strategic Communication. Retrieved from http://csc.asu.edu/2013/03/21/the-difference-between-story-and-narrative/.

Correia, A. (2006). Interpreting Jeremy Deller's 'The Battle of Orgreave'. *Visual Culture in Britain, 7*(2), 93–112.

Cox, M. (Ed.). (1992). *Shakespeare comes to Broadmoor: The performance of tragedy in a secure psychiatric hospital.* London, UK: Jessica Kingsley.

Craig, E.G. (1911). *On the art of the theatre.* London, UK: Methuen.

Croyden, M. (2003). *Conversations with Peter Brook, 1970–2000.* New York, NY: Faber & Faber.

Csikszentmihalyi, M. (1975). *Beyond boredom and anxiety: Experiencing flow in work and play.* San Francisco, CA: Jossey-Bass.

Csikszentmihalyi, M. (2009). A systems perspective on creativity and its implications for measurement. In E. Villalba (Ed.), *Measuring creativity: Proceedings for the conference "Can Creativity be Measured?" Brussels, May 28–29* (pp. 407–414). Brussels: European Commission Joint Research Centre. Retrieved from http://bookshop.europa.eu/en/measuring-creativity-pbLBNA24033/.

Dalrymple, L. (2005, April). Dramaide: An evaluation of interactive drama and theatre for HIV/AIDS education in South Africa. Paper given at the *Fifth International Conference on Researching Drama and Theatre Education*, University of Exeter, UK.

Damasio, A. (1995). *Descartes error: Emotion, reason and the human brain.* New York, NY: Penguin.

Damasio, A. (1999). *The feeling of what happens: Body and emotion in the making of consciousness.* New York, NY: Harcourt.

Delgado, M. & Heritage, P. (Eds.). (1996). Augusto Boal. In *Contact with the gods? Directors talk theatre* (pp. 15–35). Manchester, UK: Manchester University Press.

Dennill, B. (2014, November 3). What's theirs is mine, or documentary theatre gets a community out of a hole [Web log post]. Retrieved from http://www.brucedennill.co.za/whats-theirs-is-mine-or-documentary-theatre-gets-a-community-out-of-a-hole/.

Denzin, N. (1997). *Interpretive ethnography.* London, UK: Sage.

Dewey, J. (1933/1971). *How we think.* Chicago, IL: Henry Regnery.

Diamond, D. (2007). *Theatre for living: The art and science of community-based dialogue.* Victoria: Trafford.

Djikic, M., Oatley, K., Zoeterman, S. & Peterson, J. (2009). On being moved by art: How reading fiction transforms the self. *Creativity Research Journal, 21*(1), 24–29.

Doll, W. (1993). *A post-modern perspective on curriculum.* New York, NY: Teachers College Press.

Donelan, K. (2007, July 18). Drama in the 21st century curriculum: An Australian perspective. Keynote paper presented at *International Drama in Education Association World Congress*, Hong Kong.

Dutlinger, A. (2001). *Art, music and education as strategies for survival: Theresienstadt 1941–45*. New York, NY: Herodias.

Eagleton, T. (2008). Coruscating on thin ice. [Book review]. *London Review of Books, 30*(2), 19–20.

Edson, M. (1999). *Wit*. New York, NY: Broadway Play Publishing.

Eisner, E. (2007). Interlude 26: Assessment and evaluation in education and the arts. In L. Bresler (Ed.), *International handbook of research in arts education* (pp. 423–426). Dordrecht, The Netherlands: Springer.

Ellis, A. (2000). The art of community conversation. *Theatre Topics, 10*(2), 91–100.

Epskamp, K. (2006). *Theatre for development: An introduction to context, application and training*. London, UK: Zed Books.

Esslin, M. (1976). *Anatomy of drama*. New York, NY: Hill and Wang.

Eyre, R. & Wright, N. (2001). *Changing stages: A view of British theatre in the twentieth century*. London, UK: Bloomsbury.

Favorini, A. (2013). Collective creation in documentary theatre. In K. Mederos Syssoyeva & S. Proudfit (Eds.), *A history of collective creation* (pp. 97–112). New York, NY: Palgrave Macmillan.

Fichman, N. (Producer) & Girard, F. (Director). (1998). *The red violin* [Motion picture]. Canada: Lionsgate.

Filewod, A. (1987). *Collective encounters: Documentary theatre in English Canada*. Toronto, ON: University of Toronto Press.

Foreman, R. (1976). *Plays and manifestos*. New York, NY: New York University Press.

Forsyth, A. & Megson, C. (Eds.). (2009). *Get real: Documentary theatre past and present*. New York, NY: Palgrave Macmillan.

Fraden, R. (2001). *Imagining Medea: Rhodessa Jones and theater for incarcerated women.* Chapel Hill, NC: University of North Carolina.

Freire, M. (2007). A different kind of community theatre: Performance projects with GLBT adolescents. *Teaching Artist Journal, 5*(4), 243–252.

Freire, P. (2000). *Pedagogy of the oppressed: 30th anniversary edition* (M.B. Ramos, Trans.). New York, NY: Continuum. (Original work published in 1970).

Fulford, R. (1999). *The triumph of narrative; Storytelling in the age of mass culture.* Toronto, ON: House of Anansi.

Gallagher, K. (2006). Pondering ethics: Viewpoints. *RIDE: Research in Drama Education, 1*(1), 96–98.

Giannachi, G. & Luckhurst, M. (1999). *On directing.* New York, NY: St. Martin's Griffin.

Gibson, F. (2006). Introduction. In P. Schweitzer (Ed.), *Reminiscence theatre: Making theatre from memories* (pp. 11–12). London, UK: Jessica Kingsley.

Giesekam, G. (2006). Applied theatre/drama: An e-debate in 2004: Viewpoints. *Research in Drama and Education, 11*(1), 90–95.

Gladwell, M. (1999). The physical genius. *New Yorker*, August 2, pp. 57–65.

Goleman, D. (1995). *Emotional intelligence.* New York, NY: Random House.

Goleman, D. (2006). *Social intelligence.* New York, NY: Random House.

Goodwin, J. (2004). The productive postshow: Facilitating, understanding and optimizing personal narratives in audience talk following a personal narrative performance. *Theatre Topics, 14*(1), 317–338.

Gray, R. (2003). *Prostate tales: Men's experiences with prostate cancer.* Harriman, TN: Men's Studies Press.

Gray, R. (2004). Performing for whom? Spotlight on the audience. In A. Cole, L. Neilsen, J.G. Knowles & T. Luciani (Eds.), *Provoked by art: Theorizing arts-informed research* (pp. 238–249). Halifax, NS: Backalong Books & Centre for Arts-informed Research.

Gray, R., Fitch, M.I., LaBrecque, M. & Greenberg, M. (2003). Reactions of health professionals to a research-based theatre production. *Journal of Cancer Education, 18*(4), 223–229.

Gray, R. & Sinding, C. (2002). *Standing ovation: Performing social science research about cancer.* Walnut Creek, CA: Alta Mira Press.

Greene, M. (1988). *The dialectic of freedom.* New York, NY: Teachers College Press.

Greene, M. (1995). *Releasing the imagination: Essays on education, the arts, and social change.* San Francisco, CA: Jossey-Bass.

Greene, M. (2001). *Variations on a blue guitar: The Lincoln Centre Institute lectures on aesthetic education.* New York, NY: Teacher College Press.

Grotowski, J. (1968). *Towards a poor theatre.* New York, NY: Simon & Schuster.

Haedicke, S. (2003). The challenge of participation: Audiences at Living Stage Theatre Company. In S. Kattwinkel (Ed.), *Audience participation: Essays on inclusion in performance* (pp. 71–87). Westport, CN: Praeger.

Hafler, M. (2012). Operating theatre: A theatre devising project with fourth-year medical students. *Journal of Applied Arts & Health, 3*(3), 309–319.

Halverson, J. (2011). Why story is not narrative. Retrieved from http://csc.asu.edu/2011/12/08/why-story-is-not-narrative/.

Hamel, S. (2013). When theatre of the oppressed becomes theatre of the oppressor. *RiDE: The Journal of Applied Theatre and Performance, 18*(4), 403–416.

Hart, H. (2000). Religious conflicts, public policy, and moral authority. In J. Olthuis (Ed.), *Towards an ethics of community: Negotiations of difference in a pluralistic society* (pp. 91–126). Waterloo, ON: Wilfred Laurier University Press.

Hartley, J.S. (2012). *Applied theatre in action: A journey.* Stoke-on-Trent, UK: Trentham.

Harvey, M. (2010). Staging the story. Retrieved from http://storytelling.research.southwales.ac.uk/media/files/documents/2010-03-01/Staging_the_Story_Final_version.pdf.

Hennessy, J. (1998). The theatre in education actor as researcher. *RIDE: Research in Drama Education, 3*(1), 85–92.

Heritage, P. (2004). Taking hostages: Staging human rights. *TDR: The Drama Review, 48*(3), 96–106.

Hughes, C., Jackson, A. & Kidd, J. (2007). The role of theatre in museums and historic sites: Visitors, audiences, and learners. In L. Bresler (Ed.), *International handbook of research in arts education* (pp. 679–696). Dordrecht, NL: Springer.

Jackson, A. (Ed.). (1993). *Learning through theatre: New perspectives on theatre in education.* London, UK and New York, NY: Routledge.

Jackson, A. (1995). Translator's introduction. In A. Boal (Ed.), *The rainbow of desire: The Boal method of theatre and therapy* (pp. xvii–xxvi). London, UK: Routledge.

Jackson, A. (1999). The centrality of the aesthetic in educational theatre, *Drama Australia, 23*(2), 51–63.

Jackson, A. (2000). Interacting with the past: The uses of participatory theatre at heritage sites. *RIDE: Research in Drama Education, 5*(2), 199–215.

Jackson, A. (2002). Between evaluation and research: Theatre as an educational tool in museum theatre. *Stage of the Art, 15*(1), 6–9.

Jackson, A. (2005). The dialogic and the aesthetic: Some reflections on theatre as a learning medium. *Journal of Aesthetic Education, 39*(4), 104–118.

Jackson, A. & Kidd, J. (2008, November). Executive summary. *Performance, learning and heritage.* [Research report]. Retrieved from http://www.plh.manchester.ac.uk/documents/Performance,%20Learning%20&%20Heritage%20-%20Executive%20Summary.pdf.

Jackson, A. & Kidd, J. (Eds.). (2011). *Performing heritage: Research practice and innovation in museum theatre and live interpretation.* Manchester, UK: Manchester University Press.

Jackson, A. & Lev-Aladgem, S. (2004). Rethinking audience participation: Audiences in alternative and educational theatre. In V.A., Cremona, P. Eversmann, H. van Maanen, W. Sauter & J. Tulloch (Eds.), *Theatrical events: Borders, dynamics, frames* (pp. 207–238). Amsterdam, NL and New York, NY: Rodopi.

Jackson, A. & Rees Leahy, H. (2005). "Seeing it for real...?" Authenticity, theatre and learning in museums. *RIDE: Research in Drama Education, 10*(3), 303–325.

Jackson, A. & Vine, C. (Eds.). (2013). *Learning through theatre: The changing face of theatre in education* (3rd ed.). London, UK: Routledge.

Jellicoe, A. (1987). *Community plays: How to put them on.* London, UK: Methuen.

King, N. (1981). *A movement approach to acting.* Englewood Cliffs, NJ: Prentice-Hall.

King, T. (2003). *The truth about stories: A Native narrative.* Toronto: Anansi.

Kirby, M. (1965). *Happenings. An illustrated anthology.* New York, NY: E. P. Dutton Inc.

Knowles, D. (1989). *Armand Gatti in the theatre: Wild duck against the wind.* London, UK: The Athlone Press.

Kostelanetz, R. (1968). *Theatre of mixed means.* New York, NY: Dial Press.

Kuppers, P. & Robertson, G. (Eds.). (2007). *The community performance reader.* London, UK and New York, NY: Routledge.

Kushner, T. (1993). *Angels in America: Parts one and two.* New York, NY: Theatre Communications Group.

Kushner, T. (2001). "In praise of contradiction and conundrum:" How do you make social change? *Theater, 31*(3), 61–64.

Lamden, G. (2000). *Devising: A handbook for drama and theatre students.* Abingdon, UK: Hodder & Stoughton.

Le Guin, U. (1989). *Dancing at the edge of the world: Thoughts on words, women, places.* New York, NY: Harper & Row.

Lehmann, H-T. (2006). *Postdramatic theatre* (K. Jürs-Munby, Trans.). New York, NY: Routledge.

Leonard, R.H. & Kilkelly, A. (2006). *Performing communities: Grassroots ensemble theaters deeply rooted in eight U.S. communities.* Oakland, CA: New Village Press.

Little, E. (2008). Editorial: Ethics and aesthetics. *alt. theatre, 4*(1), 3.

Lyotard, J. (1979/1984). *The postmodern condition* (G. Bennington & B. Massumi, Trans.). Minneapolis, MN: University of Minnesota.

MacIntyre, A. (1981/2007). *After virtue: A study in moral philosophy* (3rd ed.). Notre Dame, IN: University of Notre Dame Press.

Magelssen, S. (2006). Making history in the second person: Post-touristic considerations for living historical interpretations. *Theatre Journal, 58*(2), 291–312.

Maiter, S., Simich, L., Jacobson, N. & Wise, J. (2008). Reciprocity: An ethic for community-based participatory action research. *Action Research, 6*(3), 305–325.

Malcolm-Davies, J. (2004). Borrowed robes: The educational value of costumed interpretation at historic sites. *International Journal of Heritage Studies, 10*(3), 277–293.

Martin, C. (2013). *Theatre of the real.* New York, NY: Palgrave Macmillan.

Maslow, A. H. (1968). *Toward a psychology of being.* Ann Arbor, MI: University of Michigan Press.

McDonnell, B. (2005). Towards a theatre of "little changes:" A dialogue about dialogue. *RIDE: Research in Drama Education, 10*(1), 67–73.

McDonnell, B. (2006). Theatre, resistance and community – some reflections on "hard" interventionary theatre. In M. Balfour & J. Somers (Eds.), *Drama as social intervention* (pp. 2–11). Concord, ON: Captus Press.

McKenzie, J. (2001). *Perform or else: From discipline to performance.* London, UK and New York, NY: Routledge.

Meirelles, F. (Director) (2005). *The constant gardener* [Motion picture]. London, UK: Potboiler Productions.

Morell, A. (2006). El teatro como herramienta para la contrucción. In L. McCammon & D. McLauchlan (Eds.), *Universal mosaic of drama and theatre: The IDEA dialogues* (pp. 213–220). City East, QLD: IDEA Publications.

Morgan, N. & Saxton, J. (1987). *Teaching drama: A mind of many wonders.* London, UK: Hutchinson Education.

Morgan, N. & Saxton, J. (1995/2006). *Asking better questions* (2nd ed.). Markham, ON: Pembroke.

Munier, A. & Etherton, M. (2006). Child rights theatre for development in rural Bangladesh: A case study. *RIDE: Research in Drama Education, 11*(2), 175–183.

Mutnick, D. (2006). Critical interventions: The meaning of praxis. In J. Cohen Cruz and M. Schutzman (Eds.), *A Boal companion: Dialogues on theatre and cultural politics* (pp. 33–45). London, UK: Routledge.

Myerhoff, B. (1992). *Remembered lives*. Ann Arbor, MI: University of Michigan Press.

Nagel, E. (2007). An aesthetic of neighborliness: Possibilities for integrating community-based practices into documentary theatre. *Theatre Topics, 17*(2), 153–168.

Napp-Schindel, D. (2002). Museum theatre: Telling stories through objects. *Stage of the Art, 14*(4), 10–16.

National Health and Medical Research Council. (1996). *Promoting the health of Indigenous Australians. A review of infrastructure support for Aboriginal and Torres Strait Islander health advancement.* Section 2, p. 4. [Final report and recommendations, rescinded March 3, 2005]. Canberra: NHMRC. Retrieved from https://www.nhmrc.gov.au/_files_nhmrc/publications/attachments/hp3.pdf

Neelands, J. (1984). *Making sense of drama: A guide to classroom practice*. Portsmouth, NH: Heinemann.

Neelands, J. & Goode, T. (1995). Playing in the margins of meaning: The ritual aesthetic in community performance. *NJ: Drama Australia Journal, 19*(1), 40–57.

Newman, P. (2008). Memorial retrospective. *Weekend Edition* with Lianne Hanson (September 28). *National Public Radio* (KPLU).

Nicholson, H. (1999). Aesthetic values, drama education and the politics of difference. *NJ: Drama Australia Journal, 23*(2), 81–90.

Nicholson, H. (2005). *Applied drama: The gift of theatre*. New York, NY: Palgrave Macmillan.

Niemi, I. (1973). Peter Weiss and documentary theatre: Song of a scarecrow. *Modern Drama, 16*(1), 29–34.

O'Connor, P. (Ed.). (2010). *Creating democratic citizenship through drama education: The writings of Jonothan Neelands.* Stoke on Trent, UK: Trentham.

O'Connor, P. & Anderson, M. (2015). *Applied theatre: Research: Radical departures.* London, UK: Bloomsbury.

Oddey, A. (1996). *Devising theatre: A practical and theoretical handbook.* London, UK: Routledge.

Odhiambo, C. (2001). What has TfD got to do with it? Fixing, un-fixing and refixing of positions and conditions. *Drama Research: The Research Journal of National Drama, 2,* 85–94.

O'Toole, J. (1976). *Theatre in education: New objectives for theatre – New techniques for education.* London, UK: Hodder & Stoughton.

O'Toole, J. (2004). Illuminated texts: From Homer to the home-page. *NJ: Drama Australia Journal, 28*(2), 5–13.

Paterson, D. (2001). The TASC is: Theatre and social change: How do you make social change? *Theater, 31*(3), 65–67.

Paulus, D. (2006). It's all about the audience. *Contemporary Theatre Review, 16*(3), 334-347.

Pavis, P. (1998). *Dictionary of the theatre: Terms, concepts, and analysis* (C. Shantz, Trans.). Toronto, ON: University of Toronto Press.

Petheridge, J. & Kendall, D. (2012). The process and impact of intergenerational theatre making. *Quality in Ageing and Older Adults, 13*(4), 301–306.

Plastow, J. (2014). Domestication or transformation? The ideology of Theatre for Development in Africa. *Applied Theatre Research, 2*(2), 107–118.

Prendergast, M. (2008). *Teaching spectatorship: Essays and poems on audience in performance.* Amherst, NY: Cambria Press.

Prendergast, M. & Saxton, J. (2015). Seduction of the real: The significance of fiction in applied theatre. *RIDE: The Journal of Applied Theatre and Performance, 20*(3), 280-284.

Prendergast, M. & Saxton, J. (2013). *Applied drama: A facilitator's handbook for working in community.* Bristol, UK: Intellect.

Prentki, T. (2015). *Applied theatre: Development.* London, UK: Bloomsbury.

Prentki, T. & Preston, S. (Eds.). (2009). *The applied theatre reader.* London, UK: Routledge.

Prentki, T. & Selman, J. (Eds.). (2000). *Popular theatre in political culture: Britain and Canada in focus.* Bristol, UK: Intellect Books.

Preston, S. (2009). Introduction to participation. In T. Prentki & S. Preston (Eds.), *The applied theatre reader* (pp. 127–129). New York, NY: Routledge.

Price, J. (2011). To teach and to delight? Examining the efficacy of popular theatre forms in radical theatre practice. *Studies in Theatre and Performance, 31*(1), 75–93.

Prior, R. (2005). Looking around in awareness: Playbuilding on HIV/AIDS. *RIDE: Research in Drama Education, 10*(1), 54–64.

Randall, W.L. (1997). *The stories we are: An essay on self-creation.* Toronto, ON: University of Toronto Press.

Rokem, F. (2000). *Performing History: Theatrical representations of the past in contemporary theatre.* Iowa City, IA: University of Iowa.

Rosestone, S. (2012). Thought-provoking experiences for secondary students. *Ethos, 20*(3), 20–22.

Saldaña, J. (2005). *Ethnodrama: An anthology of reality theatre.* Walnut Creek, CA: AltaMira Press.

Sato, S.M. (2005, January). The audience as art. *American Theatre,* 50–58.

Saxton, J. (2006). [Personal notes on Smithsonian Institute visit]. Unpublished raw data.

Saxton, J. & Miller C. (2006). The relationship of context to content in the medical model: Exploring possible paradigms. In M. Balfour and J. Somers (Eds.), *Drama as social intervention* (pp. 129-141). Concord, ON: Captus.

Schechner, R. (1997). Believed-in theatre. *Performance Research, 2*(2), 76–91.

Schechner, R. (2002). *Performance studies: An introduction.* New York, NY: Routledge.

Schechner, R. (2003). *Performance theory* (2nd ed.). New York, NY: Routledge.

Schechner, R. & Delamont, S. (2013). *Performance studies: An introduction* (3rd ed.). New York, NY: Routledge.

Schechter, J. (Ed.). (2003). *Popular theatre: A sourcebook.* London, UK: Routledge.

Schön, D. (1984) *The reflective practitioner: How professionals think in action.* New York, NY: Basic Books.

Schweitzer, P. (2006). *Reminiscence theatre: Making theatre from memories.* London, UK: Jessica Kingsley.

Schweitzer, P. (2013). Reminiscence in dementia care. *The International Journal of Reminiscence and Life Review, 1*(1), 42–47.

Shaughnessy, N. (2005). Truth and lies: Exploring the ethics of performance applications. *RIDE: Research in Drama Education, 10*(2), 201–212.

Shaw, G.B. (1906/2004). *The doctor's dilemma.* Fairfield, IA: 1st World.

Shepherd, S. & Wallis, M. (2004). *Drama/theatre/performance.* London, UK: Routledge.

Siegel, D. (2007). *The mindful brain: Reflection and attunement in the cultivation of well-being.* New York, NY: W.W. Norton & Company.

Sills, P. (1971). *Story theatre.* New York, NY: Samuel French.

Sills, P. (2000). *Paul Sills' story theatre: Four shows.* New York, NY: Applause Books.

Somers, J. (1998). Interview in "Trusting paradoxes" by Chris Johnston. In J. Thompson (Ed.), *Prison theatre: Perspectives and practices* (pp. 127–148). London, UK: Jessica Kingsley.

Somers, J. & Roberts, G. (2006). "On the edge:" Reflection on an interventionist theatre programme. In M. Balfour & J. Somers (Eds.), *Drama as social intervention* (pp. 26–39). Concord, ON: Captus.

Stein, J. (Ed.). (1966). *Random House dictionary of the English language: Unabridged edition.* New York, NY: Random House.

Stephens, S. (2010, June 25). Drama in the wings: Why theatre in prisons matters. *The Guardian.* Retrieved from http://www.theguardian.com/stage/theatreblog/2010/jun/25/theatre-in-prisons-country-music.

Stuart Fisher, A. (2011). 'That's who I'd be, if I could sing': Reflections on a verbatim project with mothers of sexually abused children. *Studies in Theatre and Performance, 31*(2), 193–208.

Sullivan, J. (2004). Community environmental forum theatre: A dramatic model for dialogue and participatory research among citizens and scientists. *Stage of the Art, 16*(1), 17–23.

Swartz, L. (2014). *The new dramathemes* (4th ed.). Markham, ON: Pembroke.

Swartz, L. & Nyman, D. (2010). *Drama schemes, themes and dreams.* Markham, ON: Pembroke.

Swortzell, L. (1993). Trying to like TIE: An American critic hopes TIE can be saved. In A. Jackson (Ed.), *Learning through theatre* (pp. 239–250). London, UK: Routledge.

Talbot, R. & Andrews, N. (2011). Triangle's immersive museum theatre: Performativity, historical interpretation and research in-role. In A. Jackson & J. Kidd (Eds.), *Performing heritage: Research practice and innovation in museum theatre and live interpretation* (pp. 172-188). Manchester, UK: Manchester University Press.

Tannahill, J. (2015). Prologue. In J. Tannahill, *Theatre of the unimpressed: In search of vital drama* (pp. 9–20). Toronto, ON: Coach House.

Target Theatre. (n.d.). Retrieved from http://www.targettheatre.ca/.

Tarlington, C. & Michaels, W. (1995). *Building plays: Simple playbuilding techniques at work.* Markham, ON: Pembroke.

Taylor, C. (2004). *Modern social imaginaries.* Durham, NC: Duke University Press.

Taylor, L. (2011). The experience of immediacy: Emotion and enlistment in fact-based theatre. *Studies in Theatre and Performance, 31*(2), 223–237.

Taylor, P. (2003). *Applied theatre: Creating transformative encounters in the community.* Portsmouth, NH: Heinemann.

Taylor, P. (2006). Applied theatre/drama: An e-debate in 2004: Viewpoints. *RIDE: Research in Drama and Education, 11*(1), 90–95.

Thompson, J. (1998). *Prison theatre: Perspectives and practices.* London, UK: Jessica Kingsley.

Thompson, J. (2001). Making a break for it: Discourse and theatre in prisons. *Applied Theatre Researcher*, 2, unpaginated. Retrieved from http://www.griffith.edu.au/__data/assets/pdf_file/0010/54982/making-break-for-it.pdf.

Thompson, J. (2003). *Applied theatre: Bewilderment and beyond.* New York, NY: Peter Lang.

Thompson, J. (2005). *Digging up stories: Applied theatre, performance and war.* Manchester: Manchester University Press.

Thompson, J. (2009). *Performance affects: Applied theatre and the end of effect.* New York, NY: Palgrave Macmillan.

Thompson, J. & A. Jackson. (2006). Applied theatre/drama: An e-debate in 2004: Viewpoints. *Research in Drama and Education, 11*(1), 90–95.

Times Colonist (2000). "New play teaches art of dealing with dying," December 11, p. D2.

van Erven, E. (2001). *Community theatre: Global perspectives.* New York, NY: Routledge.

Vine, C. (1993). TIE and the theatre of the oppressed. In A. Jackson (Ed.), *Learning through theatre* (2nd ed., pp. 109–130). London, UK and New York, NY: Routledge.

Wagner, B.J. (1976). *Dorothy Heathcote: Drama as a learning medium.* Washington, DC: National Education Association.

White, G. (2015). *Applied theatre: Aesthetics.* London, UK: Bloomsbury.

Willett, J. (Ed.). (1964). *Brecht on theatre* (J. Willet, Trans.). New York, NY: Farrar, Strauss & Giroux.

Williams, M.P. (2000). *How the raven stole the sun.* New York, NY: Abbeville Press.

Wilson, J. (2013). Agency through collective creation and performance: Empowering incarcerated women on and off stage. *Making connections: Interdisciplinary approaches to cultural diversity, 14*(1), 1–15.

Wilson, M. (2006). *Storytelling and theatre: Contemporary storytellers and their art.* London, UK: Palgrave.

Wojciehowski, H. & Gallese, V. (2011). How stories make us feel: Toward an embodied narratology. *Journal of California Italian Studies*, *2*(1), 1–35.

Yashinsky, D. (2005). *Suddenly they heard footsteps.* Toronto, ON: Vintage Press.

Author Index